AROUND GREECE
IN 80 STAYS Hotels and guesthouses of character

AROUND GREECE

IN 80 STAYS Hotels and guesthouses of character

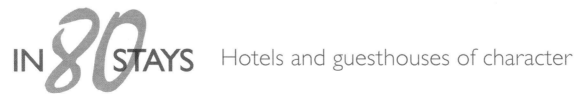

Jacoline Vinke

photography by **André Bakker**

EDITIONS

1st edition: February 2006

ISBN: 960 8189 721

In the course of preparing this book, the following have collaborated with the author:

Christina Moraki: editing

Olga Kodoni: graphic design and pagination

To my mother

My first and foremost debt of gratitude is to a group of extraordinary people, the creators and owners of Greece's most wonderful small hotels and guesthouses included in this book, for the trust they put in me to write about their places, without ever trying to interfere. This book exists thanks to them.

I am indebted to many other people who supported me in the process of making this book. I would like to thank the team at Road Editions: Yannis Tegopoulos, Stefanos Psimenos, Katerina Bardaka and Olga Kodoni. We had a seamless cooperation. Also, the encouragement I got from my partners at yourGreece, Aris Ikkos, Agathi Natsi and Philip Nielsen was of great value to me.

I would like to thank Valie Voutsa and Konstantina Zafiri for their invaluable assistance – Valie in the early stages of the project, and Konstantina in the last-minute frenzy. I am grateful as well to many others who helped me along the way: Diana Arapakis, Aliki Barnstone, Marcus Bonturi, Petra Brand, Lucas van Hasselt, Monique Korzelius, and – last but not least – Elna Kleopa. Huge thanks go to Athos Damis, dear friend and lawyer-extraordinaire. And a very special thank you to Stamatia Gotsi. I'd also like to express my gratitude to Christina Moraki for her diligent text editing. If there are any remaining errors in the text, they are mine.

It was a privilege to work with André Bakker. When we started this project, I didn't know much about him apart from the fact that he was a talented photographer, and that I expected him to do good work. But he did much more. Seeing the results of his work, I felt as if he had been looking through my eyes and my mind, and had captured my own feelings in his images.

How can I thank the three men in my life, George, Nicolas and Stefanos, for their endless love and support, and for standing by me throughout this project, even when it meant that family life was turned upside down? I could not have done this without knowing they were there for me. Thank you so much. I am home again.

Jacoline Vinke

I would like to thank:

Stamatia, my best friend, my wife, my advisor. I could not have done this book without her input, patience, love and support;

Eleni Armau and Vassilis Paparounas, for giving me shelter, the best Greek food, and for their help and friendship;

Jacoline Vinke, for her trust and a million other things;

Valie Voutsa at yourGreece for organising my often hectic and confusing travel schedule;

Yannis Tegopoulos, Stefanos Psimenos, Olga Kodoni and Katerina Bardaka at Road Editions for being so interested in the quality of the book;

And last but not least: all the great people of all the great small hotels I visited. I could only spend a limited time at each hotel and their help and support was vital to the success of the project.

André Bakker

CONTENTS

Introduction	....	15
Your Feedback	....	16
Online Information and Bookings	....	17
The yourGreece Network	....	18
Maps	....	20

Hotel and Guesthouses

Sifnos	Patriarca Boutique Hotel	....	36
Syros	Xenon Apollonos	....	40
	Lila	....	44
Mykonos	Apanema	....	48
	Geranium Residence Moonlight Hotel	....	52
Paros	Petres	....	58
	Anthippi	....	62
Santorini	The Tsitouras Collection	....	66
	Perivolas	....	72
	1864 – The Sea Captain's House	....	78
	Heliophos	....	84
Crete	Aspros Potamos	....	88
	White River Cottages	....	92
	Villa Arhanes	....	96
	Villa Kynthia	....	100
	Rodialos	....	104
	The House of Kouriton	....	108
	Suites Pandora	....	112
	Metohi Kindelis	....	116
	Milia	....	120
	Elia	....	124
Kythira	Pitsinades	....	128
	Nostos	....	132
Monemvasia	Ardamis	....	136
	Byzantino and Hammam	....	140
Lakonia	Geodi	....	144
Mani	Kyrimai	....	148
	Notos	....	154
Arkadia	Arhondiko Isari	....	158
	Hellenikon Country Club	....	162
	Trikolonion Country Club	....	166
	Kazakou	....	170
	Pyrgos Xeniou	....	174
	Traditional Guesthouse 1821	....	178
Nafplio	Ilion Suites	....	182

	Kyveli Suites	....	186
Korinthia	Helydorea	....	190
Spetses	Orloff Resort	....	194
Poros	Sto Roloï & the Anemone Residence	....	200
Parnassos	Generali	....	206
	Kiriaki	....	210
	Dadi – Arhondiko Parnassou	....	214
Evia	Eleonas	....	218
Karpenisi	Korys and Anatoli Houses	....	222
	Hellas County Club	....	226
	Anerada Inn	....	230
Lefkada	Pavezzo Country Retreat	....	234
	Pelecas Country Club	....	240
	Villa de Loulia	....	244
Zagori	Saxonis Houses	....	248
	Papaevangelou	....	252
	Archontikon Country Club	....	256
	Primoula	....	262
	Porfiron	....	266
	Arhondiko Dilofo	....	270
Kastoria	Arhondiko Alexiou Vergoula	....	274
Florina	La Moara and La Soare	....	278
	To Liakoto	....	284
Edessa	Varosi	....	288
Serres	Viglatoras	....	292
	Granitis	....	296
Kavala	Imaret	....	298
Halkidiki	Alexandrou Traditional Inn	....	304
Grevena	Valia Nostra	....	308
Trikala	Pyrgos Mantania	....	312
	Arhondiko Hatzigaki	....	316
Larissa	Arhondiko Soulioti	....	320
Pelion	Arhondiko Vogiatzopoulou	....	324
	Arhondiko Tzortzi	....	328
	Santikos Mansion	....	332
	The Lost Unicorn	....	338
	The Old Silk Store	....	342
	Despotiko	....	346
	Arhondiko Pandora	....	350
Hios	Perleas Mansion	....	354
	Argentikon	....	358
Leros	Arhondiko Angelou	....	364
Rhodes	Marco Polo Mansion	....	368
	Nikos Takis Fashion Hotel	....	374
	Melenos Lindos	....	378

INTRODUCTION

Writing this book has obviously been a lot easier than Phileas Fogg's journey around the world, even without a Passepartout to lend a hand. Travelling around Greece in search of hotels and guesthouses of character required no railways, carriages, yachts, trading-vessels, sledges, or elephants. Just a car, some ferry crossings and the occasional plane ride.

Is then the title of this book nothing more than a clever jeu de mots? Actually, it is. Jules Verne's character had made a wager at his gentlemen's club that he could complete a trip around the world in 80 days. I on the other hand, had set a wager with myself that I could find the 80 most wonderful and unique small hotels and guesthouses on the Greek mainland and islands. Unlike Phileas Fogg, I was in no particular hurry; what preoccupied me instead was whether I would be able to capture in my writing what sets these places apart.

What made my task much easier was meeting the owners (or sometimes caretakers) of the hotels and guesthouses. During my travels I got to know all of them personally, and became friends with many. It was fascinating to hear their stories and to learn about the dreams they had, their determination to realise them, the problems they encountered and the perseverance with which they overcame them. These are not people driven by visions of profits. Passion is their sole motivation: to revive an abandoned family property or restore a dilapidated building, and to create a perfect little getaway to be shared with others.

Many of us (myself included) sometimes think: "wouldn't it be nice to run a little hotel somewhere". I have seen up-close that reality is not always all that 'nice'. It is extremely hard work to keep up a small hotel, to create an environment where guests feel happy and at home, and to always be there for them, with a smile.

So, to the rhetorical question posed by Jules Verne at the end of his book, I have an easy answer. What I brought back from this long, but not-so-weary journey is an understanding of what makes these extraordinary people accomplish what they set out to do; and a newfound confirmation of what an amazing place Greece is, when nature, people and place conspire.

YOUR FEEDBACK

It goes without saying that I have personally visited all the hotels and guesthouses that appear in this book. I chose them because they were places that I genuinely liked, and that I would happily, and confidently, recommend to my friends. It would of course be ideal if I could try every one of them in different seasons so as to get the full picture, and stay longer than just a couple of nights. In practice, of course, with a group of 80 hotels, this is just not feasible.

If you have stayed in any of the places featured in this book, I would love to hear about your experiences. I have done my best to be frank and sincere in my descriptions, but of course everything I wrote is a reflection of my personal views and taste. I welcome your feedback, which you can send to **info@yourgreece.gr**.

A book like this one is only up to date at the moment of printing. All the hotels and guesthouses featured in it were last visited during the months leading up to the publication, and all factual information was verified in the weeks before the book went to print. But of course, there are always things – room rates, meals, services, and so on – that can change.

It is therefore not a bad idea to visit the website **www.yourgreece.com** if you are planning to stay at the establishments you read about in this book. This site offers reliable and up-to-date information, including detailed pricing and links to the hotels' own websites, while it also allows online bookings.

The *yourGreece* website also offers personalised travel services. These include customised tours, as well as leisure activities, like outdoor sports, eco-tourism, cooking lessons, art and photography courses or even a spa treatment, which can be pursued while travelling "Around Greece in 80 Stays".

your
GREECE
NETWORK OF GREAT SMALL HOTELS

www.yourgreece.com

When I first started looking for small, charming hotels and guesthouses in Greece, all I wanted to do was write a book about them. As I discovered one amazing little place after the other, I kept being surprised that nobody else had already done this. I also found it hard to understand how little known these places were outside Greece.

I started talking about this with a small group of people from diverse backgrounds sharing my passion for the 'real Greece'. Together we developed the idea to give a higher visibility to small hotels and guesthouses offering style, character and friendly service, and to help the 'discerning traveller' discover them through the creation of a network: the *yourGreece Network of Great Small Hotels*.

Today, *yourGreece* is the only network of its kind in the country to include a large number of exceptional establishments throughout the mainland and the islands. Its members, featured in this book, are all unique, but they share some common characteristics: they are small (usually with no more than 20 rooms); they have character (in terms of architecture, interior decoration, attention to detail); they have a warm and friendly atmosphere (most are owner or family-run); they offer good service and facilities (reasonable value-for-money); and they are set in attractive, unspoilt locations.

The hotels and guesthouses that were invited to join the network definitely represent a new trend in Greece. They offer something that combines the best of several worlds: the comfort of first-class hotels; the charm, authenticity and warm welcome associated with Greek traditions; and the aesthetics, tasteful interior decoration and little touches that the modern traveller with an eye for beauty and an aversion for mass tourism is looking for.

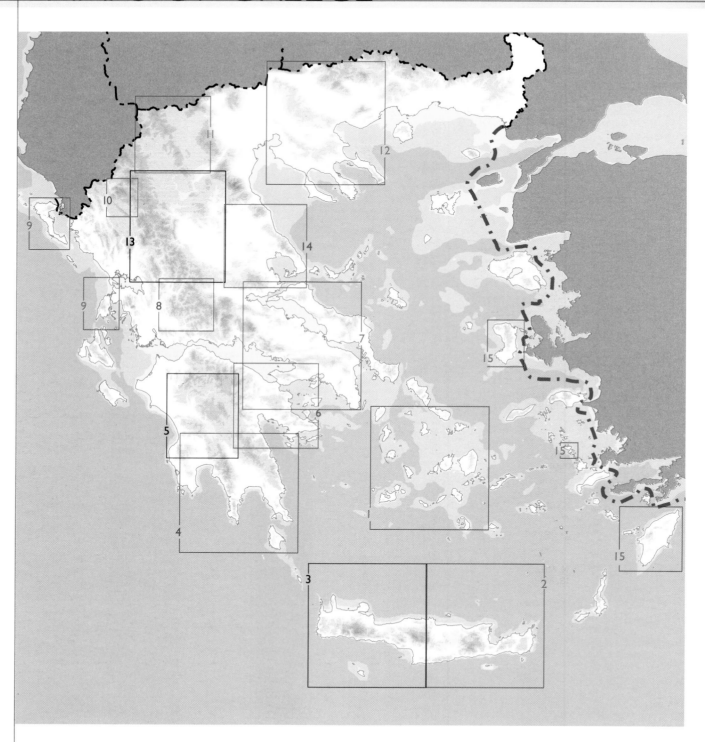

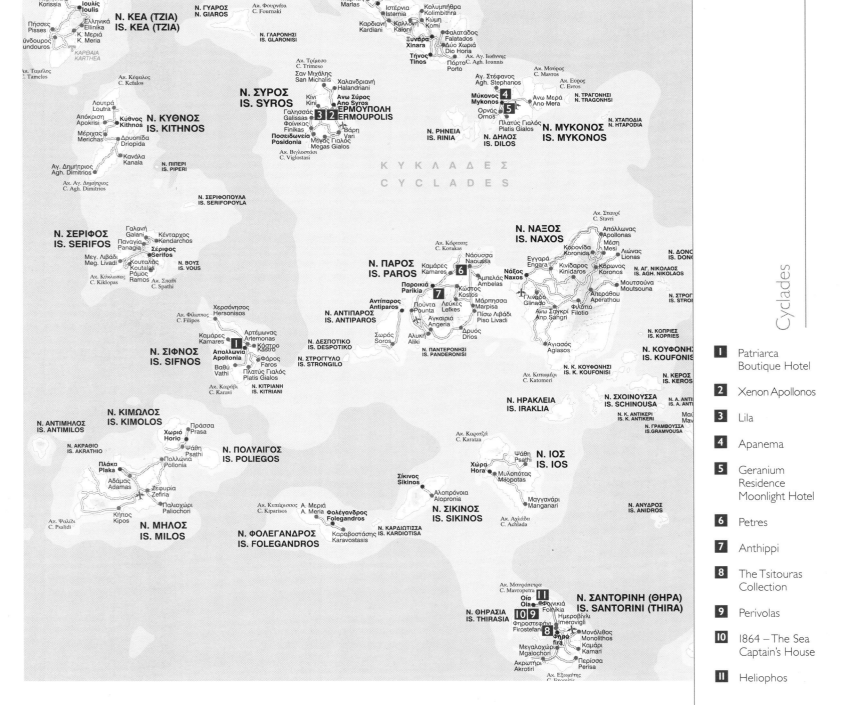

Cyclades

1 Patriarca Boutique Hotel

2 Xenon Apollonos

3 Lila

4 Apanema

5 Geranium Residence Moonlight Hotel

6 Petres

7 Anthippi

8 The Tsitouras Collection

9 Perivolas

10 1864 – The Sea Captain's House

11 Heliophos

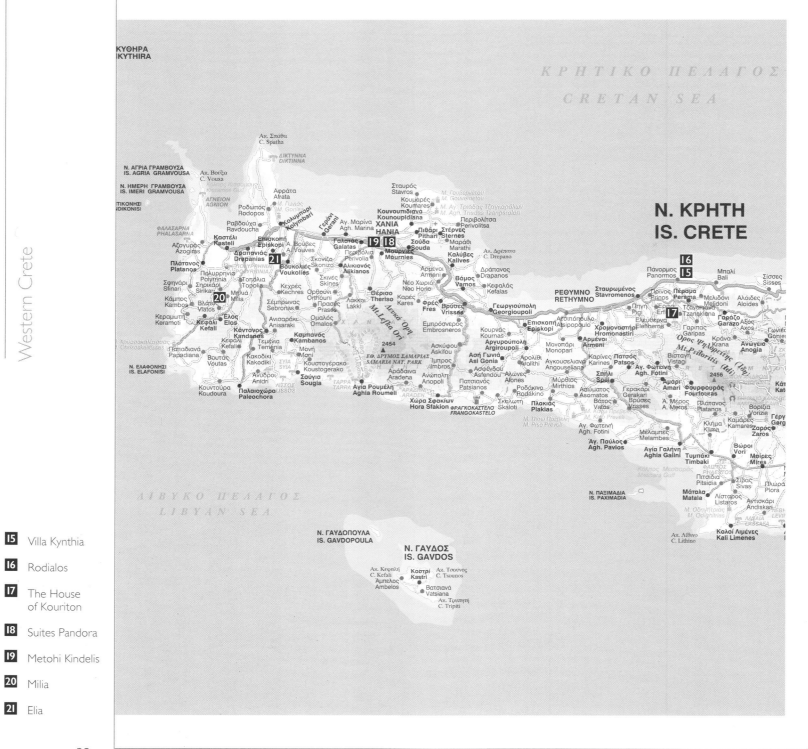

15 Villa Kynthia

16 Rodialos

17 The House of Kouriton

18 Suites Pandora

19 Metohi Kindelis

20 Milia

21 Elia

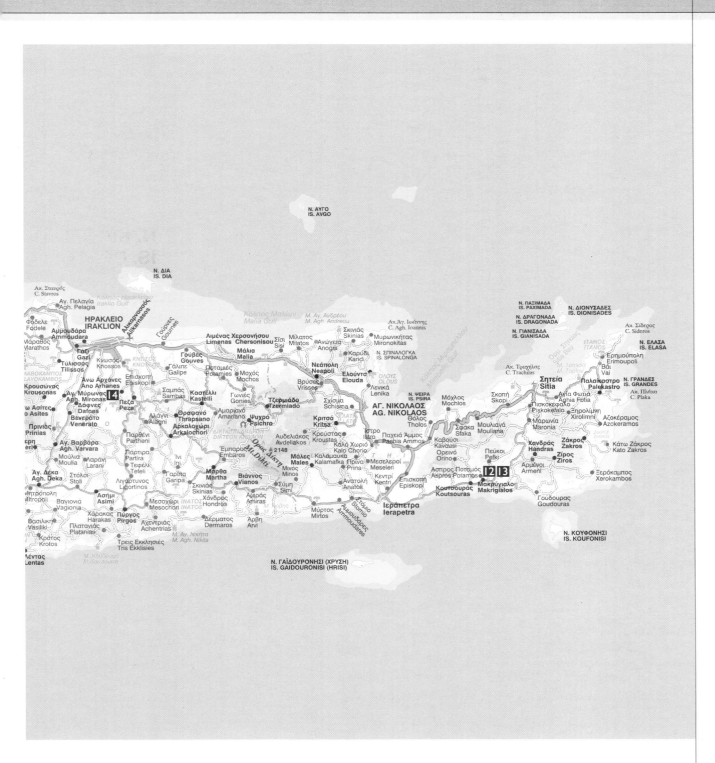

Eastern Crete

12 Aspros Potamos

13 White River
Cottages

14 Villa Arhanes

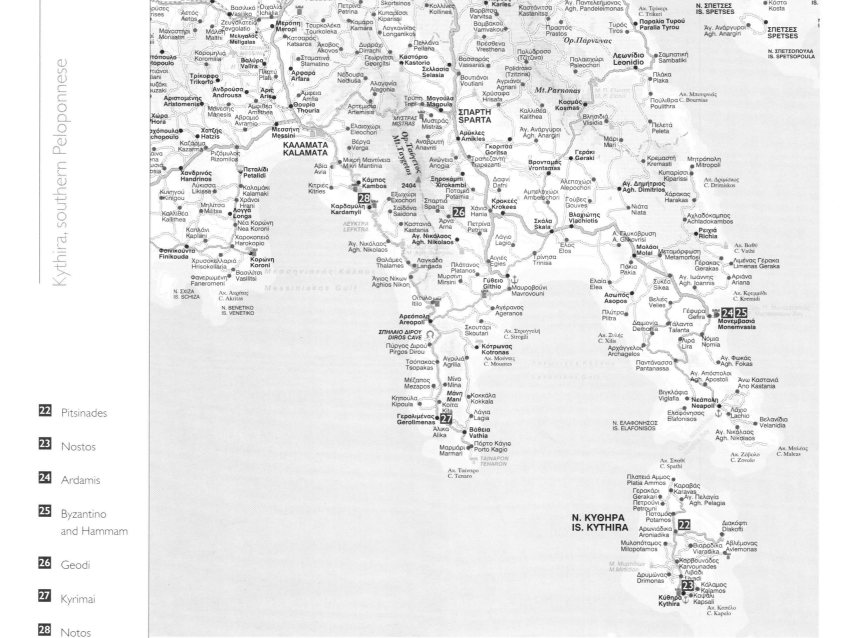

22 Pitsinades

23 Nostos

24 Ardamis

25 Byzantino
and Hammam

26 Geodi

27 Kyrimai

28 Notos

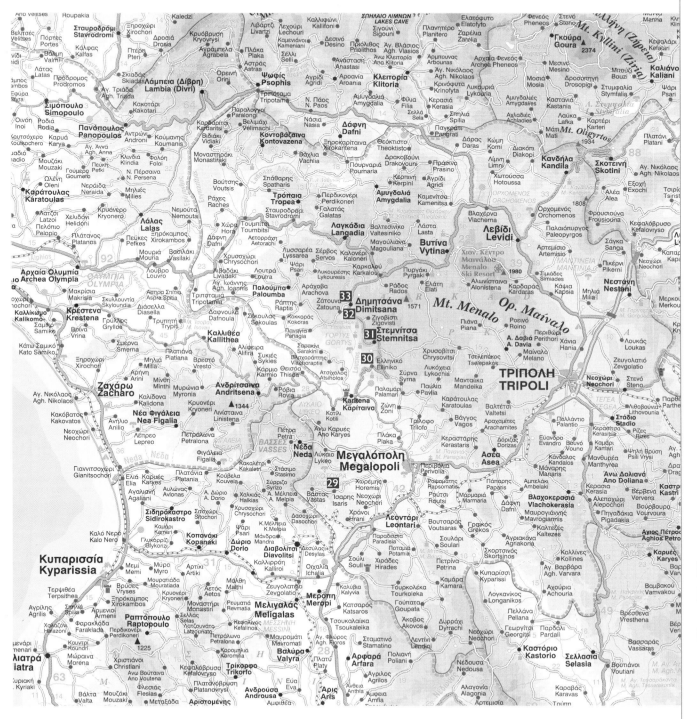

29 Arhondiko Isari

30 Country Club
Hellenikon

31 Trikolonion
Country Club

32 Kazakou

33 Pyrgos Xeniou

Northeastern Peloponnese, Spetses, Poros

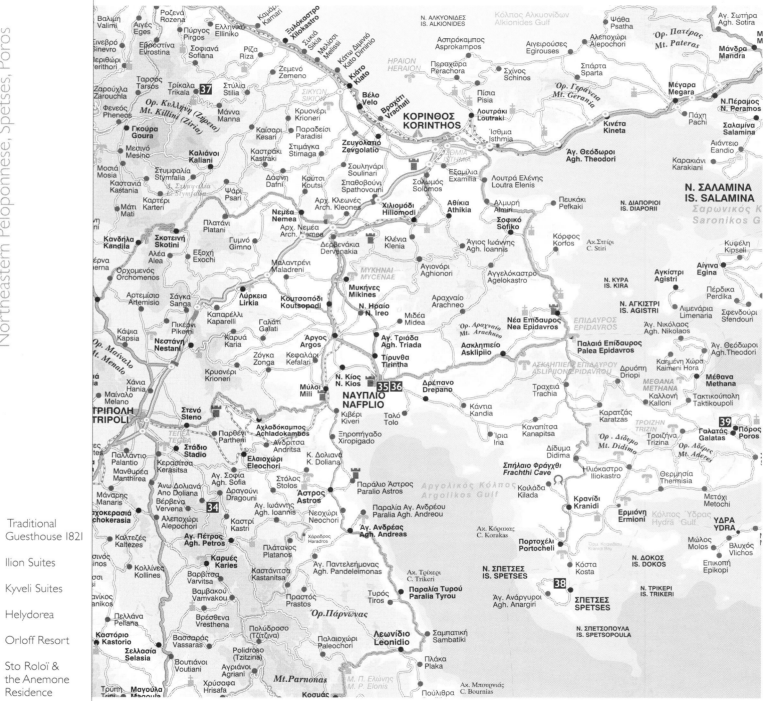

34 Traditional
Guesthouse 1821

35 Ilion Suites

36 Kyveli Suites

37 Helydorea

38 Orloff Resort

39 Sto Roloï &
the Anemone
Residence

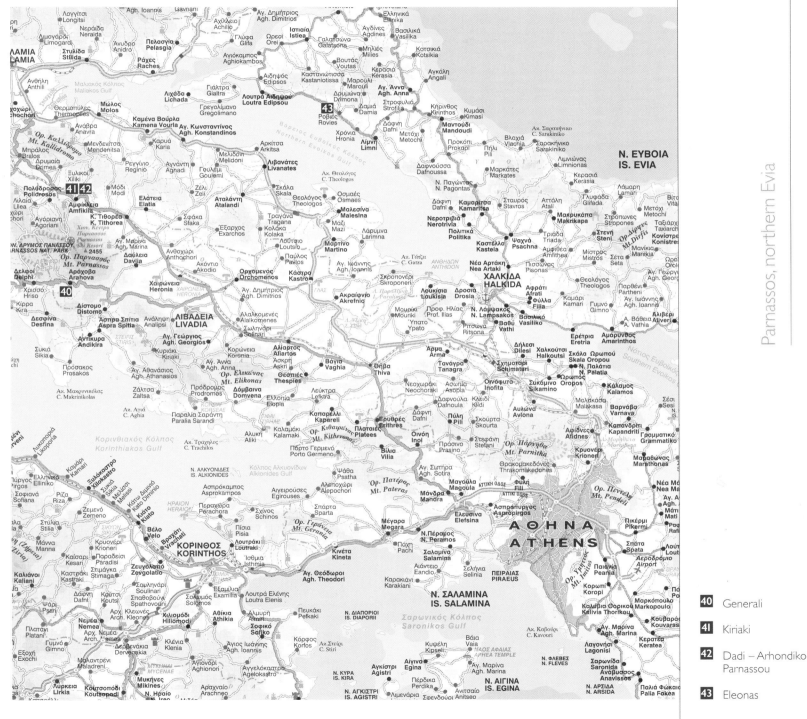

40 Generali

41 Kiriaki

42 Dadi – Arhondiko Parnassou

43 Eleonas

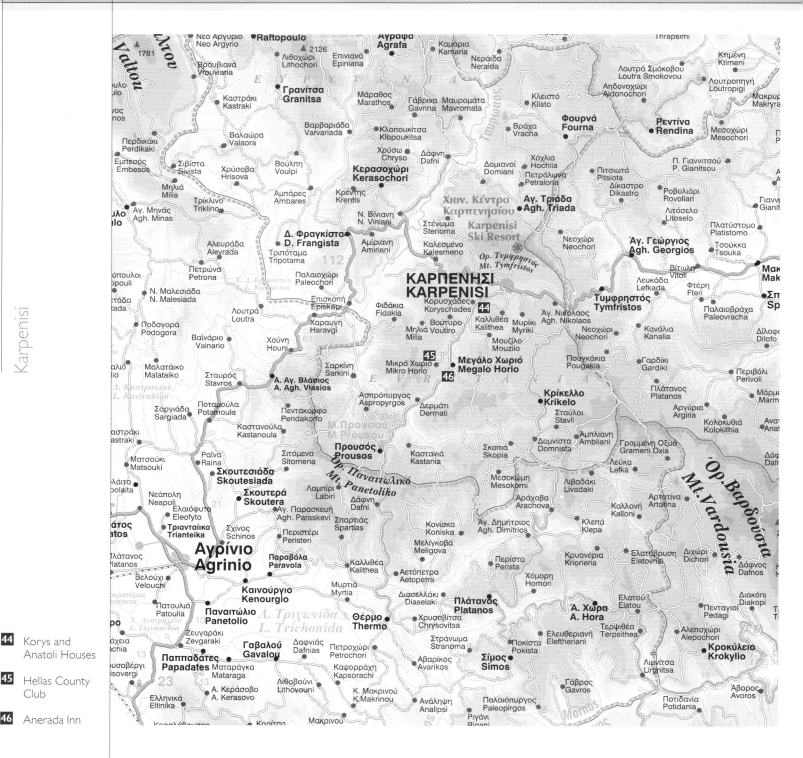

Νέο Αργύριο
Neo Argyrio
Raftopoulo
▲ 2126
Λιθοχώρι
Lithochori
Επινιανά
Epiniana
**Άγραφα
Agrafa**
Καμάρια
Kamaria
Νεράιδα
Neraida
Thrapsimi
Κτιμένη
Ktimeni
▲ 1781
Λουτρά Σμόκοβου
Loutra Smokovou
Λουτροπηγή
Loutropigi
Βρουβιανά
Vrouviana
**Γρανίτσα
Granitsa**
Μάραθος
Marathos
Γάβρινα
Gavrina
Μαυρομάτα
Mavromata
Κλειστό
Klisto
Αηδονοχώρι
Aidonochori
Μακρυρ
Makryra
Καστράκι
Kastraki
Βαρβαριάδα
Varvariada
Κλοπουκίτσα
Klopoukitsa
Βράχα
Vracha
**Φουρνά
Fourna**
**Ρεντίνα
Rendina**
Μεσοχώρι
Mesochori
Βαλαώρα
Valaora
Χρύσω
Chryso
Δάφνη
Dafni
Δομιανοί
Domiani
Χόχλια
Hochlia
Πιτσιωτά
Pitsiota
Π. Γιαννιτσού
P. Gianitsou
Περδικάκι
Perdikaki
Σιβίστα
Sivista
Χρύσοβα
Hrisova
Βούλπη
Voulpi
**Κερασοχώρι
Kerasochori**
Πετραλώνα
Petralona
Δίκαστρο
Dikastro
Ροβολιάρι
Rovoliari
Γιανν
Giani
Εμπεσός
Embesos
Μηλιά
Milia
Τρίκλινο
Triklino
Αμπάρες
Ambares
Κρέντης
Krentis
Χιον. Κέντρο
Καρπενησίου
**Αγ. Τριάδα
Agh. Triada**
Λιτόσελο
Litoselo
Αγ. Μηνάς
Agh. Minas
Ν. Βίνιανη
N. Viniani
**Karpenisi
Ski Resort**
Νεοχώρι
Neochori
**Άγ. Γεώργιος
Agh. Georgios**
Πλατύστομο
Platistomo
Τσούκκα
Tsouka
**Δ. Φραγκίστα
D. Frangista**
Αμίριανη
Amiriani
Στένωμα
Stenoma
Καλεσμένο
Kalesmeno
Αλευράδα
Aleyrada
Τριπόταμα
Tripotama
Ὀρ. Τυμφρηστός
Mt. Tymfristos
Βίτωλη
Vitoli
Μακ
Mak
Πετρώνα
Petrona
Παλαιοχώρι
Paleochori
112
Λευκάδα
Lefkada
Ν. Μαλεσιάδα
N. Malesiada
Επισκοπή
Episkopi
**ΚΑΡΠΕΝΗΣΙ
KARPENISI**
Κορύσχαδες
Koryschades
Φτέρη
Fteri
Λουτρά
Loutra
Χαραυγή
Haravgi
44
Ἀγ. Νικόλαος
Agh. Nikolaos
**Τυμφρηστός
Tymfristos**
Παλαιοβράχα
Paleovracha
Σπ
Sp
Ποδογορά
Podogora
Βαϊνάριο
Vainario
Χούνη
Houni
Φιδάκια
Fidakia
Βούτυρο
Voutiro
Καλλιθέα
Kalithea
Μυρίκι
Myriki
Νεοχώρι
Neochori
Κανάλια
Kanalia
Δίλοφο
Dilofo
Μαλατάικο
Malataiko
Σταυρός
Stavros
Σαρκίνη
Sarkini
Μηλιά
Milia
Μουζίλο
Mouzilo
Μικρό Χωριό
Mikro Horio
45
**Μεγάλο Χωριό
Megalo Horio**
Πουγκάκια
Pougakia
Γαρδίκι
Gardiki
Περιβόλι
Perivoli
Μάρμ
Marm
**Α. Αγ. Βλάσιος
A. Agh. Vlasios**
46
**Κρίκελλο
Krikelo**
Πλάτανος
Platanos
Ποταμούλα
Potamoula
Ασπρόπυργος
Aspropyrgos
Δερμάτι
Dermati
Σταύλοι
Stavli
Αργύρια
Argiria
Κολοκυθιά
Kolokithia
Ανα
Anat
Σαργιάδα
Sargiada
Πεντάκορφο
Pendakorfo
Ἀμπλιανη
Ambliani
Δομνίστα
Domnista
Γραμμένη Οξυά
Gramenι Oxia
Ὀρ. Βαρδούσια
Mt. Vardousia
Καστανούλα
Kastanoula
Μ.Προυσού
M.Prousou
Σκοπιά
Skopia
Δάφ
Dafι
Ραΐνα
Raina
**Προυσός
Prousos**
Καστανιά
Kastania
Λεύκα
Lefka
**Σκουτεσιάδα
Skoutesiada**
Σιτόμενα
Sitomena
Ὀρ. Παναιτωλικό
Mt. Panetoliko
Μεσοκώμη
Mesokomi
Λιβαδάκι
Livadaki
Λαμπίρι
Labiri
Αράχοβα
Arachova
Αρτοτίνα
Artotina
**Σκουτερά
Skoutera**
Αγ. Παρασκευή
Agh. Paraskevi
Δάφνη
Dafni
Κονίσκα
Koniska
Ἀγ. Δημήτριος
Agh. Dimitrios
Κλεπά
Klepa
Καλλονή
Kalloni
Νεάπολη
Neapoli
Σχίνος
Schinos
Περιστέρι
Peristeri
Σπαρτιάς
Spartias
Μελίγκοβα
Meligova
**Τριανταίικα
Trianteika**
Ελαιόφυτο
Eleofyto
Κρυονέρια
Krioneria
Ελατόβρυση
Elatovrisi
Διχώρι
Dichori
Δάφνος
Dafnos
**Αγρίνιο
Agrinio**
**Παραβόλα
Paravola**
Καλλιθέα
Kalithea
Αετόπετρα
Aetopetra
Περίστα
Perista
Χόμορη
Homori
Βελούχι
Velouchi
Μυρτιά
Myrtia
Διασελάκι
Diaselaki
**Πλάτανος
Platanos**
Ελάτου
Elatou
Διακόπι
Diakopi
**Καινούργιο
Kenourgio**
**Θέρμο
Thermo**
Χρυσοβίτσα
Chrysovitsa
**Ά. Χώρα
A. Hora**
Τερψιθέα
Terpsithea
Πενταγιοί
Pedagi
Πατουλιά
Patoulia
**Παναιτώλιο
Panetolio**
Α. Τριγωνίδα
L. Trichonida
Στράνωμα
Stranoma
Ελευθεριανή
Eleftheriani
Αλεποχώρι
Alepochori
Ζευγαράκι
Zevgaraki
Δαφνιάς
Dafnias
Πετροχώρι
Petrochori
Ποκίστα
Pokista
**Κροκύλειο
Krokylio**
**Παπαδάτες
Papadates**
Ματαράγκα
Mataraga
**Γαβαλού
Gavalou**
Καψορράχη
Kapsorachi
Αβαρίκος
Avarikos
**Σίμος
Simos**
Λιμνίτσα
Lirnitsa
Ἀβορος
Avoros
Ελληνικά
Ellinika
Α. Κεράσοβο
A. Kerasovo
Λιθοβούνι
Lithovouni
Κ. Μακρινού
K.Makrinou
Ανάληψη
Analipsi
Παλαιόπυργος
Paleopirgos
Γάβρος
Gavros
Ποτιδανία
Potidania

44 Korys and Anatoli Houses

45 Hellas County Club

46 Anerada Inn

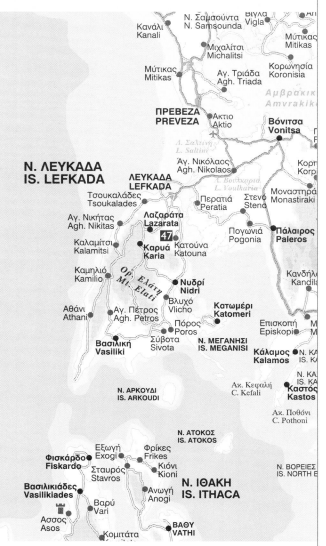

47 Pavezzo Country Retreat

48 Pelecas Country Club

49 Villa de Loulia

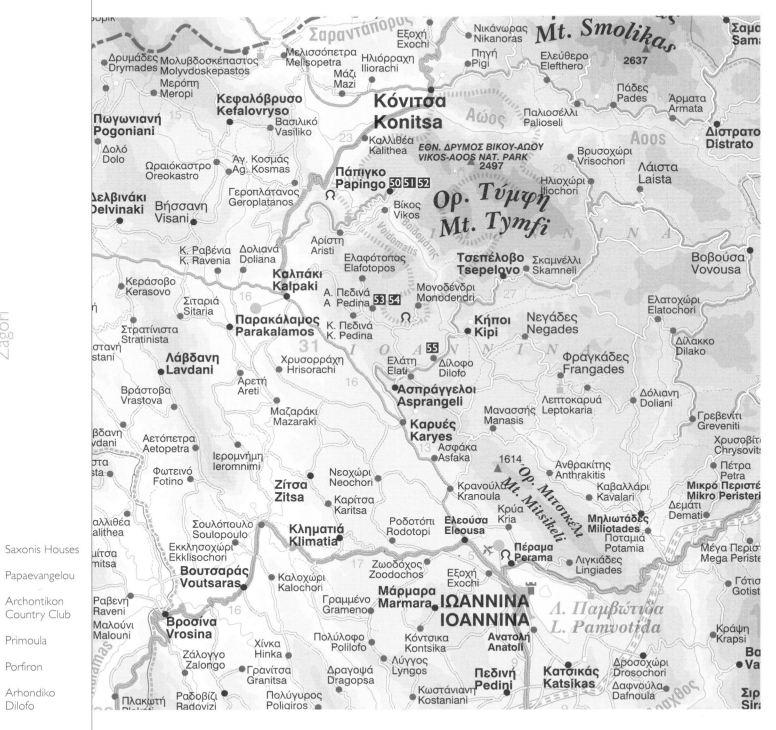

50 Saxonis Houses

51 Papaevangelou

52 Archontikon Country Club

53 Primoula

54 Porfiron

55 Arhondiko Dilofo

56 Arhondiko
Alexiou Vergoula

57 La Moara and
La Soare

58 To Liakoto

59 Varosi

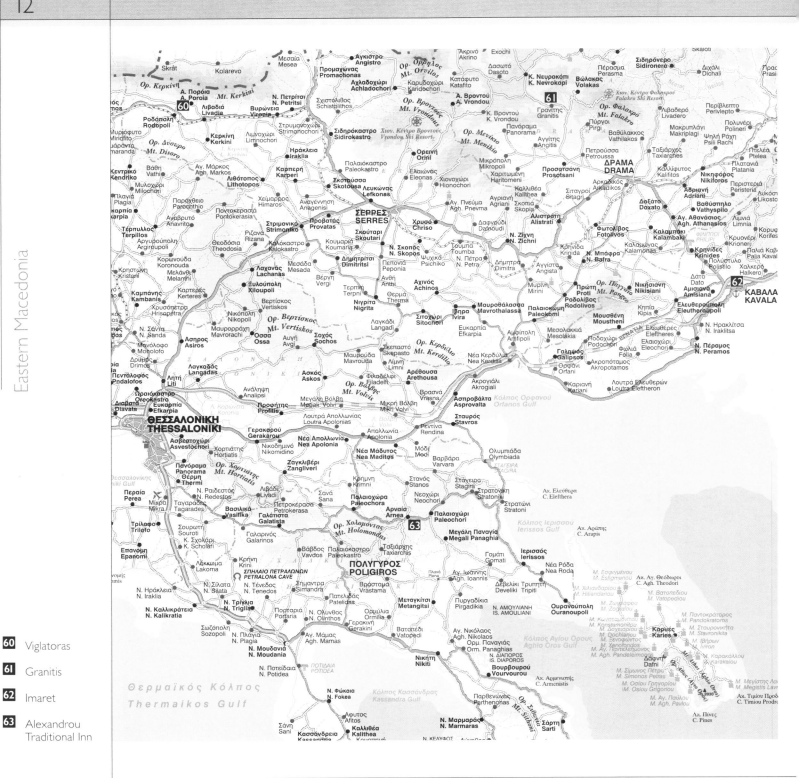

60 Viglatoras

61 Granitis

62 Imaret

63 Alexandrou
Traditional Inn

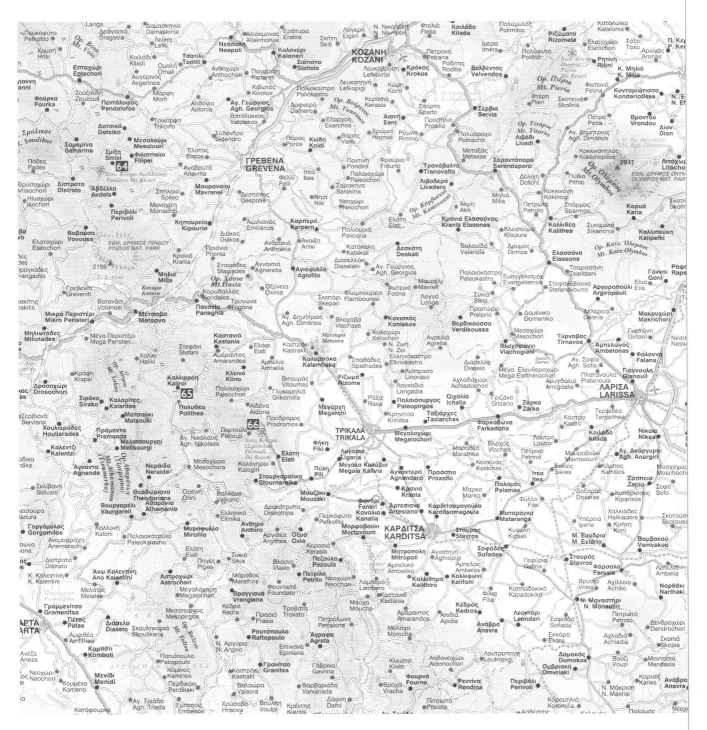

64 Valia Nostra

65 Pyrgos Mantania

66 Arhondiko
Hatzigaki

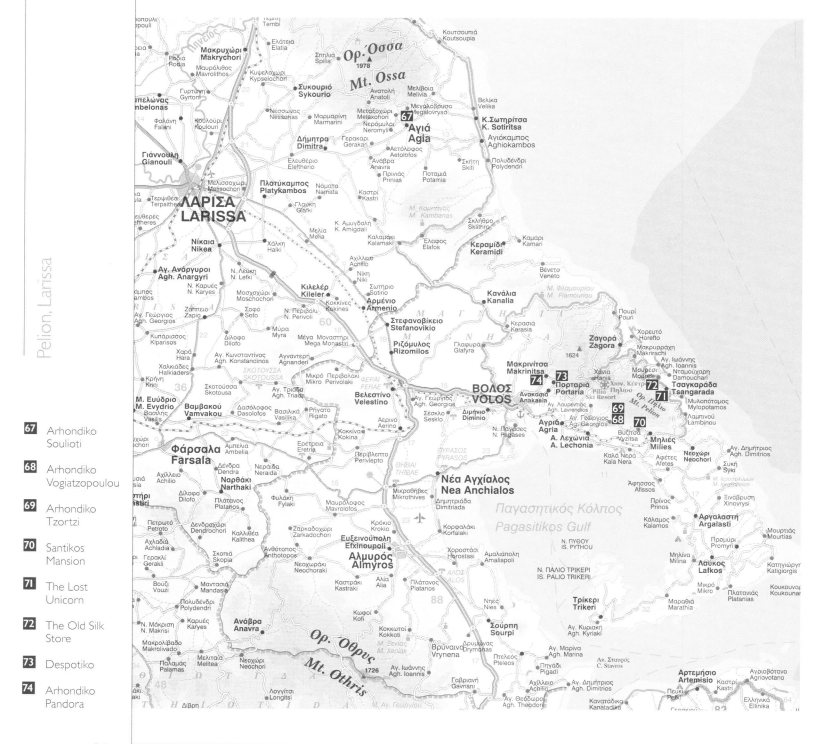

67 Arhondiko Soulioti

68 Arhondiko Vogiatzopoulou

69 Arhondiko Tzortzi

70 Santikos Mansion

71 The Lost Unicorn

72 The Old Silk Store

73 Despotiko

74 Arhondiko Pandora

75 Perleas Mansion

76 Argentikon

77 Arhondiko Angelou

78 Marco Polo Mansion

79 Nikos Takis Fashion Hotel

80 Melenos Lindos

PATRIARCA BOUTIQUE HOTEL

Famed for their great beaches, infinitely blue skies (at least in the summer) and their distinctive architecture, the Cycladic islands have an unbeatable charm. Though on the surface they have a lot in common, in fact the islands that make up the Cyclades are all different. Each has its own exceptional features, character and atmosphere, and each attracts its own crowd. Hip Mykonos draws the party animals; romantic Santorini is where honeymooners go; strategically located Paros is popular with island hoppers; and on it goes.

A bit off the beaten track, Sifnos is one for the connoisseurs. The island doesn't stand out for its beaches (though the south coast features several nice ones), but its beautiful bays, the relatively green (capers abound) and hilly landscape, topped by pretty, whitewashed villages and its excellent food – the island is famous for it – make it a wonderful holiday destination. It attracts its own pleasant little crowd of regulars. Though of course this is a blatant generalisation, its visitors do come across as a low-key, well-educated bunch, and Athenians who have summer houses on the island are by and large the types who will arrive with a pile of good books rather than a following of noisy friends.

Lefteris, Petros and George Pavlis, three brothers living in Athens, had no particular connection with Sifnos (except that they obviously liked it a lot) when they decided, a few years back, to look for an old house to buy as a summer home in Apollonia, Sifnos' picturesque, centuries-old capital in the centre of the island. They hit upon a listed, but ruined house dating from the mid-17th century, which, they were told, had been the childhood home of the patriarch of Istanbul Gregorios VII and was later used as a post-office while also housing the postman and the local schoolteacher.

Though the restoration clearly was not going to be an easy task, the brothers realised the house was a rare find, not only because of its age and historic uniqueness, but also because of its great location, towards the end of the kalderimi, the central, pedestrian alleyway, across the church of Agios Speridonos. (The only snag of the spot is the ringing of the church bells on Sunday morning.) Having a bit of a perfectionist streak, they called in the services of Angelos Angelopoulos, one of Greece's hottest interior designers of the moment. Angelopoulos proceeded to give an extra piece of advice and suggested they turn it into a little hotel; and so Patriarca Boutique Hotel was born.

PATRIARCA
BOUTIQUE HOTEL

Apollonia
840 03 Sifnos
Tel. 22840-32400

Contrary to some 'boutique' hotels of 50 rooms and over that feel more like 'department store' hotels, Patriarca, with only six rooms, is a 'boutique' true to its name. Everything is on a small scale: just one table fits in the dining room; the lounge has one sitting corner; bedrooms are compact (with, however, huge mirrors creating the illusion of space and beds so comfortable that the time spent in your room will probably be in bed anyway); and the outdoor pool is perfect if you want to break your personal record of number of laps: only four and a half metres long it doesn't take much to go from one side to the other.

Patriarca Boutique Hotel has become a breath of fresh air for Sifnos, where style is omnipresent in the traditional architecture, but seldom matched by the interior design (at least as far as tourist accommodation goes). Hidden behind a traditional white façade with blue doors and shutters, you will find carefully conceived, fresh, modern romantic interiors. The colour scheme is a merry cohabitation of flashy orange, pink and red which combines surprisingly well with the old elements of the house, just like the stylish, modern-chic furniture and fun decoration does. The atmosphere is young and informal, while service is attentive and careful.

Where you'll sleep There are five double bedrooms and one suite for up to four people. While small in size (and some a little dark), they are equipped with all mod cons: air conditioning, a television and DVD player, a CD player, a mini-bar, a hairdryer, a telephone and a wireless internet connection. The en suite showers are also small, but stylish.

When you feel hungry Breakfast is served from 9.30 to 11.30. You can help yourself from a spread including croissants, *pains au chocolat*, chocolate muffins, boiled eggs, cereals, fruits and yoghurt. During the day, cold plates can be prepared for you, and of course you will find plenty of places nearby where you can try local specialties.

Bring the children? Though Patriarca is not a typical family place (it attracts mostly young couples), children are welcome. Only the quadruple suite is suitable for families, and you can also ask for a cot. Though it would be really sad to come to an island and have your youngsters glued to the screen, you can ask for a PlayStation in your room.

To see and do A typical Sifnos holiday would be a combination of swimming, sunbathing, strolling around the villages (make sure you check out Kastro), sipping drinks on the terrace and doing a little bit of shopping. The island is known for its amazing ceramics – you can buy directly from the workshops – and in Apollonia you will find boutiques and art shops.

Good to know Patriarca is open from Easter to mid-October. (In the winter the house is available for groups.) Prices for a double room start at €100 per night in the low season, and at €120 in the high season (mid-July to the end of August), and they include breakfast. Credit cards: Amex, MasterCard and Visa.

Getting there The only way to reach Sifnos is by ferry (three to five hours from Piraeus). From the port, you take the road to Apollonia. After you pass through the small 'centre' of the village where the post office is, you turn right in the direction of Platys Gialos, Faros and Vathi. About 500 m after the turn, you will see a parking lot on your right, where you can leave your car and walk up to the Agios Speridonos church (impossible to miss) opposite to Patriarca Boutique Hotel.

It is hard to think of the Cyclades without postcard images of whitewashed houses with blue shutters and of tiny white chapels, all against a backdrop of endless blue, springing to mind. This is exactly what most Cycladic islands look like, but there is one that is positively different: Syros. Though the landscape (and the endless blue!) matches that of the other Cyclades, this island clearly distinguishes itself by its architecture: rather than whitewashed cubism, you will find splendid 19th century neoclassical mansions.

The different style is largely due to the strong historical presence of the Roman Catholic community on the island, which enjoyed the protection of France. During the Greek War of Independence from the Turks in the early 19th century, Syros managed to stay neutral and so escaped the devastation that so many other Greek islands suffered. Instead, Syros flourished during this period, when Ermoupolis was built to become the island's capital. Today it is the administrative and commercial centre of the entire group of Cycladic islands, and also the only town in the archipelago that truly qualifies as one. Life here does not evolve around the summer months and the foreign tourists they bring along. Ermoupolis is a city with an economic and cultural life of its own, where people live and work all year round.

Xenon Apollonos beautifully reflects many of the aspects that make Syros such a special island. The guesthouse is part of a larger mid-19th century building, spectacularly located right up on the rocky seaside. It is an impressive historic version of what today we call an apartment block, though obviously it has a natural charm and grandeur the modern equivalent never manages to achieve. It has

been the residence of several prominent families and from 1929 it functioned, for more than 30 years, as a girls' high school.

The largest part of the building is no longer in use (at least for the time being), but the small part that has been turned into a guesthouse does full justice to its splendour. The owners, George and Sophia Stathopoulos, are both interior designers, and it shows. The extremely tastefully styled interiors are a perfect blend of modern and old, with wooden floorboards, splendid painted ceilings, warm colour schemes, gleaming antiques as well as comfortable, more modern furniture, and a refined decoration.

XENON APOLLONOS

8 Apollonos St.
Ermoupolis
841 00 Syros
Tel. 22810-81387

There are two lounges: one with a bar and another with plush sofas and a great sea view (and a small balcony where you can sit out above the water). Especially the latter has a truly homely feel to it, just like the general ambience that permeates the guesthouse. This is not so much in the sense of a motherly type fuss over the guests (though you will be cared for very well); it is more about a generally quiet and soothing atmosphere. To give an example, you'll barely sense the need to close your bedroom door during the day, because the entire house will simply feel like yours. After all, there are only three bedrooms and with the total surface of the shared spaces being so much bigger than that of the actual bedrooms (not to say that they are small!), there is not much sharing to be done.

Where you'll sleep You will make your choice among a green, a blue or a peach coloured room. The first two look out over the water so that when you open your window you will listen to the relaxing sound of the waves washing against the rocky shore right below. The green room is on two levels, with a double bed up a flight of stairs and a sitting room downstairs, with two sofas that can be used as beds for children. The blue room is for two people and has a particularly beautiful bathroom. The peach-coloured room feels very cosy and romantic (though the canopied beds are twins!), but it looks towards the courtyard so you don't get the same "oh wow!" feeling you get in the other two. All rooms have an en suite shower, a telephone, a television, a mini-bar, air conditioning, a hairdryer and a safe.

When you feel hungry A nice breakfast (including fresh juice, croissants, scrambled eggs, cake, yogurt and fruits) is served until 12.30 and if you have a little craving during the day, you can ask for a snack. There are nice places to eat at just a few minutes' walk from the guesthouse, ranging from traditional tavernas to more funky little restaurants.

Bring the children? Though Xenon Apollonos is not the typical place to show up with children, they are welcome, and indeed the green room can function as a family room. Cots are available, and babysitting can be arranged.

To see and do A winter city break or summer holidays? Either way, Xenon Apollonos is a wonderful place to stay. In the summer it is best to rent a car to go around the island and try the various beaches; otherwise you can easily spend a few days discovering the town by foot to admire the architecture, visit museums and the beautiful 19th century Apollon theatre, and of course to do some shopping, drinking and eating.

Good to know Xenon Apollonos stays open all year round. The price of a double room is €200 in the summer, and €140 during the rest of the year, including breakfast.

Getting there To get to Syros you can either take a ferry from the port of Piraeus (the crossing takes three to five hours, depending on the ship) or you can fly from Athens. Once you are there, it is best to ask a taxi to drive you to the hotel, but if you come by boat and have your own transport, you should head towards Miaouli Square (the main square of Ermoupolis), and facing the town hall, turn right at G. Souri Street. You then turn left at Tsiropina Square into Apollonos Street, where you will find the guesthouse on your right, after about 30 m.

Ermoupolis, the capital of Syros (and of all the Cyclades), is not at all a typical Greek island town. Its grand central square and impressive neoclassical Town Hall, its beautiful 19th century architecture, its Roman Catholic churches (as well as Greek Orthodox) and the splendid Apollon theatre (modelled after La Scala of Milan, albeit on a smaller scale), give it something of a southern French or Italian feel. The waterfront is lined with terraces and behind it lies a maze of alleyways and backstreets, some quiet and peaceful, others full of life with street markets, restaurants, bars and cafés, old fashioned little stores and arty boutiques.

Guesthouse Lila is situated in a quiet part of town, a few blocks away from the seafront. It suits the Mediterranean ambience of the town perfectly, and has the feel of a little Italian *pensione* or *chambres d'hôtes* in France. There is indeed a French connection: the 150-year-old building used to be the French consulate of Syros. When Lila Papaionannou, an Athens 'escapee' looking for a quieter island life, discovered it, it was in a state of total dilapidation. Though the outside walls could be restored, the interiors had to be redone practically from scratch. That allowed Lila to do the house in a charming-old-meets-fresh-contemporary style, following much of its original layout but adding a modern aspect as well.

Both floors have wonderfully high ceilings (painted wood), and to make better use of the space, Lila added modern mezzanines in the rooms and in the café/sitting/breakfast room of the guesthouse. The furniture is also a successful mix of the old and the new. You will sleep in comfortable modern beds, but hang up your clothes in old wardrobes (very clean inside!). Similarly, you will eat your breakfast at old wooden tables but you will sit on modern, design chairs. Through a clever use of colours (soft hues that add warmth but at the same time create a light and sunny atmosphere) and nice arty touches, Lila created a fresh, charming environment. There is no space to sit outside, but the large doors to the pedestrian street are usually wide open, so that even when you sit inside, you still feel part of the life that slowly goes by.

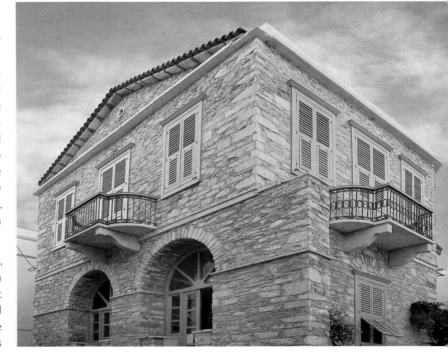

LILA

Ioannou Kosma & Fil. Etairias
Ermoupolis
841 00 Syros
Tel. 22810-82738

Where you'll sleep There are three suites on the first floor of the house. The most sought-after, the green suite, has a view to the sea and the waterfront. It features a sitting room (with two sofa beds), a bedroom and a mezzanine with two single beds. The other two suites look onto the backstreet, and can sleep up to four people. There are also three bedrooms with their own entrance from the street (no view); one is strictly double (beware – the bed on the mezzanine level is accessed via a very steep flight of steps), while the others have a double bed and a single bed on a mezzanine. Bathrooms are spacious (though the actual showers are a bit on the small side), and the rooms are comfortably equipped with a television, a telephone, an internet connection, a hairdryer, a refrigerator and facilities to make tea and coffee.

When you feel hungry Lila, who runs the guesthouse by herself, serves breakfast until 13.00. There are of course plenty of places to eat at walking distance, but should you ever not be in the mood to walk anywhere at all, catering can be arranged so you can have a meal in your own suite or in the sitting room.

Bring the children? One of the reasons why Lila, who has a little boy, moved to Ermoupolis, is that while it has all the advantages of a (small) town, the environment is quite safe for children. Local children find their way to the central square where during warm summer nights they all play together without their parents having to worry about them. The guesthouse provides a child-friendly environment and the rooms and suites are comfortable for families. (Just keep in mind that some of the mezzanines are not totally secure for very young children.) Cots are available, and in the sitting room you will find a supply of games and toys.

To see and do Syros is a great island to visit all year round, as life, especially in town, never seems to stand still. There are some nice beaches (though the island is not a typical beach destination), but you can also enjoy a performance in the splendid Apollon theatre, visit the Industrial and Archaeological Museums and discover the impressive architecture.

Good to know Lila's Guesthouse stays open all year. The price for two persons per night starts at €60 in the low season, and at €100 in the high season (mid-July to the end of August plus the Easter holidays). Note that even though it is possible to bring a car close to the house, you have to get quite lucky to be able to park nearby, but there is a large public parking space a few minutes on foot. Credit cards: MasterCard and Visa.

Getting there You can get to Syros by ferry from the port of Piraeus in three to five hours, but there also is an airport on the island and there are daily flights from Athens. The guesthouse is not too hard to find from the port: as you arrive you take a right on the waterfront boulevard Ethnikis Antistaseos and after about 200 m, right after the last palm tree, you turn left into Naxou, a very narrow alleyway with steps. The guesthouse is at the end of the fourth block on your right. It is not far, but it is a bit of a climb. Generally, however, Lila meets her guests in the port.

Mykonos is of course the ultimate holiday destination in the Cyclades. It is beautiful, it is fun and the beaches are among the best in Greece. It is a place to dance through the night, sleep late, breakfast on croissants, yogurt and fresh fruit salad, work on your tan and show it off, sip cocktails while the sun sets and choose between lobster, fresh pasta or sushi for dinner. It first became en vogue in the sixties when the gay and jet-setting crowd brought style into the island and turned it into the trendiest spot in the Aegean – a tag held until today.

Mykonos has never fallen prey to the mega hotel developments and package deal tourism that definitely scarred some other Greek islands, though it has become pretty built-up. Near the best beaches, medium-sized luxury resorts abound (catering to American Express Gold Card-holding types), as well as more plain, Cycladic style accommodations, while in 'town' you can take your pick from small hotels and rooms to let.

Apanema, a hotel situated near the sea at about ten minutes by foot from the centre of Mykonos town, doesn't really fit into any of these categories. While its standards match those of most 'glam' places, it is definitely a lot smaller (it has 16 rooms) and it has a much more personal feel to it. This is basically thanks to the young owner, Kriton Harakopoulos, who has taken an earnest hands-on approach, as he is (almost) always present on the property, welcoming his guests personally and knowing them all by name (but thankfully, not in the "*How are you today Mr Smith*" way!).

APANEMA

Tagoo
846 00 Mykonos
Tel. 22890-28590

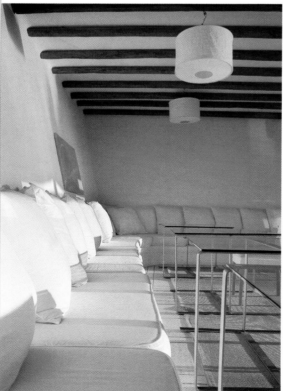

Kriton never thought he was ever going to be so closely involved with the hotel while it was under construction. He was even thinking of leasing it, so he opted for a not very original, but typical Cycladic structure of cubic shapes built around a pool, blue and white colours, a few touches of natural stone, and fairly plain interiors. But by the time Apanema neared its completion, Kriton had grown so fond of it that at the last moment he decided to run it himself. In fact, it was only after it opened that he started to develop a vision of how he really wanted the place to be, and then he instantly began a refurbishment that in the end lasted longer than the construction itself. He took it step by step, doing a few rooms at a time, giving them all a fresh, modern-romantic feel, some in a striking Cycladic white and minimalist fashion, others in soft green and blue colour schemes.

At first sight, the location of Apanema may not seem great. The stretch of coast in front of it is not the prettiest (though there are plans to build a small marina which will give it a definite lift) and you may find it a little too far from the action. Think again though: it is less time to walk to the

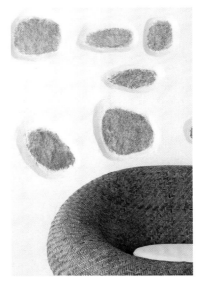

centre than it usually takes to find parking on the outskirts of the town (you can't drive further in), and also it is much quieter than many other parts of the island, where you get a fairly constant traffic din. A short walk to the town, a short drive to the beaches, no trouble parking, and a great place to be if you don't want to move anywhere – it doesn't sound too bad, does it?

Where you'll sleep There are six standard double rooms at Apanema (with a view to the pool) and six superior doubles (with a sea view), as well as two one-bedroom suites and two two-bedroom suites. They all have an en suite shower or bathroom and they are equipped with air conditioning, a mini-bar, a telephone, a television, a CD player, a safe and a hairdryer. The beds are exceptionally comfy. Each room has either a balcony or a terrace to sit out.

When you feel hungry Breakfast is served by the pool or can be brought to your room at any time from 8.30 onwards. You get a selection of fresh bread and croissants, and fresh orange juice, and you can order yogurt, cereals, fruits and cake from the breakfast menu, as well as extras (that you are charged for) like eggs, pancakes, waffles and brownies. You should of course try the restaurants in the town of Mykonos (where you will find some of the best places to eat in Greece), but from time to time you can also opt for a leisurely meal (excellent Mediterranean cuisine) by the pool of Apanema.

Bring the children? Apanema caters more to couples than to families, and is definitely not the kind of place where you will find children hanging out by the pool all day long. Older kids are welcome, but you should bring children under the age of 14 only if you feel they will fit in with the quiet ambience of this hotel. Should you come with a baby, there are cots, and occasional babysitting can be arranged.

To see and do Mykonos offers about all the entertainment you can expect on a holiday island, and it will really depend on your mood and tastes how you are going to fill your days and nights, and whether you will actually sleep during the day or during the night. Do include a trip to the nearby isle of Delos, the legendary birthplace of Apollon and Artemis, and a major spiritual and political centre of Ancient Greece.

Good to know Apanema is open usually from the Easter holidays until the end of October. Prices for a double room start at €250 per night in the summer and at €170 in the low season, and they include breakfast. Arrival and departure transfers are also included in the prices.

Getting there Mykonos can be reached either by conventional ferry (about six hours), high-speed boat (three hours) or plane (several flights a day from Athens). Apanema is situated above the coastal road between the old and the new port, at about one km from the town. You will be picked up upon arrival in the port or the airport.

While the ancient Greeks may have revealed homosexuality to the world, the modern gay crowd exposed Mykonos to the world. It was they who in the sixties put the island on the map, sparking off its transformation from a poor fishermen's island to the trendiest hot-spot in the Cyclades. Today the gay scene – a mixed crowd varying from happy honeymooners and quiet veterans, to youngish jet setters and pure scene fixtures – still has a strong presence on the island though it no longer rules it. It is stylish, but not snobbish, it is flirtatious, but there are no all-night rave parties and, well, only just a bit of late-night cruising.

There is probably not a single hotel on Mykonos that would dare not call itself gay-friendly, but some are definitely more frequented by gays than others. Alexandar Georgiev decided to go all the way with his Geranium Residence Moonlight Hotel, and made it an exclusively gay venue. The property is already 20 years old and used to be a (very) gay-friendly but nothing-special hotel. But when Alexandar took it over a few years ago, he gave it a complete make-over and turned the place into the ultimate sleek, clutter-free outpost of style.

There is lots of eye-catching white: the sofas in the large reception area/lounge, the curtains shading the terraces, the Philippe Starck outdoor furniture, the bedding, the flowerpots and even the geranium flowers. It is all extremely well taken care of; the entire scene is the epitome of gay-chic. The aesthetics of the pool area are absolutely perfect, small tables set on one side, shady corners for lazy lounging on another side, beautiful sun beds on the other two sides, and in the middle a sparklingly clean, large, almost square pool. And, a definite plus for most of the residents, naked swimming and sunbathing are allowed.

Funnily enough, while on the surface it may all look like a glitzy, smoothly and professionally managed hotel, in reality it is much more of a family-run guesthouse. Alexandar is assisted by Jordan, his partner of many years (they were high school sweethearts), his absolutely straight brother (present only part of the season), and his mother Dami, nicknamed "Mamacita" by the guys, a playful reference to her warm hearted nature. Alexandar proclaimed the property straight-friendly, not so much as an invitation for straight couples to come and stay, but more as a clear message to the guests to be nice to his family.

GERANIUM RESIDENCE
MOONLIGHT HOTEL

School of Fine Arts Area
New Ring Road
846 00 Mykonos
Tel. 22890-22867

And indeed, the ambience is totally *bon enfant*. Yes, it is flirtatious, there is lots of joking and a little bit of matchmaking going on, and if single guests want to bring back an occasional visitor for the night, they may do so. But Alexandar keeps a careful eye on what is happening and has set clear limits upon what is tolerated and what is not. The atmosphere is very much everyone-knows-everyone, though not in a suffocating way, and single newcomers usually quickly make some friends (with Alexandar's helping hand). The goodbyes are heart-warming, with vows to come back. And judging from the arrival scenes of returning guests, these are not empty promises.

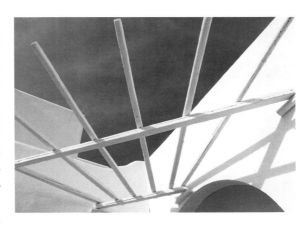

Oh, and just in case anyone wonders, did I seriously stay here? I did indeed, and I had a great time!

Where you'll sleep The eight double rooms are small but sweet, and decorated with a lot of taste. Here too, white has the overtone. Beds are superbly comfortable (with a choice of pillows). Some of the bathrooms are on the small side, but not uncomfortable. The rooms are equipped with a telephone, a television, a mini-bar, air conditioning, a safe and a telling package of condoms, earplugs and refreshing eye pads (presumably to be used in that order). There are also two double studios, two two-bedroom apartments and one two-bedroom villa. In addition to the rest, these have a fully equipped kitchen, a CD player and a DVD player. The only downside to the accommodation is its proximity to the road, but this is really not too bothersome.

When you feel hungry Breakfast is at the pool, and is served from 9.00 to 12.00 to guests staying in single or double rooms. (All the other units have their own kitchen and if you stay in one of those you can fix your own breakfast.) The table seating is arranged so that if you are lucky you'll have a gorgeous young man sitting across from you. Bread buns, croissant, cake, pie, egg, yogurt and some fruit are elegantly served and side orders (omelettes, pancakes, fruit salad…) are possible. During the day you can order light snacks from the pool bar. In the evening, everybody hits the town, usually following the spot-on recommendations of Alexandar for places to eat (he has a hotline to the greatest restaurants in town and makes reservations for everybody).

GERANIUM RESIDENCE
MOONLIGHT HOTEL

Bring the children? Um, well, no. Obviously, this is not exactly what you would call a family place. There is not, however, any explicit no-children policy and in principle, it is okay to stay with a child in the villa.

To see and do Most guests follow a daily programme that goes something like this: a lie-in, a leisurely breakfast, make it brunch, a good dose of tanning and see-and-be-seen by the pool or on the beach, freshening up and dressing up, a few drinks while watching the sunset, dinner in town and a night out.

Good to know The hotel is open from mid-April until mid-October. Prices for a double room start at €100 in the low season, and €180 in the high season. They include breakfast. The prices of the bigger units start at €170 and €280 depending on the season, but do not include breakfast. A minimum of four nights stay applies. There is private parking on the property.

Getting there You can reach Mykonos by conventional ferry (about six hours), by high speed boat (three hours) or by plane (several flights a day from Athens). The hotel is situated on the new(-ish) ring road around Mykonos town, at three km from the new port and at two km from the airport.

At a first glance, Hotel Petres does not look different from many other small hotels in the Cyclades. Cubic shapes, a few arches, whitewashed walls, blue shutters, terraces shaded by pergolas overgrown with grapevine, a swimming pool and a sea view make an attractive, but not very imaginative package. Upon closer inspection, however, you will notice a lot more to Hotel Petres than straightforward Cycladic style.

First of all, there is the interior decoration. Most hoteliers on islands like Paros operate under the assumption that people come for the beach and don't care much what the place they stay at looks like, and therefore stick to the boring basics. But that is not how Clea and Sotiris Hadjinikolakis work. Coming to Paros (they are both from Athens) was a love affair to them, and so was the hotel they built. And it shows. They decorated the sitting room, the open kitchen and the dining room with heaps of passion, and it all turned out extremely homely, warm, and island-stylish. They even installed an antique fireplace in the sitting room – barely needed but great for the occasional cosy evening by the fire early and late in the season.

But there is more than nice style that makes Hotel Petres exceptional. It is also the atmosphere Clea and Sotiris brought to the place. Living right next door, they are always around, ready for a chat with their mainly francophone guests, getting to know everyone. It is a personal (but not intrusive) approach that you don't come across often, and they are rewarded by a faithful set of customers – many return year after year. This is a place where people feel at home.

PETRES

Naoussa
844 01 Paros
Tel. 22840-52467

Where you'll sleep There are 16 double rooms, some of which can sleep a third person on a sofa-bed. They are maybe a little too functional in their set-up, but thanks to some thoughtful decorative touches (and antique brass double beds in some rooms) they have definitely more charm than most Cycladic hotel rooms. Clea took a conscious decision in keeping them this way. She does not feel like following trends and fashion when it comes to interior design and prefers to keep things in a simple island style. But she has also created an atmosphere that makes people to want to sit out on the terrace and by the pool, and not retire to their bedrooms, unless they are going to sleep.

The rooms all have an en suite shower (again functional, but without extras) and are fitted with a telephone, a television, a small refrigerator, air conditioning, a hairdryer and a safe. Each room has its own balcony or terrace. Two rooms are fully equipped for people with special needs.

When you feel hungry You can help yourself to breakfast from 9.00 to 11.30. In addition to the basics (fresh bread, homemade marmalades, cheese, ham, fruits, and yogurt), take your pick from daily varied pies and cake; sometimes omelettes are served as well. Breakfast is a leisurely affair – people fill their big wooden trays, eat out by the pool, do a bit of sunbathing and take a dip, to then eat a little more, and when they are done, many even clear the table themselves and take the tray back to the kitchen (but that is not compulsory!).

You can also have lunch and (early) dinner at the hotel. There is no formal restaurant but every day you can choose from a few traditional dishes Clea prepares. Otherwise, the little port of Naoussa is a great place to have some grilled fish (or other food) by the water, and if you don't have a car, Sotiris will happily shuttle you up and down.

Bring the children? Of course you can bring your kids to Hotel Petres, though families are generally not a majority here. Don't come under the assumption your kids will find heaps of friends at the hotel – the odds are there will be just a few more people with children. Truth of the matter is that a bit of quiet around the pool is appreciated, but then again, there are many fantastic sandy beaches just a short drive away.

To see and do Centrally located in the Cycladic island group, Paros offers beautiful sandy beaches, a hilly land-scape and picturesque little villages. The combination of a swimming pool at your doorstep, a tennis court and a gym on the premises, gorgeous beaches (you should certainly check out the perfect, white sand beaches of Kolymbithres) and a charming fishing village nearby, is not a bad package for relaxed-active holidays. You can also book a Reiki or Shiatsu therapist.

Good to know Hotel Petres is generally open from mid-April till mid-October. The price per night for a double room is €70 in the low season and €110 in the high season. Breakfast, as well as arrival and departure transfers,

is offered free. Facilities at the hotel include an outdoor swimming pool (with wheelchair access), a tennis court and a small gym with a Jacuzzi and a sauna. The hotel also offers a free mini-bus service to the harbour of Naoussa.

Getting there To get to Paros you can either take a ferry from the port of Piraeus (the crossing takes three to five hours, depending on the ship) or you can fly from Athens. Hotel Petres is situated six km from the port and 18 km from the airport. Sotiris will pick you up from the harbour or the airport, but if you arrive with your own transport you should take the road from Parikia to Naoussa, and after 6 km turn right at the sign for Petres. If you come from Naoussa, take the coastal road towards Parikia and turn left after 1.5 km.

Anthippi Kyriazanou is a young woman like no other. Free-spirited, easy-going, fun and creative, she works as an architect, runs a guesthouse, and is an artist in disguise. Her guesthouse, a small mid-19th century farm situated on the hill just outside Parikia, is an extension of her personality: it is full of character, original, playful and arty.

The farm has been in Anthippi's family for many generations – her own father grew up on it – but later on it was abandoned. When the listed property was bequeathed to her, she decided to restore it and turn it into a guesthouse. The old farmhouse was in fact tiny, offering enough space for just four studios, but Anthippi built a second house next to it and added some more. Despite their difference in age, the two houses, with their cream coloured, thick walls and small windows, stand well together. The terraces with stone and marble tables set in the shadow of wooden pergolas, the old bread oven, lush greenery and flowers and a small swimming pool (looking somewhat like a rock pool), all add up to create a scenery that is as attractive as it is unique.

Anthippi's artistic touch is traced throughout the whole property. Faced with a bare wall, most people would take a hammer and a nail and would put up a picture. That's not what Anthippi does. She takes out her paintbrush, and uses it to transform the wall into something that no longer needs decoration, and then, when the mood takes her, she adds a beautiful fresco. Similarly, old tools that lesser mortals might have chucked away are turned into art works. An old bread oven that can no longer be used as such, is filled with sea shells and lit from inside. A wooden antique refrigerator becomes a fine wardrobe. Mirror frames are made out of driftwood. The old farm mill-stone is turned into a great table for al-fresco dining. A fisherman's boat too old to brave the sea, now serves as a pool bar.

ANTHIPPI

Parikia
844 00 Paros
Tel. 22840-21601

Whenever Anthippi is done with one thing, a new idea pops to her mind. Chances that one day she will say "I'm done" are slim, as there is always something else that catches her attention. So if you're surprised that the floor tiles in some of the studios are quite 'ordinary', and that some of the bathrooms are a bit plain… just watch this space!

Where you'll sleep There are three double and two triple studios, and four one-bedroom apartments for up to four persons. They all have a shower (most are decent-sized, but some are quite small), a television and a kitchenette (a few of them are outside). Inside, the studios and apartments are not huge and they are a little dark, but they are cosy and thanks to the thick, stone walls of the houses, they provide a cool shelter from the sun. All have space to sit out.

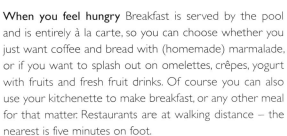

When you feel hungry Breakfast is served by the pool and is entirely à la carte, so you can choose whether you just want coffee and bread with (homemade) marmalade, or if you want to splash out on omelettes, crêpes, yogurt with fruits and fresh fruit drinks. Of course you can also use your kitchenette to make breakfast, or any other meal for that matter. Restaurants are at walking distance – the nearest is five minutes on foot.

Bring the children? Of course you will. Paros is a great island to go with children and they will be happy at Anthippi's, where they can play outside and swim in the pool. Cots are available.

To see and do You will never get bored on Paros. There are beautiful villages to visit, mountains to explore, and many fantastic sandy beaches to choose from. If you want to add a creative or sporty dimension to your holidays, just ask Anthippi. She will have plenty of suggestions for you like painting courses, sailing, surfing, waterskiing or scuba diving. She can also book you a shiatsu therapist should you need to recover afterwards. The nightlife in Parikia and Naoussa is quite animated, and it is also fun to catch an open air cinema screening in Parikia.

Good to know Anthippi is open from April to October. Prices for a double studio start at €70 per night in the low season. From late July to late August rates start at €100 per night. Breakfast is not included in the prices. Credit cards: all major.

Getting there Coming from the port of Parikia, turn right onto the main road (follow signs for Aliki and the airport). Take a left after you pass two petrol stations (there is a small sign for Anthippi) and you will see the entrance after about 100 m on the right.

There is no place like Santorini. Once a circular, volcanic island, most of it collapsed into the sea around 1650 BC, after a literally earth-shattering eruption. The whole Minoan city of Akrotiri was buried in ash and there was nothing left but a crescent-shaped rim and a smaller fragment around the world's largest, sea-filled caldera. No human remains were ever found; it is believed that early signs of the imminent danger led the inhabitants to flee the island, though no one knows what their fate was at the end.

Much of the architecture we see today on Santorini has its roots in the 19th century, when the island enjoyed a period of maritime prosperity. In the beginning of the 20th century however, the island's golden days were over, and after a serious earthquake in 1956 destroyed large parts of the settlements on top of the cliff, many people left for good.

The revival of Santorini began in the late seventies, when tourism started to develop on the island. The utter beauty of the caldera, the staggering black, grey and red cliffs rising from the sea, whitewashed villages perched on top, rapidly established its reputation as one of the most romantic destinations in the world.

THE TSITOURAS COLLECTION

Firostefani
847 00 Santorini
Tel. 22860-23747

Most people who know Santorini will agree that Oia is *the* place to stay. The capital Fira is just too much of everything (especially in the summer when during the day, cruise-ship-loads of tourists cram into the narrow alleyways) and the quieter alternative, Imerovigli, though spectacularly crowning the highest point of the caldera, has basically turned into a jam-packed settlement of hotels. But there is also Firostefani, another village right on the caldera. It is at walking distance from the bustling centre of Fira, but infinitely more quiet, and thus perfect if you want to be near the action, but not in the middle of it. And this must have been exactly what appealed to Dimitris Tsitouras, an Athenian lawyer/art collector/jet setter, when he acquired a late-18th century mansion and turned it into a collection of absolutely exquisite houses.

When the Tsitouras Collection opened in 1988, it instantly became the ultimate glam spot to stay on Santorini, and frankly, almost 20 years later, it still is. The houses are fine

examples of the island's historical building style (long and narrow houses partly carved into the cliff side with cathedral ceilings providing an airy ambience). The Tsitouras couple furnished them with carefully chosen antiques and the odd modern, design piece, and then, one by one, turned them into something like a private museum. Every house features precious relics and works of art, ranging from amphora recovered from the depths of the sea and a collection of Tanagra figurines, to original ceramic art work by Picasso.

It may seem a bit unusual to stay in an environment like this. After all, in a museum we tend to whisper rather than talk, and touching anything is totally unheard of. But this is not how things operate at the Tsitouras Collection. Dimitris' young daughter, Eleni, is in charge, and she does everything to make you feel at ease. No one will frown at you if you plummet into the sofa and put your feet up, or if you wander around without shoes. Eleni's style is easy-going and relaxed, and she's more likely to sit and have a drink with you, rather than make you feel you have to walk on eggs. But she is also professional and efficient, and you can be assured that her staff will cater to your every whim.

THE TSITOURAS COLLECTION

Where you'll sleep The Tsitouras collection consists of five houses. The House of Nureyev is for two people, and with its own terrace it offers perfect privacy. The other four houses all open up to a shared veranda, but as there is also the large Maria Callas roof terrace, with plenty of corners to sit, you won't feel you miss your privacy. The House of Porcelain (named after a collection of 19th century Minton and Royal Copenhagen porcelain plates) and the House of the Sea are for up to three persons. The House of Portraits and the House of Winds (which has a piano) both have two bedrooms and can accommodate four and five persons respectively. Each house has its own themed art collection, and if you are the ultimate aesthete, the thing to do is to stay at least one night in each. (There is enough staff to move your luggage around!)

The houses are luxuriously equipped with one or two bathrooms (shower), a telephone, a television and a DVD player, a CD player (with a selection of CD's), an internet connection, air conditioning, a complementary mini-bar, a hairdryer and a safe.

When you feel hungry Breakfast is served as early or as late as you like, and you can pretty much order anything that takes your fancy. For lunch and dinner you can order meals from a light menu (traditional *dakos*, salads, *linguini marina*, Italian style chicken, chocolate soufflé...) and for the ultimately chic dining experience, private dining on the Maria Callas terrace can be arranged (a six-course gastronomic dinner). If you go out for the day, you can ask for a picnic basket to be prepared for you.

Bring the children? Most of the fancy hotels on the caldera of Santorini do not accept children (either for safety reasons or for preserving the peace), but at the Tsitouras Collection, the last place where you'd expect children to be allowed, they are more than welcome. The environment is reasonably safe and so far there has never been a problem with children disturbing the quiet. (Though obviously, this is not the kind of place where you'd let your kids play ball in the living room.) When parents want a moment off they can rent children's DVDs (from a selection of almost 200) and babysitting can also be arranged.

To see and do The Tsitouras Collection is a place where you could easily just sit for hours and marvel at the breathtaking views and the art surrounding you, and simply take in the quiet. But then, it is barely 10-15 minutes' walk to the lively centre of Fira, and a short drive to the island's spectacular volcanic beaches and the archaeological site of Akrotiri. And of course, anything else you may be interested in doing (a speedy private cruise in the caldera or a more stylish jaunt on a catamaran, a visit to a winery, horse riding, you just name it), Eleni will happily arrange it for you.

Good to know The Tsitouras Collection is normally open all year round. Prices for two people start at €440, and they include breakfast, arrival and departure transfer, minibar consumptions and a daily sunset cocktail. Credit cards: all major.

Getting there The easiest way to get to Santorini is by plane. Arriving by boat, however, is a wonderful experience and worth the extra hours spent at sea. Guests are met at the airport or in the port upon arrival.

Costis Psychas loves digging. It all started some 30 years ago, when his parents began the restoration of several, centuries-old, ruined troglodyte houses and stables, on a plot of land they had bought in the late sixties, on the out-skirts of Oia. They opened the tiny Hotel Perivolas, with just four houses, in 1981. When a few years later his father passed away, Costis moved to Santorini and decided to continue the restoration process. Every winter, after the hotel closed, he would work on another house, proving himself a tireless builder, a skilled architect and designer, and most of all, a gifted artist. The original dwellings were tiny inside, but Costis simply dug deeper into the rock wherever he wanted more space, designing on the spot, hand shaping every curve and every bend.

It was a process that took years, and while the digging continued, Perivolas became increasingly famous. It featured in one travel and lifestyle magazine after the other, and got nothing but rave reviews. Every writer passing by was instantly smitten by the supreme elegance of the immaculately minimalist interiors, the exhilarating caldera views, the dramatic infinity-edged pool (the first on the cliff-side), the pleasantly informal, but ever so efficient service and the mesmerising ambience pervading the place. And the thing is, that anyone who has been to Perivolas will confirm every word of praise that has ever been written about it.

It wasn't, however, a craving for fame that drove Costis, but a deep-rooted urge to create. Cringing over the hap hazardous way the new constructions were developing on the cliff, his yearning for perfection grew only stronger, and each house that was added became even more amazing than the previous. After the 17th house was completed, there was a pause of a few years and for a moment it looked like Perivolas was 'finished', though *en passant* a little more digging happened, to make some space deep inside the cliff for a large kitchen.

PERIVOLAS

Oia
847 02 Santorini
Tel. 22860-71308

But Costis had yet to produce his masterpiece, the Perivolas Suite. At the far end of his property was an old (cave) winery that so far hadn't been touched at all. Carving by hand, day after day, for an entire winter, he created something that can only be described as a cave palace. Three areas spread over 140 sq m blend into each other, their arched ceilings reaching up to six metres high in places. From one of its highest points, natural light flows in through a shafted skylight. Further inside, at the back of the cave, there is a space centred around a large, sunk Jacuzzi, and tucked in niches are a shower and a hammam. The almost complete absence of straight lines gives an overwhelming sense of spaciousness. There are no corners, no ends, just soft stretches and smooth curves. The feeling of water is omnipresent, with a swimming pool starting in the bedroom and working its way through a tunnel to the end of the private terrace. I have seen quite a few impressive hotel rooms and suites, but believe me, this place is something else...

After the suite was completed, the digging continued. The next winter, a cave gym and spa room, a sauna and a hammam were added to the complex, and the 19th house was built. It did not turn out as enormous as the Perivolas Suite, but it is also hugely impressive, with a spa-bathroom as large as the bedroom itself. Was this the last one? That is unlikely. And while many small hotels lose at least part of their charm when more rooms are added, in Perivolas "more" means more of everything, and you can only hope that Costis will never stop.

Where you'll sleep First of all, let's get something straight: you don't sleep at Perivolas, you dream. Each house, whether you stay in the smallest studio (which isn't all that small anyway), or in the enormous Perivolas Suite, is breathtakingly beautiful. The stylishly minimalist interiors are white and bright, with pillows and hand woven bedspreads adding dashes of different shades of lavender, blue, and pink. It creates a calm and peaceful feeling, matching the overall

PERIVOLAS

atmosphere at Perivolas. Mod cons like televisions and CD players would be totally out of place in such an environment – a large shower, a kitchen corner and air conditioning is all you get and once you're there, you'll realise you wouldn't want it to be any different.

When you feel hungry For breakfast you will find a well-assorted buffet in the poolside bar (from 8.30 to 11.30). Lunch and dinner are also served here. (The restaurant became fully operational in 2004.) The combination of the stunning setting by the pool and the perfectly executed, sophisticated Mediterranean cuisine is absolutely unbeatable.

Bring the children? Youngsters from 16 years and up are welcome at Perivolas, but chances are that you will enjoy this magical place more if it is just you and your other half...

To see and do You can't come to Santorini and not explore the island's cliff-hanging villages, its amazing volcanic beaches

and the archaeological site of Akrotiri. However, you will also find that when you are staying in Perivolas, you won't feel the urge to go around and do things. The place in itself is so magical, that you might feel like spending all of your time in there. Life is full of hard choices…

Good to know Perivolas is open from early April until the end of October. Prices for a double room start at €370 per night in the low season, and €450 in the high season, including breakfast as well as arrival and departure transfers. Guest facilities are the outdoor pool, as well as a hammam, a sauna, an outdoor Jacuzzi and a gym. You can book massage treatments. It is unlikely that anyone has ever thought of checking in with a dog at Perivolas, but just for the record, they are not allowed. Credit cards are not accepted.

Getting there Perivolas is situated below the road at the beginning of Oia. Upon arrival, guests are met at the airport or in the harbour.

For many Americans, Santorini is the epitome of Greek scenic beauty and a must-visit-once-in-a-lifetime kind of place. But when US born Tony Mosiman came to the island, he felt that one time just wasn't enough. He returned time and again, made friends, and in the end decided to stay, transforming himself in the process from IT manager to restaurateur – together with a Greek partner he opened two restaurants. Next, he started dreaming about having a little hotel.

The opportunity came when a slightly dilapidated captain's house, situated near his two restaurants, was put up for sale. The listed property, built in 1864 by a prosperous ship-owning family, was one of the few historical mansions on the cliff that withstood the 1956 earthquake without as much as a scratch. It was just perfect for what Tony had in mind: a tiny hotel where guests can feel totally spoiled and completely at home.

It took two years to bring the two-storey house back to its former glory and to furnish it with lovely antiques and locally crafted items. During the restoration process, Tony's primary concern was to retain the atmosphere of the old house, and he was careful not to add any frill at the expense of character. As a result, the house has become the perfect low-key luxury antidote to the many flashy hotels that increasingly claim space on the caldera. It is actually one of the very few places that manage to combine impeccable service and elegance with a homey, relaxed and friendly atmosphere.

1864 – The Sea Captain's House has also become one of the few places to stay in Santorini where you truly get the feeling you are in a real house. The two-storey mansion is partly caved into the cliff, while its façade is a combination of a renaissance-inspired upper level, made out of dark, volcanic stone and a more traditional, island style lower level, washed in a creamy colour. The interiors are a blend of characteristic elements of Cycladic cave-houses and of 19th century mansions. The wide plank floors are quite rare for Santorini (you only find these in the mansions built by rich sea captains, who brought the wood on their boats) and the cross-vaulted ceilings, while more representative of the island, are among the highest in Oia.

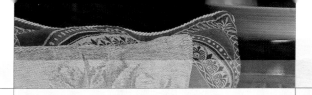

1864 - THE SEA CAPTAIN'S HOUSE

Oia
847 02 Santorini
Tel. 22860-71983

Where you'll sleep 1864 – The Sea Captain's House is a tiny hotel, with only three suites. The Venetian and the Sailing Sea Suites on the upper level are both doubles. The Captain's Suite, on the level below, has room for up to five people. The top-floor suites enjoy the best view, but the Captain's Suite, which used to be the reception/party room in the heydays of the captain's family, is probably the most impressive. Its cathedral ceilings are close to six metres high. The suites have all large, marble-clad bathrooms with Jacuzzis, and are fitted with a television and a DVD player, a telephone, a CD player, a wireless internet connection, a complementary mini-bar stocked with soft drinks, air conditioning, a hairdryer and a safe.

When you feel hungry Eating well is not something you'll have to worry about when you are in Santorini, especially when you stay at a hotel that has its own two excellent restaurants just a couple of minutes' walk away. Ambrosia is the fancier of the two and in this one it is recommended you book a table before showing up. The other one, Ambrosia Nectar, is a place where you can more easily just drop in. If you prefer to eat in privacy, you can order your meals from either of the two restaurants and have them in the mansion. Breakfast is served until early afternoon, the idea being that basically you can ask for anything you're in the mood for.

Bring the children? It is not recommended you come to the Sea Captain's House with kids. The place is simply not suitable for young children, and if you travel with teenagers, you'll be better off in Thira, where all the action is.

To see and do The whole point of staying in a place like the Sea Captain's House is that you shouldn't feel compelled to do anything at all. For some wonderful slow-paced activity, Tony can arrange for you to go on a sailing trip on a 41-foot catamaran, where your participation in the action on board remains limited to sunbathing, eating and taking in the incredible Caldera scenery. If upon return you need

1864 - THE SEA CAPTAIN'S HOUSE

to recuperate from so much activity, you can get a full massage at the mansion.

Good to know The Sea Captain's House stays open all year, but keep in mind that from December to March things are very quiet in Oia, and most restaurants and shops are closed. (But when this is the case, Tony cooks for his guests.) Room rates for two people start at €195 in the low season, and at €365 during the summer months (breakfast included). Facilities at the hotel include a small library, sauna, massage and pedicure treatment. Credit cards: MasterCard and Visa.

Getting there The hotel is located towards the end of Oia, close to the 'sunset castle', just under the main marble-paved pathway that crosses the village. You will be dropped off at a small parking space near the bus stop, where you will be met by Tony. If you arrive with a lot of luggage, your bags will be carried by a strong little fellow called *Taxi Number One*, Oia's only fully licensed donkey taxi.

When you think of Santorini, visions of the caldera, white-washed villages poised on volcanic cliffs, and breathtaking sunsets spring to mind, together with dreams of waking up in a little cave house with exhilarating views over an endless expanse of blue. Sure, the dream exists and it isn't even hard to find, but there is a downside to it: it is a dream shared by many. So anyone who has this image of wandering all alone through the narrow alleyways of Fira, Imerovigli or Oia, occasionally stepping aside to let an old man on a donkey pass, waving *yasou* to the woman watering the flowerpots on her front yard, and smiling at children chasing each other on the village square, is in for a disappointment. You no longer come across these kinds of scenes on the caldera of Santorini.

But here is a secret. Just behind Oia, there is a little village where life hasn't changed; where you hear birds, roosters, church bells and children's voices instead of music from bars and "oh, it is so beautiful" in at least fifteen different languages. It is called Foinikia, and even though it is barely ten minutes' walk from the caldera, it seems like a world apart from it.

Sophia Adamopoulou was only 23 years old when she bought a plot of land with a few wrecked cave dwellings in Foinikia (with money saved from a few summer jobs!). Living in Paris at the time, she didn't have anything specific in mind, but years later, after she moved back to Greece and settled in Santorini, she started rebuilding the houses on her property. Halfway through, she developed the idea to open them up as guesthouses. She created an utterly charming complex of little houses, some with arched ceilings dug into the rock, others in the more cubic Cycladic tradition.

It is only fair to say that there is nothing like Heliophos on Santorini. It is the combination of beautifully styled houses, of the totally unspoilt location, the extremely warm and personal welcome and the more than reasonable prices that make it so unique. Sophia had the good sense to do the interiors in the simple, local style, but furnished and decorated them with heaps of artistic flair. A passionate traveller, she has over the years created a stunning collection of old bits and pieces from all over the world, and an eclectic mix of furniture, objects and artwork give the houses a distinctive, but not overwhelming, exotic touch.

HELIOPHOS

Foinikia,
Oia
847 02 Santorini
Tel. 22860-71886

What is perhaps even more important is that after finishing the houses, Sophia did not hire an army of staff to run the place. She does everything herself. Getting up before dawn every day to meditate while the sun comes up, she spends her days taking care of the houses and her guests, making them breakfast and drinks and sometimes even throwing impromptu dinner parties for them. You can tell Sophia is happy with the life she has here and the good thing is that she is even happier to share it with others.

Where you'll sleep You can take your pick from seven houses, all with a shower (smallish), a television, an internet connection, a refrigerator, air conditioning, a CD player, a hairdryer and a safe. Most of them are for two people, but there are a few that can take an extra bed. Some are like small studios (the smallest has the best sea view of all), while others are more spacious and have an extra sitting corner inside. The suite at the bottom of the property, with a large wooden dining table in the middle of the sitting room and a bed tucked away in a vaulted niche, is an absolute dream.

When you feel hungry Sophia serves breakfast until 11.00, but should you oversleep she's not the type to say "sorry, it's too late". Occasionally she cooks for her guests, but there is no regular restaurant service. The nearest place to eat is just a few minutes on foot, and in Oia, at about 10-15 minutes' walk, you have a large choice of restaurants.

Bring the children? Children are welcome at Heliophos, but keep in mind that there are a few danger points for kiddies who are old enough to crawl or walk around but not old enough to listen to reason, so you will have to be attentive all the time. There are two interconnecting houses that together can function as a quadruple family suite.

To see and do Foinikia is a not a village attracting people who come for a quick fix of breathtaking views, candle-lit dinners and a bit of after-dinner fun. You appreciate it more if you stay a little longer on the island and so you can use it as a quiet base from where to explore the villages on the caldera, the multi-coloured beaches and the archaeological site at Akrotiri.

Good to know Heliophos is open from the end of March until mid or late October. Prices for two people start at €70 in the low season, and €120 in the high season, and they include breakfast. Cars cannot go all the way into Foinikia; they are left at the parking lot at the entrance of the village and from there you walk. Heliophos is barely two minutes on foot from the parking area. Credit cards: Amex, MasterCard and Visa.

Getting there The easiest way is to ask a taxi to drop you off at the parking lot of Foinikia, and have the driver call Sophia so she can help you with your luggage.

Sometimes it only takes one kilometre of road to separate one world from another. Take the seaside village of Makrigialos in the southeast of Crete. Built along a nice stretch of sandy beach it has 'developed' into a small scale tourist resort, with all the advantages and the disadvantages that this entails. It has a picturesque little fishing port, but the more recently added construction is — how shall I put it — rather uninspired. There are a few nice boutiques, but shops selling plastic things to take to the beach are also prominently present. And while there are several traditional tavernas offering honest Greek food, you'll also come across quite a few pizza restaurants and the like.

But follow a dirt road inland, and one kilometre away from the coast you're in Aspros Potamos, a small verdant valley without any construction at all, except for a few clusters of small stone cottages. Farmers from the village of Pefki used to take refuge in them during the olive harvest — we're talking 50-150 years back. They were abandoned at the end of the Second World War and stayed like that until the mid eighties. It was then, long before Makrigialos turned into the tourist hangout it is today, that Aleka Chalkia, a strong-willed mother with an eight-year-old daughter, bought the entire settlement and single-handedly started doing the cottages up. It was a long process, which was later taken over by Myrto, Aleka's daughter, who now runs the place.

The beauty of Aspros Potamos lies in its utter simplicity. The cottages today probably don't look much different from what they did a hundred years ago. Nothing has been modernised and everything reflects the nature around it, from the insulation on the roof and the cane ceilings, to the uneven, whitewashed stone walls inside (with chunks of rock dramatically protruding in some of the cottages) and even the ochre coloured (natural) wash the external walls get every two years.

On the inside, some adaptations were made to provide a few essentials: stone-paved floors (in the old days the floor was just the earth ground), a solar panel that generates enough electricity for a low-voltage refrigerator and a bathroom light in each cottage, gas-fired boilers so you can have a hot shower, as well as gas cooking facilities. And that's it. Staying in Aspros Potamos is the ultimate romantic, back-to-nature experience. In the morning you'll be woken by the birdsong, in the evening you will light candles and oil lamps, and if you come in winter and it is chilly, rather than turning up the heating, you will warm yourself by the fire.

ASPROS POTAMOS

Aspros Potamos
720 55 Makrigialos
Crete
Tel. 28430-52292

Where you'll sleep There are ten cottages, all clustered together. Some are just for two; others are a little larger and can accommodate up to three, four or five people. Each cottage has its own shower (most cottages have the bathroom inside, but in a few it is located right outside), as well as a fireplace and a simply equipped kitchenette. There is no electricity (except for that bathroom light and the refrigerator), but you get candles and oil lamps. It is not a bad idea to bring your own flashlight. Keep in mind that you can't charge your mobile phones in the houses (good excuse to switch them off!), though Myrto will be happy to do it for you in the village.

When you feel hungry Stock up on groceries and you can do your own cooking, either in your kitchenette, or in the shared, wood-burning oven outside. You can of course also eat out in the village, where you can choose between simple tavernas or places that cater to less Greek-oriented taste buds (the aforementioned pizza places!).

Bring the children? This is a great place to go to with children who love the outdoors, especially if they like to go for walks and play in nature. The nearby beaches are very child-friendly. Teenagers will probably appreciate the lively atmosphere at the coast, but may get a little bored staying in a place like Aspros Potamos.

To see and do This spot is for anyone looking for peace and quiet, and for hikers and nature lovers in particular, but it is also ideal for beach bums! You can use your cottage as a base and spend your days on the beach or going around, but it may be even better to get here with a pile of books (and a good companion), and just unwind.

Good to know Aspros Potamos is open all year. The price for two people starts at €35 per night. Credit cards are not accepted.

Getting there The drive from the airport (or port) of Iraklion is quite enjoyable and takes about two hours. First you follow the signs for Agios Nikolaos and Sitia, and about 20 km after Agios Nikolaos you turn towards Ierapetra. From Ierapetra you take the coastal road towards Sitia. After you pass through Makrigialos (about 20 km from Ierapetra) and enter Analipsi, you should look for a small sign on your left for Pefki village. Follow this road and after one km you'll find two small signs. Turn left at the sign for Aspros Potamos and you will find the settlement after 500 m. There is a parking lot.

WHITE RIVER COTTAGES

The sheer back-to-nature experience you get at Aspros Potamos is absolutely great, but what if you prefer to just turn the wall switch on in the evening rather than light the oil lamp, or if you like having a little boost of air-con on a hot day, or want to be able to plug in a charger or a laptop; and how about having a swimming pool practically at your doorstep? If this sounds more like what you are after, you may prefer to stay at the next door neighbour: the White River Cottages. Like the Aspros Potamos cottages, these too were used in the past as a shelter by olive farmers and became abandoned some 50 years ago. They were bought in the late eighties by Vangelis Mavrakis, an economist from Iraklion, who went on to restore and convert them into a wonderful collection of little holiday homes.

The cottages nestle on the hillside amidst olive, carob and pine trees and blossoming oleanders. It is an idyllic setting, matched by the flawless, minimalist interiors. Heavy wooden doors (with huge, old keys to match), white-washed stone walls with bits of exposed natural rock, wood-beamed ceilings, stone-paved floors, old fireplaces (in some cottages), simple traditional wood furniture and stone-built beds overlaid with brightly coloured bed-spreads, make it all just… perfect! The look is clean and uncluttered without feeling sterile, the style is traditional but not folkloristic, and you get a level of comfort that may be without any excess, but it's perfectly adequate.

The cottages are entirely self catering and you don't get the full range of hotel services, but the approach is per-sonal nevertheless. You will be welcomed by Iris van der Kaay, a lovely Dutch woman who will help you with any-thing you might need. But the odds are you won't need all that much: you have your own little dream place to stay, a great swimming pool with terraces and sun beds for lazy days, and a quiet and relaxed atmosphere and nature all around you; so even if you have to get your own drink and prepare your own sandwich, you are still in the ideal setting for relaxing holidays.

WHITE RIVER COTTAGES

Aspros Potamos
720 55 Makrigialos
Crete
Tel. 28430-51120

Where you'll sleep There are 12 White River Cottages. The smallest function as studios and can accommodate a couple, whereas the bigger cottages have a separate bedroom and one or two additional single beds in the living room. The cottages are very correctly equipped with decently sized bathrooms (shower), a neat kitchenette, fans, air conditioning (and heating), telephone, an iron (!), and a safe (against a small insurance charge). Cleaning and change of linen is provided twice a week.

Built on a fairly steep and rocky slope, the cottages are connected by stone paths and steps, but as you can leave your car either at the top of the property, or down near the reception, you won't have to negotiate too many steps. If you get one of the cottages higher up, you will have a view over the sea.

When you feel hungry If you get your supplies in the village you can cook your meals in your cottage (and eat on your private, shaded terrace…). The kitchenettes are very clean and functional, with a cooker with two electric rings, an oven/grill, a toaster and a kettle, and all the necessary pots and pans. And when you don't feel like cooking, you can walk or drive to the village, where you will find plenty of places to eat. Ask Iris for suggestions. If you plan to arrive late at night, it is not a bad idea to pack a few things for breakfast, as upon arrival you will find an empty refrigerator.

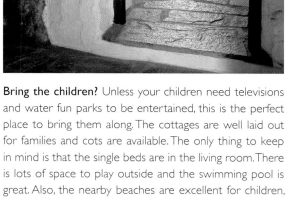

Bring the children? Unless your children need televisions and water fun parks to be entertained, this is the perfect place to bring them along. The cottages are well laid out for families and cots are available. The only thing to keep in mind is that the single beds are in the living room. There is lots of space to play outside and the swimming pool is great. Also, the nearby beaches are excellent for children, with 'castle-quality' sand gently sloping down to the sea.

To see and do If you want to do the swim and lie-in-the-sun thing, you have the pool and nearby beaches at your disposal, and for a bit of activity, you can go hiking in the mountains or through fantastic gorges. If you have a car while you are there (which is recommended anyway) there are some great routes for excursions. You can also ask Iris to make an appointment for you with a shiatsu specialist for a treatment in the privacy of your cottage.

Good to know White River Cottages are open from the beginning of April until the end of October. Prices for two people range from €65 to €115 per night, irrespective of the season. A minimum stay of three nights applies, except in the case of a last-minute booking. Credit cards: Amex, MasterCard and Visa.

Getting there Coming from Ierapetra, you will take the coastal road towards Sitia. After you pass through Makri-gialos (about 20 km from Ierapetra) and enter Analipsi, you should look for a small sign on your left for White River Cottages. After one km you'll find the parking area and the reception of White River Cottages.

Most people who come to Crete do not fail to visit Knossos – the archaeological site with the palaces of the Minoan civilization. Busloads of tourists descend on the site every day, and return to their hotels near the sea in the afternoon. If, however, they drove on a little further, they would discover Arhanes, a beautifully preserved (and protected) village in a lovely rural area that is famous for its wine production. But tourists rarely come this way.

On the outskirts of Arhanes, a 19th century mansion was recently converted into a small hotel. It consists of six (attached) houses, facing an inner courtyard with a swimming pool and the cutest little *kafenion*. Quite surprisingly, for such a small place so full of character, Villa Arhanes is actually part of a bigger hotel chain (the Maris Hotels), but this is something you barely notice while you are here (the only give-away is the Maris Hotel bathroom products). The houses are furnished in a no-nonsense, traditional style, which may be lacking a personal touch, but they do have plenty of charm, while comfort is guaranteed.

The personal touch is definitely present in the welcome you get at Villa Arhanes. Yannis Gonianakis, who has been running the little hotel since it opened in 2001, takes care of it as if it was his own. He used to work in big resort hotels, where, as he has put it, "you have a smile on your face, without really smiling". At Villa Arhanes, where he is the receptionist (without a reception), the manager, the administrator, the waiter and the cook, all at the same time, the smile on his face is sincere. He is a perfect host and takes a real interest in his guests. Proud of his origin, he loves to show what Cretan hospitality is all about, and you should absolutely let him spoil you with some of the meals he cooks.

All in all, Villa Arhanes is a wonderful place to stay, with a very peaceful and almost surreal ambience. In fact, when you walk through the entrance door, it feels like you step into the opening scene of a theatre play about people living in a village. You can just imagine the characters stepping out of their houses to meet up in the small *kafenion*. It is rather a privilege to become part of this play where fortunately, all that is expected from you is to relax, have a cool drink by the pool and try some Cretan delicacies. And thankfully, there are no spectators, but just you and a few other guests.

VILLA ARHANES

Ano Arhanes
701 00 Iraklion
Crete
Tel. 2810-390770

Where you'll sleep Villa Arhanes has two one-bedroom houses for two persons and three houses with two bedrooms (for up to six persons). They are spacious and well laid-out with a fully equipped open kitchen, a sitting room with a fireplace for the winter (only the Dionysis House does not have one), a large bathroom (with a shower), a telephone, an internet connection, a television, air conditioning, a hairdryer and a safe.

When you feel hungry Since you have a fully functional kitchen at your disposal you may want to cook a few meals yourself, but you should not miss out on those that Yannis prepares. A great Cretan breakfast is served in the morning from 7.00 to 10.00, and if you ask for it in advance, you can also get lunch and dinner at the little *kafenion*. Yannis is an excellent cook (he learned everything from his mother) and prepares all dishes with locally produced organic ingredients (and lots of herbs), following the oldest Cretan recipes; his meals are as healthy as they are delicious.

Bring the children? Children are welcome at Villa Arhanes and the layout of the apartments is indeed very practical for families (and cots are available). Kids will love the pool, but as the houses are quite close to it and people come to Villa Arhanes to enjoy the quiet, it is recommended not to let them 'run and scream' around the pool all day.

To see and do Villa Arhanes is the perfect place to stay if you want to visit the Minoan palaces of Knossos in the quiet of the early morning before the tour buses arrive (or later in the day after they leave), because the site is only at about a quarter of an hour's drive from the mansion. Otherwise, it is a wonderful spot to unwind and relax by the swimming pool and to explore the lovely countryside. In the evening you will surely enjoy the lively atmosphere in the village.

Good to know Villa Arhanes stays open all year round. (It is in fact a fantastic place to go to in the winter: you will be able to see Knossos at its best, without the tourists, and the houses are large enough so you won't feel cramped if it is cold outside.) Prices for a couple start at around €85 per night, excluding breakfast. It is possible to book half- or full-board packages. Dogs are not allowed. Credit cards: all major.

Getting there To get to the village, follow the signs for Knossos from Iraklion. After you pass Knossos, you follow the road and look out for signs for Arhanes. You will first pass through Kato Arhanes, and then you will enter (P)ano Arhanes, where after the first few buildings, you will see a sign to your left for Villa Arhanes. Follow the signs (they take you around the village) and after quite a few turns you will see the hotel on your right.

Situated in the centre of Panormos, a small and quiet coastal village, Villa Kynthia is a mixture of a family-run *pensione* and a small, luxury retreat. Look at it from the street, and you see a charming, unpretentious village inn, accessed from a slightly eighties-style café-bar. Open the back gate and enter the enclosed garden, and you're in a small oasis of tranquillity and well-being: terraces with potted flowers, sitting corners in the shade of a massive, century-old pine tree and a swimming pool lined with wooden sun beds. It is this unique combination of a low-key, unpretentious atmosphere, and reclusive luxury that makes Villa Kynthia a very special place to stay.

The village itself is also quite exceptional. In the 19th century, it was a flourishing trading port. For the past 25 years (or so) it is as if time has stood still, and Panormos has – miraculously – escaped the fate of so many other Cretan seaside villages: ugly tourist development. Surely, there are some – only a few – bigger resort hotels on the outskirts of the village, but they are out of sight, and, as they provide full board to their customers and thereby keep them on their premises, there has not been an 'invasion' of foreign tourists in the village. So Panormos has remained quiet and unspoilt, with a handful of grocery stores and craft shops, and a few small cafés and tavernas with tables out in the pedestrian streets.

Villa Kynthia sits at the beginning one of those streets, just a couple of minutes' walk from the port and the adjacent (very nice) sandy beach. It is a late 19th century merchant house which in the eighties was almost torn down to make way for a supermarket. Thankfully, Korinna Milaraki, who was (and still is) involved in the cultural activities in the village, stepped in, together with her brother Andonis, with a much better idea. They bought the place, restored the house and turned it into a very charming little hotel with just five rooms, an attractive dining room and a bar/café. (Admittedly, the latter could do with a little revamping.) Villa Kynthia is the kind of place that never needed much advertising: it has always left such a positive impression to its guests, that the word of mouth has done the trick.

VILLA KYNTHIA

Panormos
740 57 Rethymno
Crete
Tel. 28340-51102

Where you'll sleep Villa Kynthia consists of two rooms, two suites and one small apartment. Rea, the apartment, has a charming double bedroom and a small sitting room with two single beds. It opens up directly onto the garden. The other four rooms are on the first floor of the house. The two suites (Artemis and Odysseas) are quite striking with wooden floors and ceilings, romantic murals and gleaming antique furniture. The Artemis Suite looks out over the garden and has a canopied double bed, comfy sofas and *trompe l'œil* wall paintings. Odysseas has the advantage of a balcony. The other two first-floor rooms (Pandora and Nefeli) are smaller but they are cosy and comfortable. Pandora has its own veranda. All units have a nice en suite bathroom (only Nefeli, for the time being, has its bathroom just across the corridor), a telephone, an internet connection, a television, a refrigerator, air conditioning, a radio and a cassette player, a hairdryer and a safe.

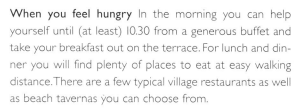

When you feel hungry In the morning you can help yourself until (at least) 10.30 from a generous buffet and take your breakfast out on the terrace. For lunch and dinner you will find plenty of places to eat at easy walking distance. There are a few typical village restaurants as well as beach tavernas you can choose from.

Bring the children? If you have the feeling that your children will 'fit' in the calm ambience that reigns in Villa Kynthia, you will very much enjoy being here with them. With the beach nearby, the pool in the garden and the easygoing village atmosphere, families will definitely feel in the right place. The Rea apartment which is accessed directly from the terrace is particularly handy for people with children, as is the combination of Nefeli and Pandora which together can be used as a family unit. Cots are available (for a small charge).

To see and do You are probably going to spend most of your time relaxing by the water (the swimming pool or the sandy village beach), enjoying the quiet village ambience, but Panormos is also 'strategically' located for taking excursions. Rethymno is only a short drive away, as is the ceramics village of Margarita, and even Knossos makes an easy daytrip.

Good to know Villa Kynthia is open from early April until the end of October. Room rates for two persons start at €90 in the low season, and at €115 in the summer. Dogs are not allowed at the hotel (with the exception of Andonis' dog that occasionally comes and visits at weekends). Credit cards: MasterCard and Visa.

Getting there Follow the national road towards Rethymno and turn off at the exit for Panormos (about 55 km from Iraklion). There are signs for Villa Kynthia in the village.

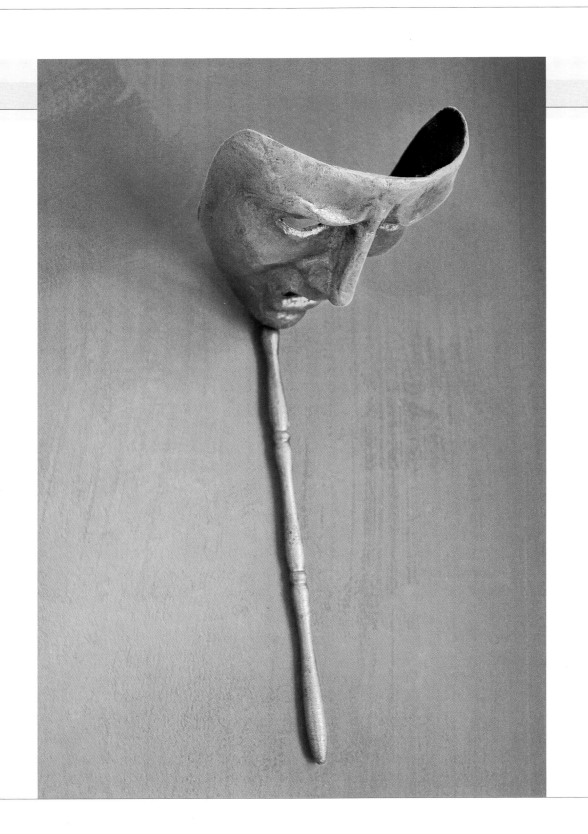

Low-fat, low-carb, low-this, low-that – while the debate about the 'perfect diet' seems never-ending, Cretans must wonder what all the fuss is about. Their ancestors figured out the key to health and longevity thousands of years ago, simply eating the goods their land offered them: lots of fresh fruit and vegetables, virgin olive oil, cereals, herbs and honey, and smaller amounts of dairy products, meat, fish and wine. It is a simple diet, which thanks to the quality of the ingredients and the inspired way they are combined, is as tasty as it is healthy.

There is no doubt that if you spend holidays in Crete and you are lucky enough to have a few genuine Cretan meals, you'll be tempted to try and reproduce some of the wonders you've eaten back at home. You can always pick up a cookbook at the airport, but if you want to learn the real tricks of the trade, you should stay at Rodialos where during 'alternative holiday programmes', you can discover the ins and outs of Cretan cooking.

Rodialos is not a hotel or guesthouse. It is a house. You can't just check in for a few days and take some cooking courses *en passant*. You either rent the entire property or otherwise you enrol in a holiday programme. Renting the house with a bunch of friends must be great; but to come here for a week and be guided by owner Mary Fragaki and her childhood friend and professional cook, Jenny Vassilaki, through the world of the Cretan cuisine, is an experience that is hard to match. You will shop in local markets, harvest organically grown fruits and veggies, collect herbs from the fields, choose fish, fresh off the fishermen's boats, and then, you will learn how to transform all these, the purest of ingredients, into beautifully tasting meals, using ancient recipes adapted to modern lifestyles.

For Mary, an economist by training and a TV producer by profession, Rodialos is a return to her roots and also an expression of her passions: art, creation, ecology and natural lifestyles. The house, a recent construction on the rocky shore just outside Panormos, is a contemporary interpretation of the Minoan palace. Built with natural materials around a small patio shaded by a pomegranate tree (*rodialos*, in ancient Greek, means "pomegranate from the sea"), its colours are reminiscent of the palaces of Knossos, and with large windows looking out over the sea, and doors opening to terraces all around, the house seems filled with energy, while exuding an atmosphere of calm and an aura of optimism.

It is in this spirit that Mary started inviting groups to the house and developed courses. The cooking has become a way to both satisfy her creative urge and to honour her Cretan heritage, and it brings her immense joy to share this with her guests. Her attitude is relaxed and easy-going. The 'programmes' are flexible and adaptable to what the guests feel like doing and learning. Nothing is planned in a strict manner – in the morning Mary and her guests decide together how the day will be filled. This spontaneous approach has led to many impromptu parties, concerts and dances.

RODIALOS

Panormos
740 57 Rethymno
Crete
Tel. 28340-51310

Where you'll sleep There are four bedrooms in the house. The master bedroom is a splendid large bedroom-cum-bathroom. Its windows are small but it has a large skylighted ceiling and at night you can gaze at the stars up above from your bath. The other three rooms are smaller and rather basic and share two bathrooms (both with shower).

When you feel hungry If you come to Rodialos for a 'Cretan cuisine' programme you are in for a continuous culinary feast. If you are renting the house however, you won't totally miss out on this, because Mary will come by at least once to prepare a *grand repas*. Otherwise you will have the large open kitchen at your disposal and you are free to harvest some organic veggies from the garden. If you do not feel like cooking you can just walk over to Panormos. When you first arrive at Rodialos, the refrigerator is stocked with ingredients for breakfast.

Bring the children? The courses at Rodialos are not for children and while they last, all rooms are kept for participants. If, however, you rent the entire property, your kids are more than welcome and they will enjoy the space in and around the house. Young children should not be left unsupervised around the garden as there are some steep cliffs plunging down into the sea.

To see and do If you come to Rodialos for an 'alternative holiday programme', you will be kept as busy as it pleases you, not only with cooking lessons, but also, if you wish, with yoga, tai chi, massage and shiatsu sessions, as well as sailing, mountain biking, walks and excursions. If you rent the house to yourself, you can arrange for the occasional cooking lesson or yoga, massage or shiatsu session. To go for a swim you can climb down the rocks beneath the house to the sea (there are some nice flat rocks for sunbathing) or you can walk for a couple of minutes to a tiny beach where you will have easier access to the water.

Good to know The house is available all year round. Usually programmes are organised in May, June and September. In all other periods (also in between the seminars) the house can be privately rented. Prices for the seminars start at €75 per person per day, on the basis of a shared double room. The price per night for the entire house is €250 in the high season, or €210 in the low season (for a maximum of eight persons). Normally, the minimum rental period is two weeks. Facilities in the house include the fully equipped kitchen, a washing machine, a telephone, an internet connection, a television and a CD player. Credit cards are not accepted.

Getting there Rodialos it about 800 m west of Panormos (off the national highway about 20 km from Rethymno, or 55 km from Iraklion). The terracotta-coloured house sits all by itself and is hard to miss, but new arrivals are met in the village.

THE HOUSE OF KOURITON

Staying at the House of Kouriton is quite an experience. It is not the place to go to if you are looking for a romantic little getaway where you close your door and you don't get to see anyone else but your beloved. But if you are interested in Cretan customs and you'd like to experience what it is like to stay in a historical village house, you will like it a lot.

When you walk into the house, you may wonder for a moment if you are in the right place, because it definitely does not look one bit like an ordinary guesthouse (which indeed it isn't). Welcomed by an intense scent of herbs, you enter a décor that could come straight out of a 'country living' coffee table book. It is country cosiness taken to the extreme. Bunches of dried herbs and flowers dangle from the wood-beamed ceilings, shelves are stocked with jars with homemade preserves and bottles of aromatised olive oil, a large wooden table is covered with history books, freshly picked flowers and herbs, and another table displays a collection of very beautiful ceramics.

Hostess Anastasia Friganaki is a retired history schoolteacher with wide-ranging interests (philology, architecture, Minoan culture, local traditions, arts and crafts…), which she is keen on sharing with others. And this was exactly what she had in mind when she bought the listed stone-built country manor. The building, dating from 1750, was in bad need of repair, but Anastasia saw its potential to become a place where people could get a glimpse of the traditional ways of life on Crete.

The design and the construction are purely Cretan. Unlike many other historical buildings on the island, the house does not display any Venetian or Turkish influences. It is what people used to call a *fournospito* – a house with a big bread oven inside where bread was baked not only for the (relatively wealthy) family that lived there but also for the workers in the family's employ. Another distinctive feature of the house is its labyrinth-like layout – a remarkable

Minoan inspiration found in 18th century Cretan architecture. Even though the house is not huge, you can easily get disoriented by the structure of the interconnected rooms and the confusing stairways. All in all, the combination of an intriguing building with an inspiring hostess, make Kouriton's House a fascinating place to spend a few days.

THE HOUSE OF KOURITON

Tzanakiana, Margarites
740 52 Rethymno
Crete
Tel. 28310-92359

Where you'll sleep The six bedrooms (one double and the rest for three or four persons) are furnished with locally crafted furniture (there's an antique brass double bed in one of the rooms) and are decorated with dried flowers, little icons and artworks, and ceramics. They have a nice traditional and cosy look, though they are a bit dark. They have a small refrigerator and a television. The en suite showers are tiny!

When you feel hungry Eating in the House of Kouriton is all part of the immersion into Cretan tradition. In the morning pots of herbal (dittany) tea will welcome you (though there is coffee too!), together with a selection of local products such as *dakos*, olives, yogurt, free-range eggs, fresh butter, homemade marmalades and thyme honey. If you are hungry during the day, Anastasia will be delighted to let you taste her homemade 'spoon sweets' or other little traditional bites, though for your meals she will direct you to the village restaurants. They all have their own specialty and it would be a shame not to try them. Sometimes Anastasia too, will cook for her guests (and you can help and learn a few tricks of the trade), but you have to ask her in advance.

Bring the children? Children are very welcome. During the winter, Anastasia regularly lets in school children on day excursions, and gives them brief seminars about local traditions such as ceramic production and the various uses of herbs. So, if you come and stay with your children you can be sure that the lady of the house will teach them a thing or two.

To see and do Though of course you are free to just hide away in a little corner with a book, Anastasia is not the kind of person to easily leave you on your own. She will encourage you to explore the sites in the area (monasteries, Byzantine churches, caves) – often she even accompanies her guests to give them a private tour. She also organises activities 'at home', ranging from spontaneous cooking classes and demonstrations on how to make aromatic olive oils, to seminars on Cretan traditions and ceramics workshops. Whenever she hears there is a *panigiri* (a traditional feast at a church to celebrate its saint's name day) or a Cretan wedding in the area, she offers to take her guests there herself.

Good to know The House of Kouriton is open all year. From mid-July until the end of August the price for a double room is €100; during the rest of the year prices start at €70, including breakfast. Credit cards are not accepted.

Getting there Follow the national road between Iraklion and Rethymno and turn off at the exit for Panormos (about 20 km from Rethymno, or 55 km from Iraklion). From here you should follow signs for Perama. In Perama, turn right and continue straight until you see a sign to the left for Margarites. The House of Kouriton is in Tzanakiana, the village just before Margarites. There is no sign, but it is hard to miss the impeccably restored stone house right above the road.

Set within centuries-old fortifications and built amphitheatrically around its picturesque old harbour, the town of Hania is a living testimonial of Crete's turbulent past. Its history dates back to the Minoan period, and throughout the centuries it has been under Roman, Arab, Byzantine, Venetian and Turkish rule. The old Venetian harbour is always full of life. The only lull is in that short interval between the ending of the last animated discussions on the terraces lining the waterfront, and the arrival of the first fishermen that come to take their brightly painted *caiques* out to the sea. The narrow, pedestrian backstreets are a tad quieter, but with little boutiques and art shops, cafés and small restaurants, they too are usually bustling with life.

Hotel Suites Pandora is situated towards the end of the Venetian harbour, in a quiet dead-end street. You access the 1870 neoclassical house from a charming courtyard shaded by an enormous lemon tree. The entrance hall is quite striking: one of its walls is entirely covered with a colourful modern fresco, with marble sculptured chairs that are literally part of it! With the exception of the courtyard and the roof terrace (with stunning views over the harbour), there are no other common areas where you can sit – this is a hotel you use more as a base to explore the city, and less as a place to pass your days or stay for long. It doesn't provide full services: breakfast is served in the morning and during the day there is always someone at the reception, but at night you just get the key to enter the building. It does, however, have an undeniable charm and if you are looking for accommodation with character, you won't be disappointed.

SUITES PANDORA

27-29 Lithinon St.
731 32 Hania
Crete
Tel. 28210-43588

Where you'll sleep The eleven rooms and suites are light, airy and elegant in their décor. All of them are equipped with an en suite shower or bathroom, a telephone, air conditioning, a refrigerator and a safe. The suites have a sitting room, a little kitchen unit and one or two bedrooms. The rooms that overlook the water are the most attractive, but at night you might sometimes get the noise from a nearby nightclub. If you feel that the occasional throbbing won't bother you (or you have good earplugs) you should ask to stay in Aphrodite or Dias, the one-bedroom suites with a large private veranda overlooking the old port.

When you feel hungry Breakfast (fresh orange juice, perfectly boiled eggs, bread buns, home-baked cake) is served from 9.00 to 10.30 on the roof terrace, and you have an almost unlimited choice of restaurants at walking distance.

Bring the children? The question is not so much whether the hotel is a good place to come with children, but, rather, whether the town is appropriate for them. Though most of the alleyways in the old city are car-free and thus relatively safe, you probably shouldn't spend more than one or two days in Hania with small kids. Anyhow, teenagers with some interest in history and culture, or (more likely) shopping and nightlife, will enjoy the town.

To see and do The old town of Hania is a place where you could easily spend several days wandering around the narrow alleyways and sitting by the sea. Your walks will take you past the old fortifications, Turkish hammams and minarets, churches and monasteries, and several museums worth a visit (the Archaeological Museum and the Naval Museum are particularly interesting).

Good to know The hotel is open from early April until late October. Prices for a double room start at €85 in the low season, and at €100 in July and August. They include breakfast. Credit cards: Diners, MasterCard and Visa.

Getting there From the central Sindrivani Square in the old town of Hania, facing the sea, turn right into Kanevaro Street and take the first left at Lithinon Street.

Metohi Kindelis is a beautiful, centuries-old farmhouse just outside Hania. The estate has been in use during the past 400 years for olive and fruit production. Manolis Kindelis grew up on the farm (he only left for a few years to study in Italy), and has been working it for the past two decades. Some years ago, he decided to open it to guests. The idea itself wasn't all that original – agro-tourism is definitely on the rise in Greece – but the way he went about it was. His concern was not how to fit the maximum number of rooms at minimum cost (as unfortunately it often goes) but quite the opposite. He started with just one unit, converting the old olive press into a beautiful, spacious guesthouse, and the land in front of it into a garden, complete with a swimming pool. He did it all with such finesse and good taste, that his one-room 'hotel' became an instant hit.

Enjoying the company of his guests, Manolis decided to also do up the old living quarters of the farmhouse and opened a second guesthouse. Both units stand out because they are done with the greatest respect for the historical character of the farm, without however being too traditional. They almost have a designer look (though everything is Manolis' own vision) and the comfort level equals that of the best hotels.

Obviously there are no staff dashing around the premises (unless you count a handful of farm workers who quietly go about their business). Manolis is usually there, and while he is helpful and kind, his presence is discreet. There is no restaurant, but you have your own kitchen. There is no room service either, but your refrigerator is stocked with drinks and a bottle of wine, and should you want something fruity, you are welcome to collect strawberries from the field or pick peaches, oranges or apricots. How much more perfect can it get? Frankly, the only thing that is not absolutely perfect in Metohi Kindelis is the distant hum of the road, but the singing of the birds (and at night the croaking of the frogs) is definitely a lot louder.

METOHI KINDELIS

Perivolia
731 00 Hania
Crete
Tel. 28210-41321

Where you'll sleep The lower house, Danae, in the old olive press, is essentially one large space (with a double bed in a cosy niche that can be shut off from the rest of the room). The look is tastefully bare: exposed stone walls, arches, beamed ceilings, an old fireplace and simple wood furniture; the feel is traditional yet modern, minimalist yet warm and cosy. It is a great space, matched by the private garden that lies in front of it: a large lawn, a swimming pool and a shaded dining corner.

There's no need to be jealous though if you stay in the upper house, Kynthia, where you have your own garden just 30 m away from the house. Here you also have a pool, a terrace and even a summer kitchen and a music installation, so that if you wish, you can spend your entire day by the pool. Inside, Kynthia has a double bed in the main room and a small extra bedroom with its own little shower. Ochre coloured walls and stylish furniture give it a warm, country-style feel.

Both houses can accommodate a couple and two children, and have a fully equipped kitchen, an en suite bathroom with shower and bath, a telephone, a CD player with an extensive music collection, a hairdryer, and, upon request, a television.

When you feel hungry Throughout your stay Manolis supplies the ingredients so you can make your own breakfast and if you do some shopping, you can prepare all other meals in your house. There are also a few places to eat in the village of Perivolia, at just a 15-minute walk, and many more in the Venetian harbour of Hania, only a few kilometres away.

Bring the children? The rural setting, the gardens and the swimming pools make Metohi Kindelis a heaven for kids. Danae is great if you come with very young children because of the easy walk-in walk-out situation (but keep an eye on your toddlers so they don't go near the pool unsupervised). With slightly older kids you may prefer to stay in Kynthia which has a separate bedroom with bunk beds. Cots are available and babysitting can be arranged.

To see and do Metohi Kindelis is a great little hideaway to just do nothing, but it is also an excellent base for getting around. If you are in the mood for some shopping or nightlife, you have the bustling old town of Hania (almost) at your doorstep. You feel like a day by the sea? There are several nice beaches nearby (15 minutes by car), and if you drive on, you will find some of the most beautiful beaches in Crete. And for a complete change of scenery you also have the mountains – if you bring your hiking shoes you should definitely walk through the famous Samaria Gorge (the starting point is at about 40 km).

Good to know Metohi Kindelis stays open all year but keep in mind that there is no central heating and during the winter you will have to use the wood burning stoves (and in Danae the fireplace) to keep warm. During the winter months a minimum stay of three nights applies. Prices for two persons start at €130 per night; during July and August the price for two goes up to €200. There is just a small extra charge for children over ten. Credit cards: MasterCard, Visa.

Getting there The farm is situated off the road that goes parallel to the main road towards Kissamos. If you arrive at the port or the airport of Hania, you will be met there; otherwise you will be met in Hania and accompanied to the farm. Manolis will give you a map and directions, so that next time you will manage to find your way to the farm by yourself as well. But be careful: simple as that may seem, it does require a bit of practice. (Yes, I got lost the first time I drove back alone!)

When I hear about eco-tourism, little alarm bells start ringing in my head. I instantly have visions of eating funny vegetarian food, served by people wearing grey woollen socks and sandals, who talk to me about animal rights and make me feel guilty for not always taking public transport. Milia, a 400-year-old settlement of stone cottages, hidden in the forested mountains of western Crete, is a prize-winning eco-tourism venture, but there are no grey-woollen-sock-types involved. It is totally off the beaten track and it definitely offers a 'back to nature' experience, but the philosophy behind it is simple, reasonable, and most of all, admirable.

Milia was established as an environmentally sustainable operation long before 'eco-tourism' became the buzzword it is today. It all began when two local families decided to rebuild the ruins of the 16th century cottages that had been abandoned by their original inhabitants, after a cholera plague around 1650. The families had the idea to turn them into guesthouses and to combine this activity with organic farming, reforestation, and environmental protection. It took them about ten years to create a fabulous little get-away, where electricity is generated from a combination of solar and hydro energy, wood-burning stoves are used for heating (and for any tree cut at least one other is planted), and all waste is recycled.

You don't need to be a hard-core nature lover to appreciate Milia. The setting, for a start, is just beautiful: green, green and more green, as far as you can see, and not a single building in sight. The cottages, all made from natural stone and local wood, blend in perfectly with their surroundings, and inside, they are cosy and utterly country-stylish. Fitted with locally crafted wood furniture and cast-iron stoves, and finished off with starched linen curtains, cream-white duvets and a few candles tucked away in little corners, they ooze charm. It all combines beautifully with the bare stone walls (with natural rocks protruding in many of the houses) and floors made of wood and smoothed concrete.

Staying in Milia is memorable. When you arrive the first thing you notice is the silence. You're in nature. A few rules signposted at the parking lot are straightforward: no littering, no flower cutting, no noise making, no hunting and no campfires. But that is as far as regulations go. You are simply asked to realise you are inhabiting unspoilt nature and this you have to respect. You accept the basics, and you will have a wonderful time. The people running Milia are young and easy going, and happy to share their place with you and show you around, but they are never intrusive. Most of them have been here since the beginning of the operation and even though what they are doing is often hard and difficult work, they have no plans to leave. Their love for the place is immense, and as you will see, it is infectious.

MILIA

Vlatos
730 12 Kissamos
Crete
Tel. 28220-51569

Where you'll sleep The stone houses of Milia are divided into 13 units, most of them for two people, but there are a few that can sleep one or two children as well. They offer basic comfort, but you certainly don't have to 'rough it'. Each unit has its own en suite bathroom with a (hot) shower. For heating there is a wood-burning stove, and some units also have a fireplace. At night you just turn the light switch on, but there are no sockets in the rooms, so you might as well leave your hairdryer at home. Mobile phones can be charged in the main building.

When you feel hungry The nearest restaurant is six km away, and if you want to do some shopping you have to add another six. But in Milia you'll never have to go hungry: it has its own restaurant (cum-sitting room). With just a few exceptions, everything you eat or drink is prepared with homegrown products. For breakfast (served till 10.30) you can try mountain tea or coffee with fresh goat's milk, home-baked bread, fresh eggs, local honey, strawberry and

blackberry juice and yogurt. For lunch and dinner there is always a variety of dishes. There are some good choices for vegetarians, but meat is served as well. Sometimes people are shocked to hear that this also comes from the farm, but at least here you have the assurance that the animal in question has had a good life.

Bring the children? If your kids need at least a swimming pool and a television to be happy, then this is not the right place for them. (Remember: it is not easy to recharge the Gameboy here!) But if they're the types who like playing in nature and will fancy participating in some of the farming activities (feeding the animals or milking the goats), they will have a fantastic time. Coming with a baby may not be so easy (impossible to handle a pushchair over the paths) but if you do, cots are available.

To see and do You may be worried that you'll get bored in a place that is so remote. If your interests are nightlife and shopping, your concern is justified. But if you enjoy walking, mountain biking, cooking, bird watching or simply relaxing with a book or a game, then you will find all you need here. Also, by car you can easily make a day excursion to Elafonissos, one of the most beautiful beaches in Greece.

Good to know Milia is open all year. Prices for two people start at €60 per night, breakfast included. Note that the parking is 150 m far from the houses, but when you arrive you can bring your car closer to unload. Credit cards: MasterCard and Visa.

Getting there From Hania, you take the national road towards Kissamos. A few kilometres before you reach Kissamos, you take the turn-off for "Elafonissos – Hania Old Road". Follow this road in the direction of Elafonissos (the villages you pass through are Kaloudiana, Voulgaro and Topolia). Some kilometres after you pass through the Topoliano Gorge, you turn right towards Vlatos, from where you follow signs for Milia. The last two km are on a dirt road, cut into the steep mountainside – you are not to do this drive if you're not 100% sober!

Elia is a 200-year-old farmhouse that sits all by itself amidst olive groves and fruit trees in the hills of western Crete. The setting is rural and ever so quiet, with the sea only a ten-minute drive away. The house and the 15 acres around it belong to George Digrintakis, a young plastic surgeon practising in Athens. The property has always been in his family, but after George's grandmother passed away, the house stood empty for many years, and it slowly started to crumble into dereliction.

When George realised that something had to be done and that a simple facelift would not salvage the house, he decided to go for a major "reconstructive surgery" and carry out a complete renovation. With, evidently, an eye for aesthetics, and with the same dedication he must apply in his regular profession, he transformed the decaying old farm into a beautiful guesthouse. He was very careful not to compromise on the character of the house and indeed it has kept its lovely, traditional, country feel. He then went on to build a swimming pool (fortunately at a safe distance from the house) and he also added a small spa centre on the premises.

After George opened his guesthouse he still had one issue to solve: who was going to run the place? Though he found it increasingly hard to tear himself away from the little haven of peace and tranquillity he had created, he couldn't just give up his surgery practice in Athens. A shrewd man as he is, he invited his close friend Maria to come and stay for a while. As he knew she would, she fell in love with the place the moment she arrived. When he suggested her to stay on and take over the management she didn't even have to think about it – she was thrilled.

Elia has become the kind of place that is so peaceful and soothing, that the moment you arrive you feel at home. You will sleep in a room that offers the perfect combination of warm traditional aesthetics and comfort, and even luxury. Even the lightest sleepers will have a solid night's rest here: the mattresses are just perfect and the silence is complete. Days can be spent in the flower-filled gardens and on the terraces with their many little corners shaded by fruit trees, just chilling out with a book. Service is friendly and personal and the atmosphere is totally calm and relaxing.

ELIA

Ano Vouves
730 06 Kolymbari
Crete
Tel. 28240-83056

Where you'll sleep There are nine cosy and comfortable rooms, named after the trees and flowers you find in the gardens. Most are doubles, but a few can accommodate one or two children as well. They are all different, some with stone-built beds, others with romantic canopied or old iron beds. The rooms open up directly to the garden and have either a private veranda or a sitting corner nearby, that you can consider your own. All have an en suite shower or bathroom and are equipped with a mini-bar, a television and air conditioning. If you are in a position to choose, ask for the large and romantic Elia Suite – it is wonderful.

When you feel hungry A help-yourself, traditional (and very healthy) Cretan breakfast is served in the morning till 10.30. During breakfast time you will be asked if you want to have dinner in the evening (dinners are home-cooked and unless you ask for something specific you will be served the plat du jour). For lunch you can order light dishes like salads, sandwiches and typical Cretan dakos (delicious rye bread with chopped tomatoes, feta cheese, topped with oregano and the best olive oil in the world).

Bring the children? Some people are worried that their children may get bored in a place where you cannot walk to the beach or to the ice cream vendor. Maybe teenagers would prefer to be a little closer to the action indeed, but for younger children, Elia is just one big playground, with so many centuries-old olive trees to climb and 'secret' little places to hide. They will have a great time. There are a few family rooms and cots are available.

To see and do Relaxation should be the main theme of your stay in Elia, and a good way to start, is to take your pick from a full spa menu, offering 30 different one- to five-day programmes. A Turkish bath, aromatherapy and massage will sound familiar, but you can also opt for a mud therapy with enzymes in a steam bath, seaweed compresses, or a body peeling with salt, bran and olive oil, to name just a few options. There are even special spa programmes for couples.

So it might be tempting to simply not move from Elia during your stay. But then again it would be a shame to be lazy all the time. Some of Crete's most amazing beaches are at reasonable driving distance; you should spend at least one afternoon and evening in the old town of Hania, and why not, schedule an early rise one day to make the traverse of the stunning Samaria Gorge...

Good to know Elia is open all year. Prices for a double room start at €110 in the summer (€80 during the low season), and they include breakfast. Facilities at Elia include a sitting room with a fireplace, gardens and terraces, an outdoor swimming pool and the spa centre. Credit cards: MasterCard and Visa.

Getting there On the national road from Hania to Kissamos, take the exit for Kolymbari and Spilia, and turn left towards Spilia. Pass through Spilia following signs for Ano Vouves. You first come across Kato Vouves, and as you enter Ano Vouves, turn left (i.e. don't go up the hill). After you drive past a few houses, you stick to the left, and after a few hundred metres you will see a sign on your left for Elia.

There are a few things that Kythira doesn't have: frequent ferry connections, well-developed public transport or much of a tourist infrastructure, not even any neighbouring islands to hop over to. But, it is exactly *because* it lacks these things, that in fact it has it all. The roughly 280 sq. km island stands all alone, south of the Peloponnese. It may only be a one-hour boat ride from the port of Neapoli, but Neapoli is a five-hour drive from Athens. That is why it doesn't get island hopping backpackers or Athenian weekenders (except for the handful of people that fit on the little plane that makes a daily return flight). Instead, it attracts people who come to stay longer and enjoy the quiet atmosphere of this truly unspoilt island.

The picturesque south part of the island is probably the most frequented, with a lot of greenery, a pretty *hora* crowned by a ruined castle, and the scenic bays at Kapsali. Further up, the landscape has a raw beauty reminiscent of the Cycladic islands (though the forested area all the way up in the north is different again), with unspoilt villages topping the hills. One of these villages in the centre of the island is Pitsinades, a tiny, car-free settlement with only ten year-round inhabitants. There are quite a few totally ruined buildings here (with great potential…), but also several beautifully restored houses.

It is quite hard to imagine that 20 years ago Guesthouse Pitsinades was in the same condition as all those ruined houses that make up about half of the village. The guesthouse consists of two buildings that used to belong to a large family. They were abandoned in the fifties, when the owners emigrated to Australia (along with a large part of the island's population). It took Lena Yannakaki, who bought the property in 1985, seven years to restore the two houses. She followed their original layout, retaining all the beautiful old elements (like the stone window frames, the arched doors and the ovens and fireplaces) and adding some traditional details, such as pebble mosaics on the floors. A nice little courtyard with greenery and flowers completes the picture – this is a wonderful place to stay if you are looking for total peace and quiet in a charming environment.

PITSINADES

Pitsinades
Aroniadika
802 00 Kythira
Tel. 27360-33877

Where you'll sleep There are six rather traditionally styled rooms, several with arched ceilings. The décor is low-key but not plain simple — a few antiques and little arty touches nicely complement the authentic feel of the rooms. Five of them are doubles (with twin or double beds — some can take an extra bed), and one is a large triple. They offer simple comfort but the essentials are there: a large shower to freshen up and a refrigerator to chill your drinks. The rooms have no air conditioning but the thick walls keep everything pleasantly cool.

When you feel hungry A small help-yourself-style breakfast awaits you from 8.30 to 11.30. No other meals are served in the guesthouse, but in any case, most people prefer to spend their days on the beach and go out for dinner in the evening. One kilometre away there are a few small

places where you can eat (there is nothing in Pitsinades), and Lena and her husband will gladly give you directions to some other excellent restaurants on the island.

Bring the children? Children are very welcome at the guesthouse. Especially if they are young, it is great to let them roam freely in the village without having to worry about cars. They'd better, however, be capable of amusing themselves, because there is not any form of organised entertainment around. The white sandy beach with lagoon-like shallow waters at Diakofto is perfect for families.

To see and do Kythira is a place to come in order to enjoy the peaceful island life: there are lots of great beaches to choose from (some easy to reach, others involve a bit of walking but they are worth the effort!), the villages are lovely and unspoilt, and if you enjoy hiking, you will be thrilled to discover the green north and south of the island. There is not too much going on in terms of nightlife, though if you need to, you can get your fix of late night reverie in Kapsali.

Good to know Guesthouse Pitsinades is open from the Easter holidays to the end of September. During July and August (and the Easter period) the price per night for two persons is €80, and at other times it is €60. Breakfast is included. Dogs are not allowed. Credit cards are not accepted.

Getting there Kythira can be reached by plane (one daily flight from Athens) and by ferry (daily connections from Neapoli, and less frequent services from Gythio and Kissamos on Crete). When you arrive at the port at Diakofto, you just follow the road, until you reach Aroniadika, where you turn right on the island's main north-south road, in the direction of Agia Pelagia. After about 100 m, in a double bend, you turn left towards Pitsinades (one km). You can leave your car just before the village and continue on foot (for only one or two minutes): you walk into the village right where the big pine tree is, then turn right into the first alley, and you will see the guesthouse a little further on your right.

Due to its relatively isolated position, Kythira, unlike so many other Greek islands, has not been spoiled by tourism; as a matter of fact, it has hardly been touched by it. The whitewashed *hora* (the main village) of Kythira, situated near the island's southernmost point, competes in beauty and authenticity with many of the hilltop *horas* in the Cyclades, and yet, nobody has exploited this to some commercial benefit. There are just a few small cafés, shops, rental rooms and guesthouses.

Nostos is a small guesthouse on the central alleyway right in the middle of the *hora*. Dating from the mid-19th century, the listed building used to be a family home. On the ground floor, there's a charming little café and, on the other side of the alley, a quaint antique shop (which is not part of the guesthouse).

The café functions as breakfast room, lounge and reception at the same time. Its old-style furniture and decoration give it a pleasantly romantic-traditional feel. Indeed, owner Niki Foraki, who inherited the building from her grandfather, consciously created a slightly nostalgic ambience (and then called it Nostos, Greek for nostalgia). While I was having my breakfast on Sunday morning, a small group of local women dropped in for a coffee and some gossip after church (while in all probability their husbands were seeking out a smoky *kafenion* for a stronger drink). They fitted the picture perfectly.

NOSTOS

Hora
802 00 Kythira
Tel. 27360-31056

Where you'll sleep The bedrooms are all on the first floor, accessed from a separate entrance. Usually, an entrance door opening directly to a flight of stairs means bad news – chances are that it will lead you to a bare first-floor corridor with numbered doors, into the kind of rooms where you sleep, shower and then get out of as fast as you can.

But that's not what Guesthouse Nostos is like. You can tell right away that the white-painted, creaky wooden stairs must lead to a well-kept hallway – and they do – and that behind the doors, carrying names rather than numbers (the rooms are named after winds), you are going to find accommodation with character – and indeed you do.

There are six double bedrooms in total, all equipped with a mini-bar, a telephone, air-conditioning and a hairdryer. Most have parquet floors (some painted), nice timbered ceilings and antique furniture. The en suite bathrooms are small, but more than adequate. The nicest room is Zefyros – it is the largest of all, and the only one with its own veranda. The other rooms are a little smaller but also appealing, though they have no place to sit outside.

When you feel hungry A nice breakfast is served in the adorable little café, where during the day you can also order drinks and small snacks. In terms of restaurants, there is nothing worth mentioning in the *hora*. In the main alley there is only one place to eat, but sadly, it mostly serves *souvlakia*, of dubious quality. So it is better to hop into your car or on your bike and try to find something in Kapsali or in the nearby villages.

Bring the children? Even though Nostos (and the *hora* in general) may not be a typical family place, it is perfectly suitable for a not-too-long stay with children. (For longer stays, it is better to be somewhere where children can easily run in and out.) With the exception of Zefyros, the rooms cannot take extra beds (cots are possible though), but there are two double rooms – one with a double bed and one with twin beds – that can interconnect.

To see and do The *hora* of Kythira is a great place to stay if you want to be close to the liveliest part of the island (the Kapsali bays) and the best beaches, and at the same time be part of a typical Greek picture-postcard setting. In the village you shouldn't miss the 500-year-old Venetian castle; the best time to walk up there is just before sunset. Otherwise, don't expect much in terms of entertainment from the *hora* (a drink, a stroll and a bit of shopping – that's about it), but it is a charming base from where to explore the rest of the island.

Good to know Nostos is open from Easter until the end of September. Prices for a double room start at around €60 in the low season (excluding breakfast), and €90 in July and August (including breakfast). Dogs are not allowed. Credit cards are not accepted.

Getting there Kythira can be reached by plane (one daily flight from Athens) and by ferry (daily connections from Neapoli near the south-western tip of the Peloponnese, and less frequent services from Gythio in Mani and Kissamos on Crete). When you arrive at the port of Diakofto, you follow the road until you reach Aroniadika, where you turn left towards Kythira (the *hora*). Park your car at the entrance of the village, and walk along the main alley towards the castle. You will find Guesthouse Nostos about halfway through.

Built on the top of a steep rock in the sea, connected to the mainland via a long causeway, the ruined fortress of Monemvasia and the fortified 'city' – now a small community – that lies beneath it, are a monument to the Greek turbulent history of the past thousand years. This Byzantine/Venetian city castle, near the south-eastern tip of the Peloponnese, holds an inescapable magic – imagine something like France's Mont St Michel, but less touristy and on a smaller scale.

When you pass through the narrow entrance gate to the so-called Kastro (Greek for "fortress" – this is how locals refer to the settlement), you step into a different world. There are no cars or even mopeds. The few shops are either endearingly old fashioned or arty and tastefully done. A handful of restaurants and cafés, all small and cute, constitute the only nightlife spots on the rock. And, most importantly, there is not a single architectural *faux pas*. The Kastro is under strict archaeological protection and the only type of construction allowed is restoration.

Guesthouse Ardamis is among the oldest and most beautiful buildings in the Kastro. It is estimated to be at least 800 years old and was used as a governor's office during the Venetian rule and the Turkish occupation. Carefully restored, the soberly-romantic interiors display beautiful historical elements (the white marble well in one of the rooms is particularly impressive), that, combined with the owner's own stylistic touches, create an environment that is as awe-inspiring as the Kastro itself.

ARDAMIS

230 70 Monemvasia
Tel. 27320-61886

Where you'll sleep The guesthouse offers six comfortable rooms (doubles and suites for up to four or five persons). With the exception of the 'tower' room, they are all very spacious, and they open up directly outside, so they are perfectly suited for an independent stay. The Royal Suite is not located in the house itself, but above the Ardamis café in the main alley. All rooms have an en suite shower or bathroom, and are equipped with coffee and tea making facilities, a telephone, a television and a hairdryer.

When you feel hungry In the main alley, you will find several places to eat – anything from breakfast or a day-time snack, to an afternoon tea with sweets or a late night dinner. In the winter the options are fewer, and if you don't feel like going out, pizza boys can deliver your dinner at your doorstep! Also, if in the morning you prefer a lazy awakening, you can order breakfast to your room from the Ardamis café.

Bring the children? Children are welcome but keep in mind that you have to walk down a few steps to get to the guesthouse, so it is not such a good idea to come with kids that are too little to walk.

To see and do Ardamis is a wonderful place to stay for a romantic mini-break. If you come in the summer, you will have the chance to enjoy the water (there are steps that lead to the sea). Though the Kastro does not offer the full entertainment package, you will like strolling around the little alleyways and visiting the ruined Byzantine castle on top of the rock.

Good to know Guesthouse Ardamis is open all year. Prices for a double room start at about €130 per night (breakfast not included). The parking area is a few minutes on foot, over uneven paths and steps. Dogs are not allowed. Credit cards: Amex, MasterCard and Visa.

Getting there It is an approximately four-hour drive from Athens to Monemvasia (via Korinthos, Tripoli and Sparta). After you cross the causeway, you leave your car at the entrance gate of the Kastro and continue on foot (there are signs). It is just a few minutes' walk from the gate.

When she was a little girl, Anna Traïforou loved roaming around in the Kastro of Monemvasia. She was one of only a handful of children growing up surrounded by the medieval fortifications, with the cobbled alleyways and ruined houses as their playground. For Anna, the Kastro was also a storybook. Every house or ruin had its own history, and the little girl was all ears for the stories the older inhabitants had to tell. There are probably very few people like her right now in the Kastro, who are so intrinsically linked to the place, and know so much about it.

But Anna was not just a spectator. Years ago her father started restoring old ruins to turn them into guesthouses. As she grew up, she gradually became the 'soul' of the houses, furnishing them with charming antiques and traditional pieces, and giving them names according to their history and her own childhood memories. One house she called Papous (Greek for "Grandpa"), in memory of the old man who used to live there (one of Anna's story tellers), and another one, owned by a wealthy Turkish family in the past, she called Saray, Turkish for "palace".

The latest undertaking is the Hammam; this consists of two old, restored houses, built around a courtyard with the remains of a 500-year-old Turkish hammam. The plan is to bring the hammam back to its former glory and make it operational again. Also, under the houses, empty space areas were discovered that must have been miniature indoor swimming pools, and if Anna gets her way, these too will be usable again in the foreseeable future. So even though for the time being the Hammam consists simply of some charming rooms and suites to stay, a few years from now it will be an amazing little spa on the castle rock.

BYZANTINO
AND HAMMAM

230 70 Monemvasia
Tel. 27320-61254

Where you'll sleep You will stay in a historical house, and of course no two rooms are the same. Most are doubles, but there are also triples and quadruples, as well as double suites. It is best to ask lots of questions when you book, because each room has its own characteristics. Some have a sea view, while others have a view of the Kastro (which in some cases means no view). Some rooms have a private veranda, others don't. Bathrooms vary from miniscule and fairly basic to large and fitted with mod cons such as hydro massage. Some rooms are situated on the central alleyway – convenient if you want to minimise the walking, but, especially in the summer, you will hear the voices of people passing by beneath your window. Other rooms are further away and are quieter, but you'll have to walk a bit on uneven paths and go down some steps to get to them (though nothing too dramatic). All rooms have a small refrigerator, air conditioning and a telephone. Some rooms have a television as well.

When you feel hungry There are several small cafés and restaurants to eat in the Kastro and even in the winter you will always find a few places open. Byzantino has its own little café where you can go for breakfast à la carte, but you can also have it delivered to your room (from 7.30 onwards).

Bring the children? Children are welcome, and several rooms are well laid out to accommodate families. (Cots are available.) Chances are that your kids will love the slightly mystical atmosphere of the Kastro, but keep in mind that it is not the kind of place that is suitable for a prolonged stay with small children. For a few days, however, it is wonderful.

To see and do Most people consider Monemvasia a destination in itself, and stay just a few days to wander around in the Kastro (and in the summer take an occasional dip from the rocks), to visit the ruined Byzantine castle on top of the rock and to relax. But you could also use Monemvasia as a base for longer holidays and spend a few days on nearby beaches, go hiking in the beautiful mountainous inland, and spend a day on Elafonissos, a small island famous for its stunning beaches. (Elafonissos is just off the west coast of the eastern peninsula of the Peloponnese, a one-hour drive and a short crossing by ferry).

Good to know Byzantino and Hammam are open all year. Weekends and holiday periods are considered high season and prices for a double room start at €90; at all other times prices start at €75 per night. Breakfast is not included. Credit cards: Diners, MasterCard and Visa.

Getting there The easiest way to reach Monemvasia from Athens is to drive (via Korinthos, Tripoli and Sparta). The journey takes approximately four hours. You have to leave your car at the entrance gate of the Kastro and continue on foot. You will see the reception of Byzantino and Hammam in the main street, on your left, not far from the gate.

Sometimes, while travelling through the Greek countryside, to check out new hotels and guesthouses, I wonder why there are so few that have managed to 'get it right'. I've come across so many newly opened places where an effort has clearly been made to create something nice, but it just didn't work out the right way. Call me choosy, but when I spend a weekend somewhere away from home, at the very least I want the place where I stay to look pretty (and it really doesn't always need to be breathtakingly beautiful): I'd like my room to be in competition with my own bedroom at home, I'd like to have a comfortable bathroom, to find a nice place to hang out, to be welcomed by someone who is friendly and helpful, and generally, to enjoy the atmosphere.

Somehow, it is not that easy to find places that score on all counts. Geodi, a recently opened guesthouse in the mountains of Lakonia, does. Without being an awe-inspiring, absolutely amazing sort of place, it has all the characteristics of a pleasant and friendly guesthouse, conceived to make you feel at home. In addition, it enjoys a fantastic quiet location just outside the adorable village of Arna, at an altitude of about 800 m, on the eastern side of the Taygetos mountain range, with exhilarating views over the mountains and hills straight out to the sea. You can walk to the village square which most of the year, looks rather dozy, especially in the winter when it is often covered in snow, but comes to life during the summer months, when entire families with roots in Arna come for their holidays and spend late evenings on the square dining and chatting.

Eleftheria Vavouli had spent many of her summers in Arna (her mother was born in the village) when she and her partner Christos Papageorgiou decided to open a guesthouse. They found an abandoned property, dating from 1928, with an unusual and rather sad story behind it. In the late thirties, the owner, a father of two young boys, went hunting, and was killed by his own gun that went off when he tried to hang it on a tree. His wife was devastated and emigrated with her children to the United States, and the house, its doors and windows boarded up, stood empty for many decades. (After a while, villagers used it as a shelter for the occasional goat or sheep in the winter.)

GEODI

230 54 Arna
Lakonia
Tel. 27310-20703

When the couple eventually bought the property some years ago, the house was in such a poor state that the external walls were the only part worth keeping. The interiors had to be redone from scratch. They approached the restoration process with a healthy dose of pragmatism and did not try to recreate old-looking interiors, nor did they turn them into something fashionably modern. Instead they found the middle ground and created a warm and welcoming atmosphere, even though everything is unmistakably new. The warm atmosphere is further enhanced by the reception you get from Anna, the local hostess of Geodi. (Christos and Eleftheria live in Athens, but spend many weekends in Arna.) Anna keeps the house in an impeccable state and, all smiley and friendly, she will take care of you with genuine enthusiasm during those precious few days you have to relax in the mountains.

Where you'll sleep Geodi has four elegant-romantic bedrooms on the first floor, and two rooms, more rustic in style, accessed from the garden. Each (fruit themed!) room has its own character. The two most attractive rooms (Apple and Lotus) are large doubles with balconies and a view over the mountains. All the rooms have fine bathrooms (with a shower) and are all equipped with a telephone, a television and a hairdryer.

When you feel hungry In the morning (from 8.00 to 11.00) you are greeted by a nice buffet with, among other things, omelettes, smoked meat, homemade marmalades, yogurt, dried fruits, cake and fresh orange juice. Later in the day, you can ask Anna to make you an omelette or a cold snack, but for your meals you will have to walk (or drive if you feel slack) to the square.

Bring the children? Geodi offers a pleasant, family-friendly environment and your children are very welcome here. Some of the bedrooms have a third bed, and in the (newly constructed) cottage there is a room on two levels that is ideal for families with two children. Cots are available.

To see and do While the area is great for outdoor action, there are not many organised activities as of yet. With a good map at hand and a comfortable pair of shoes, however, you will have plenty of opportunities for wonderful walks and hikes. Geodi is also a good base for visiting nearby churches and monasteries, and for making day excursions to Mani and the remnants of the Byzantine city of Mistras.

Good to know Guesthouse Geodi is open all year. The price for a double room is €130. Breakfast is included. Dogs are not allowed. Credit cards: MasterCard and Visa.

Getting there Follow the road from Sparta towards Gythio. About 18 km after Sparta, turn right towards Potamia, and follow signs for Liantina, Gorani, Vasiliki, and Arna (22 km on secondary road). If you come from Gythio, you should follow signs for Sparta, and after roughly 8 km (in the village of Egies) turn left towards Petrina and follow signs for Arna (you will pass through Melitini and Agia Marina).

A visit to inner Mani, the middle peninsula of the southern Peloponnese, is always a somewhat mystical experience. This is the land that throughout Greece's history, foreign occupiers never quite managed to control. *Maniates*, men and women alike, have always been known for their fiercely independent spirit. Some hair-raising stories exist not only about their ferocious battles against the Ottoman rulers, but also about bloody family feuds. Just like its people, the landscape of this southernmost part of the Greek mainland comes across as stark and forbidding, but the spectacular coastlines and barren mountain ranges, dotted with small clusters of fort-like tower-houses, never fail to captivate those passing through.

Close to the southernmost tip of Mani lies Gerolimenas, a tiny fishing port. Its development dates back to 1870, when a local businessman foresaw that the small sheltered bay would make an ideal trading centre for the area. He constructed a stone house and several warehouses right by the water and they became the base of a flourishing business. Five generations later, two brothers, Alexander and Aris Kyrimai, turned a page in the family history and transformed the property into a unique hotel.

The conversion of the old family house and the adjacent warehouses into their current state was no easy task. A few small buildings were added, creating a castle-like complex of little stone houses and towers connected by stairways and terraces. The interiors further enhance the distinct character of the place and offer a perfect balance of style, comfort and warmth. Fireplaces in the large sitting room and restaurant are used most of the year round.

KYRIMAI

230 71 Gerolimenas
Mani
Tel. 27330-54288

The moment the sun comes out, however, even mid-winter, doors to the terrace open up and people sit outside. It is this easy flow between the indoors and outdoors that makes Kyrimai a destination as much for the summer as for the winter. The seafront location and the swimming pool make it an ideal place to just relax, swim and get a tan, while the warm country-style interiors make it wonderful for a winter break.

Alexander and Aris probably don't see much of each other these days. They take weekly turns looking after the hotel, and usually greet each other somewhere along the way between Athens and Mani. Only during the holidays they both stay in Gerolimenas, when they are also joined by their father and often other members of the family. And this is another asset of Kyrimai: while it is a fully professional operation and you will be looked after by capable staff (though not fluent in English), at the same time you get the feeling that this is a family-run hotel.

Where you'll sleep The 21 stylish bedrooms and suites (sleeping two to four persons) are spread in different parts of the complex; some are on the top floor of the waterfront warehouse, others are in the stone houses that lie behind it. One suite extends over three levels of a little tower (ask for this one only if you don't mind going up and down the stairs). The typical Mani architecture doesn't allow for big windows and not many rooms have a full sea view, but there are plenty of terraces to make up for it. This way also, the rooms stay pleasantly cool in the summer, while they have a warm and cosy feel in the winter (and most have a fireplace you can use). All rooms have a telephone, an internet connection, a television (with DVD players in the suites), a refrigerator, air conditioning, a hairdryer and a safe. The superior rooms and the suites have a Jacuzzi.

When you feel hungry The restaurant of Kyrimai is a major draw. Usually, the Greek countryside is not where you should go looking for sophisticated, modern cuisine. For most small hotels, food is a mere afterthought, if there is anything served at all. (Usually, local tavernas do the job.) Things are different in Kyrimai, which is quite a culinary destination. Exquisite meals are served in an elegant setting by the pool or in the candlelit dining room. The breakfast buffet (served every day until 11.00) could do with some originality, but the lunch and dinner menus offer a great variety of refined, creatively combined dishes, derived from Greek, Italian and French recipes, which the young chef executes to perfection.

Bring the children? Mani is not a typical family destination (no ice-cream vendors on every street corner and no abundance of sandy beaches for building sandcastles). But your children will love staying at Kyrimai (mine did!), especially if you make them believe it is a real castle

KYRIMAI

(it has the looks). The only thing your little ones may not appreciate is the menu which is really designed for grown up taste buds; it is advisable to ask the restaurant staff in advance if they can prepare some kid-friendly dishes for your children. Also, parents of young children will need to keep a watchful eye on them because of the many stairs, the different terrace levels and the waterfront location.

To see and do Mani is an area to simply take in, rather than to run around touring site to site. Wandering around its many stone tower villages is a great experience (Vathia is a must). Also, the caves of Pirgos Dirou are among the best known in Greece and definitely worth a visit. There are several nearby coves and bays with lovely beaches; the nearest is five kilometres away. But keep in mind that this intriguing peninsula is not the place for beach bums, but for those who like to walk, explore and discover in peace and quiet. If you drive all the way down past Vathia, you can make a wonderful walk to the Tainaron lighthouse, at the southernmost point of the Peloponnese.

Good to know Kyrimai is open all year round. The summer months (mid-May to mid-September) and holiday periods are considered high season. Prices for a double room start at €80 in the low season and €95 in the high season; suites start at €180 and €200 respectively. Facilities at Kyrimai include a main sitting room with a fireplace and television, a room with billiards, and of course, the outdoor swimming pool. Credit cards: MasterCard and Visa.

Getting there Inner Mani is about 300 km from Athens, but you should count four to five hours for the drive. From Korinthos, follow signs for Tripoli (all motorway up to this point), and from there go on towards Sparta, Gythio, Aeropoli and finally Gerolimenas. After turning off the main road towards Gerolimenas (about 25 km after Aeropoli) you will find Kyrimai at the end of the village on the right.

In contrast to the untamed wild beauty of the Inner Mani, the Outer Mani that lies to its north is much more friendly and lush in appearance. Set against the backdrop of the Taygetos mountain range, the area is one of the most scenic in Greece (though of course the country has many!). The landscape is marked by hills covered with olive groves and punctuated by cypresses, lovely tower house villages, wild oleanders lining the winding road south, tiny Byzantine churches, and a beautiful coastline with emerald green waters. It has remained blissfully unspoilt and is still relatively undiscovered – the tourism that makes it to this out-of-the-way corner of Greece is generally the 'good kind': people looking for natural beauty, tranquillity and a few sights rather than beach entertainment and nightlife.

A little rest in a beautiful environment was precisely what Maria Malliri had in mind when, about ten years ago, she came to Kardamyli on holidays. She found just what she was looking for, and even some more: not only did she fall for the area, she also found the love of her life, Giorgos Giannakeas (the son of Lela, owner of the 'famous' Lela's Taverna in Kardamyli). After her holidays were over, Maria vowed to come back; she did, and in the end, she stayed. As Maria and Giorgos started their life together, they began to think about building a small hotel on the beautiful plot of land on the hill overlooking Kardamyli, which belonged to Giorgos. Saddened by the development which was increasingly scarring the nearby beachfront village of Stoupa, the couple was determined to do it right, and they opted for a small group of natural stone

houses, designed to fit in harmoniously with their surroundings. Giorgos has always been very serious indeed about preserving the beauty of the area. He runs a voluntary organisation that cleans up the litter left by less considerate travellers on the roads and walking paths – an initiative that is quite rare for Greece. He also operates the country's only privately owned fire-engine (he brought it from Austria) in which he sprints away whenever there is a fire to be put out. Talking about a boyhood dream come true!

NOTOS

240 22 Kardamyli
Mani
Tel. 27210-73730

The couple succeeded in creating a wonderful, peaceful little getaway. Set in well-kept gardens, the houses are lovely to look at, and a quiet and friendly ambience pervades the whole place. Inside, they look fresh and inviting, pleasant and unpretentious. They are done in an unfussy, honest style: tiled floors, soft-coloured walls, wooden ceilings, light colours, hand-designed (and handmade) pine furniture, and simple, slightly arty decoration. There is no particular 'style signature' (if anything, it has something of a modern Scandinavian flavour), but it is all done in good taste and the houses have a very nice, clean and airy feel, just perfect for uncomplicated holidays.

Where you'll sleep Notos consists of ten open-plan studios and four apartments. The studios have a double bed or twin beds, and the apartments have a bedroom with a double bed

or twin beds, and an open plan living room with a sofa convertible into twin beds. Each unit has its own shaded terrace or veranda, an open kitchen and a very decent shower (the white-tiled, clean look), and is further equipped with air conditioning, a telephone, a television, an internet connection and a hairdryer. If you come in winter, you should ask for a studio or an apartment with a fireplace.

When you feel hungry As you have your own kitchen, you could do all your cooking yourself. The kitchens are very correctly equipped, though they have no oven (just two cooking elements). But since you're on a holiday, why bother? You can order breakfast any time after you wake up and you will get a large tray with bread, eggs, fresh juice, marmalades, cake, cereals and yogurt with fruits and honey delivered at your doorstep. For lunch and dinner you can go to Elies (700 m from Notos), a charming beachside taverna run by Giorgos' brother, where you can enjoy some excellent food in the shade of olive trees. In Kardamyli, you should try Lela's taverna, a definite 'classic' in the village, run for over twenty years by Giorgos' mother.

Bring the children? Notos is a nice place to come with children, even though there are no specific facilities – there is no pool and it might be a little too far to walk to the beach (and especially back – it's uphill). But the apartments are well laid-out for families; there is plenty of space to play; and the atmosphere is family-friendly.

To see and do Notos attracts three kinds of guests. Summer guests come for relaxing beach holidays, in spring and autumn Notos is a favourite among hikers, and during the winter months, Athenians like to come here for a few days of absolute peace and quiet. The opportunities for walking and hiking in this beautiful area are indeed numerous, and walking routes are clearly indicated by different coloured marks. They vary

from easy half- to one-hour walks in the foothills of the Taigetos Mountains, to more serious hikes, notably the six-hour trek through the Viros Gorge. Giorgos is quite a hiker himself and will be happy to give you advice, provide you with maps and arrange pick-up transport for you.

Good to know Notos stays open all year. The price per night for a couple is €85 in the low season, and €100 in the high season (beginning of July to mid-September). Breakfast is not included. Credit cards: Amex, MasterCard and Visa.

Getting there Kardamyli is situated about 35 km from Kalamata. (The town is a good four-hour drive from Athens and in summer there are international charter flights to Kalamata.) To get to Notos, you have to drive from the village in the direction of Kalamata. The first kilometre of road is a straight stretch. Just before the road bends to the right, you will see a sign for the hotel to the left. Notos is at the end of this 800-metre dead-end road.

If you like easy-to-reach but scarcely visited mountain spots, the village of Isari in Arkadia will appeal to you. It is a painless two to three-hour drive from Athens, but as most people are drawn to the villages just a little further north (Dimitsana, Stemnitsa…), the existence of Isari hasn't really registered yet.

Admittedly, it is not as picturesque as Dimitsana and the like, but it has a pleasantly laid-back and authentic feel to it, and the surrounding area is beautiful. It is the kind of village where Athenians, seeking some tranquillity in their free time, have second homes, rather than a place where the masses go on weekend excursions.

Kostas Filandros and his wife Elena, who live in Athens with their two children, also thought that Isari was a lovely place for a weekend house. But after they bought the almost 150-years-old farm house in the village, they decided to turn it into a small guesthouse. They had to carry out a complete renovation that lasted several years, and finally, in 2005, the charming Arhondiko Isari opened as a guesthouse. It is set in a quiet spot, in a garden, with a sweeping vista over the mountain and hilltops all the way to the Messiniakos Gulf. Inside, it is cosy and homey, with an inviting sitting room on the ground floor and bedrooms spread over two floors. Kostas and Elena, who are there most weekends, are helped by a local couple in the day-to-day running of the guesthouse, and, all new and fresh in the business, they are keen to please and take the best care of their guests.

ARHONDIKO ISARI

222 00 Isari
Arkadia
Tel. 27910-21101

Where you'll sleep Arhondiko Isari features 11 snug bedrooms: nine doubles (with either double or twin beds), one triple and one quadruple. They are tastefully decorated (warm colours, country-style and antique furniture), but the double rooms are on the small side (one is very small!). They are nice little cocoons to snuggle up in bed with a good book on a cold winter day, but otherwise they are too small to really hang out. The rooms on the top floor, set under the sloping roof, are particularly cosy, but as the windows are tiny, they don't have a view. All rooms have an en suite shower, a telephone, a television, a refrigerator and air conditioning.

When you feel hungry You can have breakfast from 8.30 to 10.30 (or later…). It is either served to your table, or, when the guesthouse is full, you can help yourself from a buffet with, among other things, two types of bread, pies, ham, yogurt, cake and biscuits, and eggs on order. The orange juice will be freshly squeezed for you. In the evening it is possible to have a hearty, home cooked dinner with dishes like *fasolada* (white bean soup) and traditionally cooked meat, but only if ordered in advance. Otherwise, there are two decent places to eat in the village just a couple of minutes away on foot (one proper restaurant and a simpler place serving small traditional bites, called *mezedes* in Greek).

Bring the children? Children are welcome, but keep in mind that you can't put extra beds in the double rooms (you can get a cot and it will just about fit). If your children are young, you will be comfortable in the triple or quadruple room; otherwise you can also take adjacent rooms. In the summer it is not a bad idea to ask for rooms at the ground floor, from where you can step out directly into the garden.

To see and do You can go for wonderful mountain walks and hikes in the immediate surroundings of Isari. The nature here is beautiful and will tempt even those who would not normally walk further than the first street corner. You could also use the village as a base for sightseeing (there are several small archaeological sites in the area), for outdoor activities like rafting and river trekking, and even for the occasional day on the beach (about one hour by car).

Good to know Arhondiko Isari is open all year, but the winter months are considered high season. Prices for a double room are between €80 and €120 per night, depending on the period and the length of stay. Breakfast is included. Dogs are not allowed. Credit cards are not accepted.

Getting there Follow the motorway from Korinthos to Tripoli and continue in the direction of Kalamata. After you pass Megalopoli, turn right towards Horemis and follow signs for Isari. Right after you pass the village centre (consisting of a church and a *kafenion*) you will see a sign for Arhondiko Isari on your left hand.

Faster cars, better roads, higher incomes – it is no surprise that spending weekends in the countryside has become about as common for Athenians as it has been for New Yorkers, Londoners and Parisians for decades. But in the absence of luxury log cabins, grand country mansions or *auberges de charme*, the Greek urban escapees had, for a long time, to settle for simple hotels without any luxury, grandeur or charm.

Having spent quite a few dreadful weekends himself in hotels *sans charme*, Kyriakos Griveas was among the first to start filling this gap in the market when, in the late nineties, he transformed a bland village hotel in the mountains of Central Greece, into a stylish "Country Club". It became such a hit that within a few years he applied the same recipe to several other places, thus creating a miniature "Country Club" chain.

The secret of success of the Country Clubs is a straight-forward, but for Greece quite innovative, formula. The ingredients are a beautiful location, a great level of comfort, a stylish decoration bearing a clear signature (a blend of classic, traditional, homey and ethnic elements) and professional, efficient staff. This concept is the antidote to the increasingly hyped idea of agro-tourism where guests must get the feeling they are staying on a farm. No such pretence here. You are in the countryside, but you don't have to dress down because you have left the city, or go for long walks and get mud on your shoes (though if you want to, you're in the right spot for that too!). On the contrary, no one will look surprised if you are wearing your Sunday best because that happens to be your style,

and if your idea of enjoying the countryside is to take in the views from the terrace.

HELLENIKON COUNTRY CLUB

220 22 Ellinikon
Arkadia
Tel. 27950 31700

The Hellenikon Country Club is located on a sunny spot on the mountain slopes just outside the village of Ellinikon, at an altitude of 680 m, overlooking the plain of Megalopolis. With only ten rooms, it has the smallest capacity in the Country Club family, though it is much more spacious than you'd think. The common rooms – a sitting room, a dining room, a room to play cards and an elegant meeting room – are so large that guests barely feel they are actually sharing them.

Where you'll sleep The rooms (nine doubles and a suite, extra beds possible) come in four different styles – Rhapsody, Roman White, Hunter and Montana – a reference mainly to the wallpaper patterns and the warm colour schemes. They are furnished in a classic hotel style, and the thick carpets, the wallpaper and the heavy curtains and bedspreads give them a somewhat urban look. Bathrooms are great and the rooms are equipped with a television, a telephone, an internet connection, a mini-bar, a hairdryer and a safe, and they all have a balcony with a view.

When you feel hungry If you are a fan of big breakfasts, you are definitely in the right place. You will be welcomed in the morning (until 10.30) by a buffet with everything ranging from croissants and *pains au chocolat*, boiled eggs and omelettes to yogurt, nuts and dried fruits, fresh juice and fruit salad. You can also order your breakfast in bed (for an extra charge). For lunch and dinner you can order from a 'light menu' (sandwiches, salads, cold plates, etc), and there is also a taverna at walking distance.

Bring the children? Children are absolutely welcome. The smart aspect of the Country Clubs is in no way such, that could make families feel snubbed; quite on the contrary, a few happy children's voices are very much part of the 'scene'. And after all, there is space enough for everybody so you never get the feeling that children get in the way.

To see and do Did I create the impression that Country Club guests tend to stay inside and deny the fact that they have left town? Maybe some do, but most people end up being seduced by the wonderful surroundings. There are indeed great many options for outdoor activity, varying from sight seeing, simple walks or a swim in the nearby Lousios River, to more serious action like river trekking, hikes through the Lousios Gorge and white water rafting.

Good to know The Hellenikon Country Club is open all year. Prices for a double room range from €90 (summer weekdays) to €170 (winter weekends) and they include breakfast. Facilities include a meeting room and a game room. Credit cards: all major.

Getting there Turn off the motorway between Korinthos and Tripoli just ten km before Tripoli, towards Levidi and Vytina. About 12 km after Vytina, follow signs for Dimitsana and Stemnitsa. Take a right towards Ellinikon a few kilometres after Stemnitsa. You will see the Hellenikon Country Club on your right, just before you reach the village.

TRIKOLONION COUNTRY CLUB

Built on a steep mountain slope, at an altitude of 1050 m and overlooking the Lousios River, Stemnitsa is among the prettiest villages of Arkadia. Beautiful centuries-old churches and mansions are the legacy of a prosperous past – just as neighbouring Dimitsana thrived due to its gun powder production, Stemnitsa was famous for its highly skilled metal workers, (church) bell-makers, silver- and goldsmiths. In recent times it has become a much loved destination for mini-breaks all year round: in the winter when the village is often covered in a layer of snow, in spring and autumn, when nature is at its most beautiful, and in the summer, when the fresh mountain air brings some relief from the heat.

It must have been patently evident all along to Kyriakos Griveas that Stemnitsa, at only two and a half hours' drive from Athens, would make a great location for another Country Club hotel. Not long after he opened the Hellenikon, he found out he could take over the rather old-fashioned, Trikolonion Hotel in Stemnitsa (a converted 19th century boarding school for girls). At this stage, it was probably barely a challenge for him to transform it in record time to yet another swanky Country Club, using the same success formula: stylishly decorated sitting rooms (spacious and cosy at the same time), very comfortable bedrooms, a (card) games/meeting room and, to complete the package, friendly and professional service.

In the Trikolonion Country Club, however, there was space for more, so it also features a gym (though I wonder why anyone would mount the treadmill in this area, that is so terrific for walking), a massage room (with a masseur of course!), a sauna and a Jacuzzi. The locals weren't quite sure what to make of the Jacuzzi 'hammam', with its semi-circular stained glass windows, and apparently some wild stories about what was supposedly happening behind them went round the village. Nosey local gossipers would probably be disappointed to learn what really does go on in there: some good old, simple resting and relaxing, which, after all, is the reason why people come to the Country Clubs in the first place.

TRIKOLONION COUNTRY CLUB

220 24 Stemnitsa
Arkadia
Tel. 27950-29500

Where you'll sleep The Trikolonion Country Club features 14 double bedrooms, as well as four suites with a double bed and a convertible sofa for two children. Following the Country Club 'tradition', the rooms come in specific styles. The Trikolonion has three: Gaia (earth olive green), Fos (shades of gold) and Ouranos (sky blue). The bedrooms have probably a little more character here than in the other two hotels of the 'family': the Trikolonion buildings are old and there is more variation between the rooms, while some of the architectural features like wooden ceilings and arched windows, set in thick walls, definitely add extra charm. All the rooms have an en suite shower (with hydro massage in the two superior suites) and are equipped with a television, a telephone, an internet connection, a safe, a mini-bar and a hairdryer.

When you feel hungry Like in all Country Club hotels, breakfast is a generous buffet, but you can also order it as room service. For lunch and dinner there is a menu with light meals (mainly sandwiches, salads and cold plates), but you can also

walk to the traditional tavernas in the village, and in Dimitsana, a few kilometres away, you'll find several more places to eat.

Bring the children? Children are welcome in the hotel, and both the suites, as well as the interconnecting double rooms, are convenient for families. In some rooms extra beds can be placed and cots are available as well.

To see and do Stemnitsa is generally considered a winter weekend destination, even though in terms of 'things to do' you could easily spend a week without ever getting bored, in any season. There is a great deal of touring to be done (Ancient Olympia for a day trip, and shorter drives to villages like Vytina, Magouliana, Lagadia, Karitaina and of course Dimitsana). If you're into outdoor action you can take your pick from hiking (the walk through the Lousios gorge is fantastic), (organised) river trekking, rafting and in the winter, even skiing. Other places of interest include the open-air water power museum of Dimitsana, the cliff-hanging monasteries of the Lousios gorge (some

are easily accessible), and in Stemnitsa the superb Museum of Popular Art, as well as some quite impressive 16th and 17th century churches.

Good to know The Trikolonion Country Club is open all year. Prices for a double room range from €110 (summer weekdays) to €205 (winter weekends) and they include breakfast. Facilities include a game/meeting room, a gym, a sauna, a massage room and a spa with a Jacuzzi. Credit cards: Amex, MasterCard and Visa.

Getting there Turn off the Korinthos-Tripoli motorway ten km before Tripoli, towards Levidi and Vytina. Follow signs for Dimitsana and Stemnitsa after Vytina. You will reach Stemnitsa after about 16 km. The hotel is on your left, just off the road that passes through the village. Alternatively, you stay on the motorway to Tripoli and continue in the direction of Kalamata. Turn off towards Megalopoli and then follow signs for Karitena, Elliniko and Stemnitsa. In Stemnitsa, you will find the hotel on your right.

Built amphitheatrically on a steep mountainside at an altitude of 1050 m, in the very heart of the Peloponnese, lies Dimitsana which has played an important role in the Greek war of Independence (from the Ottoman rule). While it has long been known as a beautiful historic village, it has only recently developed into somewhat of a destination for holiday-makers, and a very lovely one at that.

In the beginning of the nineties, the impressive, mid-19th century Kazakou mansion was the first in Dimitsana to be restored and converted into a guesthouse. For several years it was run by the Greek Tourist Organisation, but it was subsequently taken over by two friends, Thefi and Irini, who significantly improved the level of comfort and added a more personal style to the interiors. With small enhancements (ample supplies of candles, comfy duvets for the winter, CD players in all rooms) they managed to turn it into a much more welcoming place. The sitting/dining room in the vaulted cellar is particularly homey.

After they completed the finishing touches to the guesthouse and everything was running smoothly, Thefi and Irini started working on some other projects. They are currently in the process of restoring the house next door, where they creating some more luxurious suites and, at just a stone's throw away, they are going to open a small café. The café will not only serve coffee and snacks, but it will also function as a space for art exhibitions and live music performances (jazz rather than the *Syrtaki*!).

KAZAKOU

220 07 Dimitsana
Arkadia
Tel. 27950-31660

Where you'll sleep The guesthouse has five comfortable bedrooms (one double, two triples and two quadruples), all with en suite showers and equipped with a mini-bar, a hairdryer, a telephone and a CD player. They are furnished in an attractive, local style. Some look out over a village square and the neighbouring church. Be prepared: the local priest does not have much sympathy for late sleepers on Sunday morning!

When you feel hungry Whether you are planning a lazy day, sipping coffee on the village square, or you have a full schedule ahead of you, Thefi and Irini will make sure you don't go out on an empty stomach. They will serve you (from 8.30 to 11.00) a wholesome breakfast with excellent omelettes, stacks of mini-pancakes, yogurt, preserved fruits and freshly squeezed orange juice. For lunch and dinner you will find several tavernas in the village.

Bring the children? Children are welcome at Guesthouse Kazakou and the quadruple rooms are convenient for families. Getting around in the village with babies and toddlers is not very easy (the cobbled lanes and steps are not great for pushchairs), but for little walkers the area is paradise.

To see and do Athenians consider Dimitsana a winter weekend destination and usually stay no more than one or two nights. But the area is worth a much longer stay, and you will never get bored. There is a lot to see: Ancient Olympia makes a great day excursion and nearby you can visit traditional villages, an open-air water power museum and centuries-old monasteries. The area is also great for walking, and you can make arrangements to cross the five-kilometre Lousios gorge with a guide. You can also arrange to go for (organised) river trekking and rafting.

Good to know Guesthouse Kazakou is open all year. From September until the end of May, the price for a double room is €125 per night during weekends and €100 on weekdays, but during the summer months it goes down to €100 per night. Breakfast is included. Dogs are not allowed. Credit cards: Diners, MasterCard and Visa.

Getting there Turn off the Korinthos-Tripoli motorway just ten km before Tripoli, towards Levidi and Vytina. About 12 km after Vytina, follow signs for Dimitsana (and Stemnitsa). At the very beginning of the village, take a sharp left into a narrow street up the mountain – there is a sign for Guesthouse Kazakou. It is possible to drive all the way up to the guesthouse to unload your luggage, but parking space is limited. There is a fairly large parking area a few minutes' walk away.

In the early 19th century, about 15 years after the Greek War of Independence from Turkey, a raisin merchant from Patras moved to Dimitsana and decided to build a house in the village. At the time, a stranger from 'far away' settling down in the village was a highly unusual event, and for decades the locals stubbornly referred to his house as *to spiti tou xeniou*, "the house of the stranger". In fact, the building itself was also out of the ordinary: five storeys high, it stakes the claim of having been the tallest house at its time in Greece.

A few years ago, the house of the 'stranger' was converted into a lovely guesthouse which now carries the name Pyrgos Xeniou, "Tower of the Stranger". It is run by a young painter/writer couple, Giota and Manolis. Both are visibly happy (and very capable) in their new roles as innkeepers.

The interiors of the house are spectacular. The two top floors, which used to be the living quarters, are particularly impressive with hand-painted walls and ceilings (original in parts), and antique and traditional furniture. Even though the house is completely renovated, you still get the sense that this once was the home of a noble family. With the exception of the television, the elegant living room on the fourth floor gives out the impression that for a long time nothing has changed here. The views from this room are fantastic, and if you are lucky, one of your fellow guests will play the piano.

The three lower floors were used as a storage space and as stables in the past. On the third floor you will now find a bar/dining room. With a tall vaulted ceiling, an exposed rock (from which some plants grow) and a glass wall on one side, it is like a winter garden and a cave bar combined.

PYRGOS XENIOU

220 07 Dimitsana
Arkadia
Tel. 27950-31750

Where you'll sleep The seven bedrooms (two doubles, one triple and four quadruple rooms and suites) spread over all five levels of the building. As the actual entrance of the house is on the fourth floor (the building 'leans' against the mountainside and is partly built into the rock), staying on the top floor (where three of the bedrooms are) doesn't mean you have to climb endless flights of stairs. Only if you're in the apartment-like room that is spread over the two lowest levels of the house, you will have to exercise your legs a little. The rooms are all different in colour and style, but they are all comfortable, and equipped with an en suite shower, a telephone, an internet connection, a refrigerator, a CD-player and a hairdryer.

When you feel hungry Giota serves a full range of home-made products for breakfast (from 8.30 to 10.30), and you can choose where you want to take it: in the cave bar, in the living room or in your bedroom. For lunch and dinner you will find several places to eat nearby.

Bring the children? Pyrgos Xeniou is probably not the right place to show up with young children, unless they are the very-quiet type. That said, the large, quadruple room on the two lowest levels of the house, is very comfortable for families. It has an independent entrance.

To see and do Apart from the mountain villages, monasteries, and, a bit further away, Ancient Olympia, you should definitely visit the open-air water power museum of Dimitsana. Many victories during the War of Independence against the Turks were attributed to the watermills that grounded gunpowder and produced a constant supply of it to the partisans. The "Secret School" (*Kryfo Scholio*) of the Monastery of Phylosophos, where, during the years of the Ottoman occupation, monks taught the youth the Greek language and culture, is another must-see. Otherwise, the area is a paradise for outdoor activities. In Pyrgos Xeniou you are in good hands, because Giota and Manolis used to work as mountain guides. They can give you the insights on hiking routes and all the options you have for mountain climbing, river trekking and rafting, and if you wish, make arrangements for you.

Good to know Pyrgos Xeniou is open all year. The winter is considered high season; the prices for a double room start at €140 per night on weekends, and €100 on weekdays. In the summer, the price for a double room starts at €120 per night on weekends, and at €100 on weekdays.

Breakfast is included. Dogs are not allowed except in the ground-floor quadruple room. There is a municipal parking lot at two minutes' walk from the guesthouse (steps!). Credit cards: Diners, MasterCard and Visa.

Getting there Turn off the Korinthos-Tripoli motorway just ten km before Tripoli, towards Levidi and Vytina. About 12 km after Vytina, follow signs for Dimitsana (and Stemnitsa). Once you arrive in the village, turn right into the cobbled lane right after you pass a few small tavernas and cafes. You will find a parking lot after about 50 m. Leave your car, walk back in the direction you came from, and turn left at the steps. This takes you straight to the guesthouse. You can also call Giota and Manolis for instructions (and if you have trouble finding the place, they will come and meet you).

In the mountains of Arkadia in the Peloponnese, at an altitude of 1050 m, lies the pretty, traditional village of Ano (or upper) Doliana. In order to escape the often fierce weather conditions, the majority of its original residents now live most of the year in Kato (or lower) Doliana, but many still prefer to spend their summers in the upper village. Luckily, however, Ano Doliana was never totally abandoned, not even in the winter, (a fate that numerous other, similar villages didn't manage to escape) and it has been kept in a very good state.

With stone-built houses, cobbled lanes, far reaching views and beautiful surroundings Ano Doliana has plenty of charm to attract visitors all year round. As, however, there were no more children to fill the village school, some years ago the local community took the pragmatic step of converting the beautiful, old stone school building into a guesthouse. The classrooms made way for guestrooms, and an adjacent 150-year-old building was turned into a restaurant. Such municipal initiatives may — and do — start with the best of intentions, but unfortunately often they don't quite manage to succeed, simply because they are missing the personal touch that a place needs in order to stand out. Fortunately, this hasn't been the case with Traditional Guesthouse 1821. Here, everything was done with a lot of care and good taste, and the personal touch was added by a young couple, Dimitris and Katerina, who are now in charge of the guesthouse.

TRADITIONAL GUESTHOUSE 1821

Ano Doliana
220 13 Kastri
Arkadia
Tel. 2710-234080

When you see the gorgeous stone building and the terraces where, in the summer, drinks and meals are served, it is hard to believe this was once a school. Inside you don't get that feeling either. The warmly decorated living room has a pleasant, lived-in feel, and during the winter guests linger by the fire choosing teas and coffees from a large drinks menu. There is a friendly and unpretentious ambience throughout, which Dimitris is keen on keeping up. It so happens that nice places at a short driving distance from Athens easily become trendy weekend destinations and sometimes can even make you feel underdressed if you show up in your jeans and sneakers. Luckily, traditional Guesthouse 1821 has escaped the vogue, and you don't have to worry about having something fancy to wear. Walking shoes and a warm top are perfectly appropriate.

Where you'll sleep There are ten bedrooms to choose from, ranging from simple doubles to maisonettes for up to four or six persons. The rooms have an appealing look with simple wood furniture (nice canopied beds) and walls that are partly stone, partly painted in deep colours, while the high windows and ceilings are a vague reminder of the building's past. All rooms have an en suite shower (two in the maisonettes) and are equipped with a telephone, a television, a hairdryer, a refrigerator, and a CD player.

When you feel hungry The guesthouse has its own restaurant, "the Old School", serving typical Greek, seasonal dishes. It is open for lunch and dinner, and in the morning (8.00-10.30) there is a buffet breakfast for guests.

Bring the children? How could an old school not be appropriate for children? The maisonettes are luxuriously spacious, just ideal for families, and there is a lot of space for children to play outside.

To see and do Ano Doliana is an off-the-beaten-track spot; it is just perfect to relax and immerse in the slow rhythms of village life. The surroundings are excellent for walking and you may wish to follow some part of the E4 European trekking route, which passes through Ano Doliana. If you come for a longer stay, you can also use the village as a base for excursions to the sea, to Nafplio and to the Lousios gorge where you can visit centuries-old monasteries.

Good to know Traditional Guesthouse 1821 is open all year. Winter weekends and holiday periods are the high season, with room rates starting at around €140 per night. On weekdays and throughout the summer the price for two people per night starts at €100. Credit cards: MasterCard, VISA.

Getting there From Athens, follow signs for Korinthos and Patras. After Korinthos (about 80 km from Athens), follow signs for Tripoli. When you drive by Tripoli, look for the motorway exit towards Sparta and follow signs for Stadio, Rizes, Dragouni and Ano Doliana. Once you get to the centre of the village, follow the road up towards the guesthouse (there are signs). If you come from Nafplio, the fastest way to go is to follow the coastal road towards Kiveri and Astros. Just before you reach the centre of Astros, you follow signs for Tripoli (signs may also mention Kato Doliana, and Rizes). About 1.5 km before Rizes, you turn left towards Dragouni and Ano Doliana.

Greeks don't really do 'city escapes'. In the winter people prefer trips to the mountains, and as soon as the weather turns summery, weekends are spent on the beach. This is not all that surprising: most Greeks who take a mini-break every now and then, already live in the city and they'd rather escape *from* it than *to* it – unless of course they're heading towards Rome, London, Paris and the like.

The only town in Greece that is much appreciated as sort of a city weekend-break destination is Nafplio. Steeped in history, it is one of Greece's most fascinating towns. Its development dates back to the Neolithic period and through the centuries it has been under Minoan, Roman, Byzantine, Franc, Venetian and Turkish rule. In 1828 it became the first capital of the modern Greek state until 1834, when the administration was moved to Athens. Today the Venetian influence remains most apparent in the historic part of town, with the odd mosque as the testimony of the Turkish presence.

It is not difficult to explain why Athenians happily drive over on Friday night for a (romantic) weekend in Nafplio. It is barely two hours away by car from Athens, and apart from its beautiful architecture and its great setting by the sea, it also has an excellent choice of restaurants, bars, cafés, boutiques and little art shops. Truth be told, Nafplio is only a small town and compared to Athens, it seems like a village: everything is on an infinitely smaller scale, the atmosphere is easy-going and – what a relief – the air you breathe is clean.

Tucked away in a narrow street in the historic part of Nafplio, Hotel Ilion Suites perfectly fits the bill of a romantic escape. The 300-year-old mansion, once the mayor's residence, was crumbling into dereliction when Themis and Mimi Papaioannou decided to restore it and convert it into a hotel – just a few years after opening the tiniest of hotels, with only four rooms, in the adjacent house.

Mimi, who also owned an antique and art shop, took charge of the interior decoration. Happily ignoring the going trend of stylish minimalism, she just did her own thing and made up her hotel in a wildly romantic style. If you believe that hotels should be done either in a traditional or in some sleek design or elegant country style, then forget about Hotel Ilion. You won't like it. But if you are a bit open-minded and have a taste for the extravagant, you are in for a treat.

ILION SUITES

4 Efthimiopoulou & 6 Kapodistriou St.
211 00 Nafplio
Tel: 27520-25114

Where you'll sleep There are ten rooms and suites in the hotel, each with its own theme (Renaissance, Passion, Love and Soul, Sky, Dreams...). The rooms are smaller than the suites, but they are all are very comfortable. Antiques like beautifully restored fauteuils, small desks, bedside tables and mirrors fill up the place, and in every little corner you'll find paraphernalia like dried flowers, framed black-and-white pictures, a straw hat, an antique radio, or a small art-deco object. In addition to the usual amenities (television, telephone, hairdryer, air conditioning) there are also lots of little 'extras' to make you feel pampered – you will find satin sheets, bathrobes and ample supplies of beauty products, soaps and shampoos next to the Jacuzzi baths or hydro-massage showers.

A little further down the road, are the Ilion Suites Studios. Make sure not to mistake these for the hotel itself: the studios are in a modern, plain building and even though their decoration is similar to that of the hotel, they are not quite as charming.

When you feel hungry Breakfast (priced separately) is available until 11.30. It is fairly standard, but the nostalgic atmosphere of the small dining room where it is served makes it worthwhile anyway. There is an enormous choice of restaurants within walking distance from the hotel, and it is not a bad idea to ask the staff for some recommendations.

Bring the children? The Ilion Suites are more of a romantic getaway for couples, but children are accepted, and some rooms can take an extra bed (but there are no cots).

To see and do The old town of Nafplio is first of all a place to just stroll around, to take in the unique atmosphere and discover its little shops, art galleries and restaurants. There are several small museums worth a visit (from the archaeological museum on Syntagma Square and the Folk Art Museum displaying a beautiful collection of Greek costumes to the komboloi museum for worry-beads!). You should also visit the old Venetian fort on top of Palamidi and the Acronafplia battlements that lie beneath it. In the summer you can cross by boat to the fortified island of Bourtzi, in the middle of the bay. Also, if you stay a little longer in Nafplio, you can use the town as a base to visit Mycenea and the ancient theatre of Epidavros. There, you can even catch a summer festival performance of an ancient Greek tragedy.

Good to know Hotel Ilion is open all year. Prices for a double room start at €95, but do not include breakfast. Dogs are not allowed. Credit cards: Diners, MasterCard and Visa.

Getting there Hotel Ilion is in the higher part of the historic district of Nafplio. The easiest way to find it is on foot. From the big central square of Syntagma (which is hard to miss), turn into Efthimiopoulou St. (northwards, uphill), and take the second street to the right (Kapodistriou St.). You will find the hotel on your left. It is possible to drive up to the hotel, but the streets are narrow and most are one way, so it is not always very easy. There is a public parking space at just a few minutes on foot.

The days when the choices for a stay in a Greek provincial town were limited to scruffy traditional hostels or larger hotels without character are still fresh in my memory. Small and charming was not an option. In most places there has been no change in this respect, but Nafplio, where quite a few historical buildings have been converted into guesthouses and hotels, is definitely on the move. Hotel Ilion was the first to make an impression with its extravagant retro style; recently, Leonidas Lambrinakis, a painter and mosaic artist, and his sister Ioanna have given a whole new twist to the small hostel 'concept', with their newly opened Kyveli Suites.

The two adjacent 150-year-old buildings stand out because of their sea green and salmon colours. If, however, it wasn't for this unusual colour palette, your first impression might have been that of an ordinary city hostel, with just a tiny reception area as you come in and a staircase leading up to the bedrooms. But here you will not be handed a room key by an over-aged receptionist upon check-in, nor will your room be the kind where you'd rather spend as little time as possible. In Kyveli Suites things are done a little differently.

You will be welcomed by Leonidas or Ioanna, who run their guesthouse in a way that allows you to be fully independent and use your suite as a self-catering apartment, while at the same time they add a warm and personal touch with their presence. The suites offer a level of comfort that approaches luxury, nothing like the bare basics provided in traditional hostels. Every suite has a comfortable sitting corner (though small), beds are superb and the bathrooms are large and modern. The décor is refreshingly contemporary, even though the furniture is a mix of modern and classic.

KYVELI SUITES

18-20 Vas. Alexandrou St.
211 00 Nafplio
Tel. 27520-96230

Where you'll sleep There are nine suites in total, two of which are strictly doubles, and the other seven have an extra double sofa bed. All suites are equipped with a telephone, a television, an internet connection, a mini-bar, facilities to make tea and coffee, and air conditioning. The large en suite bathrooms have a bath with hydro massage.

When you feel hungry There is no breakfast service in the Kyveli Suites, but the mini-bars in the rooms are stocked with some (complimentary) provisions so you don't have to go out with an empty stomach in the morning. If you want a proper breakfast, you will find nice cafés just a short walk away; as for the choice of restaurants, in Nafplio it is enormous.

Bring the children? Nafplio is not the kind of place to spend more than a couple of days with children, but your little ones are welcome in the Kyveli Suites. If you travel with a baby you will have to bring your own cot.

To see and do With the old town of Nafplio literally at your doorstep, you will never be short of things to do – shopping, sightseeing, visiting museums, climbing up to the castle – Nafplio has enough on offer to keep you entertained for several days, and if you make excursions to Epidavros and Mycenae, you can add a couple more to your schedule.

Good to know The Kyveli Suites remain open all year. Prices for two persons start at €85 on weekdays, and €100 on weekends. Reductions apply for stays of three nights and over. Dogs are not allowed. Credit cards: MasterCard and Visa.

Getting there As you approach Nafplio, follow the signs for the old town. At the beginning of the old town, turn left into Singrou St and then right again into Amalias, where you will usually find space to park your car. Take the second or third street on your right – Vas. Alexandrou St, where the hotel is, runs parallel to Amalias and is two blocks down towards the sea.

The first time I visited the village of Trikala in the mountains of the northern Peloponnese, there was not much to it. It was just a little village (actually, three villages, as Trikala is divided in a lower, middle and upper part) in a beautiful area, with a limited choice of tavernas and a few not-so-special hotels. But there was also Helydorea, the place where I stayed and instantly fell in love with for its tasteful country-style decoration, comfy bedrooms and easy-going feeling. It had been built some years before by Stathis and Eleni Triantafyllou, an Athenian couple who liked the idea of spending weekends at Trikala and having friends over. As it happened, they enjoyed having guests so much that they eventually turned the house into a hotel.

When after an absence of several years (during which I travelled around in the hunt for other special places to stay in Greece), I finally made my way back to Trikala, the village had changed quite a bit. Several more decent hotels had opened; the choice of restaurants had definitely increased, and I even came across some new, vaguely trendy little bars. Clearly, Trikala had been discovered and was on its way up. (The recent opening of a miniature ski resort nearby – so far with just one lift – will probably accelerate this process.)

Helydorea had also changed. Some suites had been added (they are nice and stylish, though the finishing is a little rough on the edges), the living room had been enlarged, and also a sort of log cabin had been built to function as a meeting hall or small conference room. But despite these additions, the hotel still has a pleasant and friendly feel to it, especially during the holiday periods and weekends, when Stathis and Eleni are there to personally welcome you.

HELYDOREA

Helydorea
204 00 Mesea Trikala
Korinthia
Tel. 27430-91444

Where you'll sleep Helydorea now has 16 rooms and suites (doubles, triples and quadruples). Most rooms are located in the main house, and the rest are in the recently extended garden house. Each one is different, but they are all done in an attractive country style with wood or stone-paved floors, bare stone walls, built-in or antique brass beds, a working fireplace in some, and nice bathrooms (with bath or shower). All rooms have a telephone and a television, and some also have a refrigerator, a CD player and/or a DVD player. Most rooms have a balcony or a veranda with far-reaching views.

When you feel hungry The hotel does not have a restaurant, but in the evening it is possible to get a meal (though if you arrive on a weekday, it is better to ask for it in advance). There is no menu; you just get a traditional, home-cooked meal. There are also several places where you can eat at in the village. For breakfast you will find a buffet (from 8.00 to 11.00) with a good variety during weekends and holidays, while on weekdays the choice is a bit more limited.

Bring the children? The area is great to go to with children, and so is Helydorea. Children are welcomed with wide open arms (sometimes literally) and the quadruple rooms and suites are comfortable for families.

To see and do Helydorea is a great place to spend a few lazy, relaxing days. The mountains are wonderful for walks and hikes (and also for excursions by car…). When there is snow, you can go on a snowmobile trip, rent a sleigh and do a bit of skiing. In other seasons you can rent mountain bikes, or, if you are the adventurous type, climb to the summit of Mount Ziria (with certified guides) and make a descent into the Flambouritsa Gorge.

Good to know Helydorea is open all year. Prices for a double room start at €60 in the low season (summer and weekdays in May and September), and at €120 in the high season (winter weekends and holidays) and they include breakfast. A meeting/conference room for up to 70 persons is available. Credit cards: Amex, MasterCard and Visa.

Getting there Follow the national road between Patras and Korinthos. Turn off at a town called Xilokastro (about 30 km from Korinthos or 105 km from Patras) and follow the road signs for Trikala. The hotel is on your left in Mesea Trikala (Middle Trikala, there is also Ano, or Upper, and Kato, or Lower, Trikala) about 24 km from where you get off the national road.

Spetses is to Athens, a bit like what Ile de Ré is to Paris. It has a unique charm that in the summer attracts a cosmopolitan crowd from the city – not so much those in search of a hot beach and nightlife scene, but a more discerning lot, people who appreciate the laid-back and refined atmosphere that reigns in this pinewood-covered little island just off the coast of the Peloponnese. Many have second homes in the 'town' of Spetses, renowned for its elegant 18th and 19th century mansions, idyllic gardens and pebble-mosaic courtyards. Only a few cars are allowed to circulate on the island – those of the local residents, and luckily then again their use is restricted to the absolutely necessary; people in Spetses go around on mopeds or bicycles.

Christos Orloff belongs to one of the oldest families of the island. He spent most of his childhood on the island, and even though he didn't always live there, he is a *Spetsiotis*, heart and soul. Since the beginning of the nineties he has been running one of the best-known restaurants on Spetses, but a few years ago he and his brother Vassilis engaged in yet another project: to create a small hotel in the gardens of the mid-19th century Orloff mansion. They had no intention to convert their family home into a hotel, but the gardens offered space for several separate residences.

Christos enlisted the help of his good friend and architect Eliza Manolas, with whom he worked closely together, from the initial conception of the idea, all the way through to the final touches. They erected five houses, each with its own architectural features, in the traditional local building style, distinguished by simple elegance and pure lines.

ORLOFF RESORT

Old Harbour
180 50 Spetses
Tel. 22980-75444

There was no attempt to create a *faux* impression of period buildings – the aim was just to blend in harmoniously with the surroundings. Inside, rather than opting for a traditional kind of styling, they took a refreshing, contemporary approach. The interiors are stylishly minimalist and clutter free. Every detail is deliberate and thought through, from the materials (all of the highest quality) and the colour schemes (white has the overtone, with the occasional splash of vibrant colours), to the furniture (modern and comfortable) and the decoration (minimal, but just right). Lamps were all individually designed, cotton summer blankets are the softest ever, and bathrooms are spacious and light. Nothing was left to chance by Christos, who remained involved in every step of the process.

The walled gardens are no less attractive than the interiors. Here too, tradition blends with modernity: terraces made of smoothed concrete and pebble mosaics, a pool that is large but not too flashy, modern design garden furniture, greenery and potted flowers, and four striking olive trees. Christos lovingly calls them 'his four old ladies' and while he is the last one to brag about what he has achieved with the Orloff Resort, he is openly proud of them: he did not sacrifice a single tree during the construction. The ones that had to be removed were carefully replanted elsewhere in the gardens and they are all doing extremely well.

Where you'll sleep The Orloff Resort has a total of 18 guest units. Most are double rooms – those that are on the top floor are labelled 'superior'. There are also four studios for up to three people, as well as a suite and two maisonettes sleeping four or six people respectively. Every room has its own balcony or veranda. The rooms have a bathroom with a shower (the suite and one of the studios have a Jacuzzi bath) and are equipped with a telephone, a television, an internet connection, a refrigerator, air conditioning, a hairdryer and a safe. The studios, maisonettes and the suite have an equipped kitchenette. There is also one entire house for rent with five bedrooms, four bathrooms (one with a Jacuzzi), a large sitting room with an open kitchen and a private garden.

When you feel hungry There are plenty of restaurants you could try in the old harbour (just a few minutes on foot), including the Orloff restaurant in a 200-year-old building, in the past the island's first port police quarters. It is a beautiful spot right on the water, and it is famous for its excellent *mezedes* (the Greek version of the Spanish *tapas*). If you'd rather eat at the hotel, you can have a meal brought over to you from the Orloff restaurant. Breakfast is served till late in the morning: you can either help yourself from a generous buffet including fresh bread, croissants and *pains au chocolat*, pies, cake, yogurt and fresh fruits, or ask to have it brought to your room.

ORLOFF RESORT

Bring the children? Spetses is a nice island to visit with children. They will enjoy roaming about in the little alleyways of the town, riding a horse-drawn carriage and taking a water taxi or caique to the beach. The best way for families to go around is by bicycle – you can rent them everywhere and most places have children's bicycles too. Even though the Orloff Resort doesn't have a typical family atmosphere, your kids are welcome and the maisonettes in particular are well laid-out for families. Cots are available and babysitting can be arranged.

To see and do It is not a bad idea to start by renting a bicycle so you can pedal around the island to explore the pine tree forests and the many beaches and coves. At the Orloff Resort, however, you'll probably end up spending a lot of time relaxing by the pool. There is also a small, organised beach just five minutes on foot. If you feel like a little shopping spree, you won't be disappointed in the town of Spetses, and at night the Old Harbour comes to life and you will find some great places to go for a drink.

Good to know The Orloff Resort is open from April to November. Prices for a double room start at €90 in the low season and €160 in the high season, breakfast included. Facilities include a computer room, an outdoor swimming pool with hydro jet, as well as massage, shiatsu and face treatments. Credit cards: Amex, MasterCard and Visa.

Getting there Every day several hydrofoils leave from Piraeus for Spetses. It takes roughly two hours, but if you prefer to travel by conventional ferryboat (less choppy!) you should count double the time. The Orloff Resort is located at about five minutes' walk from the waterfront at the Old Harbour. If you inform the hotel which boat you arrive on, you will be picked up at the port.

A weekend break on an island is just what the family needs to recuperate from the hectic first few weeks of the new school year. The kids are tired, so are we, and we don't want to spend too much time travelling. Poros is the perfect choice. Separated by a narrow channel from the shores of the Peloponnese, this small island is only a one-hour trip by hydrofoil from the port of Piraeus, but offers a complete change of scenery and a real away-from-it-all feeling. Maybe not as eye-catching as its neighbour Hydra, where boatloads of tourists disembark nearly every day, Poros still has plenty of charm. It is blessed with dense pine tree forests, sheltered beaches and a picturesque little town, but does not get a lot of tourism.

Our stay in Poros is in the Anemone Residence, one of several buildings owned by Marie Louise Andoniadou, an Austrian architect living and working in Greece. When, in the early nineties, she came to the island for the first time, she instantly knew that this was the place for her. She has since bought and restored two 19th century houses, and is currently working on a third one. Sto Roloï ("at the clock") was the first one, which she converted into two apartments and a studio. After she finished those, she started on the Anemone Residence, which she split into two apartments, one of which has a small garden and a small pool. She worked with a lot of respect for the old character of the houses, and furnished them with charming antiques and country-style pieces. But she also added a modern hint to them, using fresh colours and touches of luxury.

STO ROLOI &
THE ANEMONE RESIDENCE
13 Hatzopoulou-Karra St.
180 20 Poros
Tel. 22980-25808

Upon arrival at the port, we are met by Kostas, a local restaurateur, and a friend and assistant of Marie Louise. After a quick exchange of greetings, he whisks us off in a taxi. The driver negotiates the narrow alleyways of the town of Poros at maximum speed (but with an astounding level of precision) and I only just manage to yell "seatbelts" at the kids before we arrive, barely a minute later, at the house. When Kostas shows us around, I can only be grateful that a minute more hasn't been wasted on travelling. Our weekend is short, and I can't wait to stretch out on one of the sun beds by the pool.

In the end, of course, little time is spent on that sun bed. A leisurely lunch in Kostas' restaurant, walks through the town, coffee by the water, some more exploring, and time just flies. At night it is a bit chilly to sit outside, but our little house is cosy and we feel totally at home. This is a place where I could easily imagine myself spending a few weeks on holiday.

Where you'll sleep Sto Roloï is divided into three units. The street-level Garden Apartment has a living room with an open kitchen, two double bedrooms and a small sauna. It opens directly onto the alleyway and a small courtyard shared with the Studio. The Studio is a small all-in-one unit for up to two persons. The Terrace Apartment is on the upper level of the house and has a living room, a large kitchen and two bedrooms. It is accessed from a private courtyard.

In the Anemone Residence you can choose between the Little Tower and the Anemone House. The Little Tower is on two levels, and has one double bedroom, a small living room with a convertible sofa-bed (for one person) and a kitchen corner. The Anemone House, also on two levels, has a double bedroom and a larger living room with a convertible sofa (for two children or one adult), and an open kitchen. It also has a private garden with a swimming pool (3 × 6 m).

All units have a comfortable bathroom, with a hydro-massage shower or bath (except the studio, which has a regular shower) and are equipped with a television, a telephone, a CD player and air conditioning.

When you feel hungry When you arrive, you will find your kitchen stocked with supplies for breakfast (except for bread). There are several mini-markets and a bakery at walking distance from either house, but if you don't feel like carrying anything, grocery shopping can be done for you. You will also find plenty of traditional restaurants on the waterfront. Most guests end up taking many of their meals at Kostas' restaurant (To Kathestos tis Gefsis – loosely translated as "the foundation of taste"!) which has become

STO ROLOI &
THE ANEMONE RESIDENCE

sort of a meeting point for people staying at Sto Roloï and the Anemone Residence. Kostas serves excellent fish and traditional dishes, and he can also arrange for meals to be brought to your house.

Bring the children? Poros is not a typical island for family holidays, but for kids who love swimming and walking it is a great place to go to, plus they can roam around in the alleyways of the town of Poros (just make sure that they watch out for mad taxi drivers!). Marie Louise welcomes children in her houses, and the layout of the Garden Apartment and the Terrace Apartment nicely suits families with children. The Anemone House and the Little Tower also have space for one or two children, but are more comfortable for couples. If you travel with a baby, keep in mind that the alleys of Poros are not ideal for pushchairs. In any case, cots are available.

To see and do Poros gives you the rare chance to enjoy island life, while, at the same time, you can also go sightseeing. The ferry puts you across to the Peloponnese in just a few minutes, so if you rent a car, the ancient theatre of Epidavros, the famous Mycenae and the historic town of Nafplio make easy day excursions. Other wonderful daytrips can be done to Hydra, Spetses and Egina, and why not, to Athens! Poros itself has ample beaches (most are pebble beaches with trees for shade and incredibly clear waters). The nearest is about ten minutes away on foot; to get to the others it is best to rent a bicycle or a motorbike, or take either a land taxi or a water taxi. There is a school for water sports on the island and you can also rent a sailboat. Marie Louise can arrange for you to accompany a local fisherman during a night fishing trip.

Good to know Sto Roloï and the Anemone Residence are open all year. Prices for two people range from €75 to €250 during the summer months, and from €50 to €175 during the rest of the year. Credit cards: MasterCard and Visa.

Getting there The hydrofoils and ferries to Poros leave from Piraeus and take respectively one or two hours to get to the island. You can also go by car via the Peloponnese (about 2,5 hours from Athens) and cross at Galatas (the ferry leaves every half hour and the crossing takes a few minutes). You will be met upon arrival at the port. Sto Roloï is just one minute away on foot from where you get off the ferry (up a flight of stairs), and the Anemone is about five minutes' walk.

If you come to Greece in the winter or in the early spring, you can go skiing. Before you laugh, read on. Three quarters of the land are covered by mountains, many of which reach over 2000 m high, and there are about 20 ski centres in the country. Surely, they can't compete with those in the Alps (some have just a handful of lifts and open up only on weekends), but there are quite a few centres where you can get some decent skiing done.

Mount Parnassos is the largest ski area in Greece. At just a two-hour drive from Athens, it attracts a fair amount of skiers during winter weekends, but as few Athenians will actually take days off work to go skiing (and there are no Greek school vacations between the New Year and Easter), on weekdays the slopes are practically empty.

The Parnassos ski crowd typically stays in Arahova, which during most of the year is just a traditional and picturesque little mountain town, but comes to life during the ski season, when the cafés fill up with youngish types, showing off their hippest ski gear. Not surprisingly, there is a wide array of lodgings in and near the little town, varying from little traditional pensions to fancy design hotels. But hidden in a narrow pedestrian street, is a place that is one of a kind: Guesthouse Generali. From the outside, it has the simple looks of just a charming, traditional house. Inside though, it is full of surprises.

Your first impression will be of the living room, small, cosy and a tad cluttered, but ever so sweet and full of character. Owner Stamatis Generalis didn't call in a designer to add flair to the house where he was born and raised, but instead, he did it all himself. A carpenter by profession, but also an inspired painter, his house is his playground and he has created a décor that is personal and fun. Every detail

in there will bring a smile on your face. And that smile will get even bigger when you discover the indoor relaxing area with a swimming pool, a hammam, a spa and a sauna. It is not just somewhere to get steamed and/or freshened up; with the deckchairs, music playing and again a great décor, you might end up spending more time in there than on the slopes!

GENERALI
320 04 Arahova
Tel. 22670-31529

Where you'll sleep Guesthouse Generali has nine completely different, themed rooms. The smallest, Erotas (Greek for "love"), is an evocatively decorated, dreamy little love nest furnished with just a large bed. The others (doubles, triples, one quadruple suite and a family room on two levels) have comfortable country style furniture, a working fireplace and lots of fun details in their décor. All rooms have an en suite shower with hydro-massage, and are equipped with a telephone, a television, a CD player, a refrigerator, air conditioning, facilities to make coffee and tea, and a hairdryer.

When you feel hungry Breakfast at Generali is a grand affair. Served from 8.00 to 13.00, it includes great omelettes, crêpes, croissants, chocolate cake and fresh juice. You help yourself to some of the basics, and whatever tastes better prepared fresh, you order from a menu resembling a comic book. For lunch and dinner, Arahova has a good choice of places to eat, and there are many restaurants along the road to the ski centre.

Bring the children? Children are welcome, but you should keep in mind that everything in the guesthouse, the sitting room in particular, is small. So if you come with young children in the winter and you're unlucky with the weather, you may not feel totally at ease. Having said that, the people in the guesthouse love children (Stamatis' own little ones are around regularly as well) and as long as you know what to expect, you and your children will be fine. Companionship and Helicopter are good family rooms, and you can ask for a cot. And of course children can have some real fun in the pool, but only until 18.00. After that the pool area is for quiet grown-ups only!

To see and do So yes, in the winter you can ski, but Arahova is also a perfect base from where to visit the ancient site of Delphi and the picturesque seaside town of Galaxidi, or to simply enjoy the beauty of the mountains all year round.

Good to know Guesthouse Generali is open all year, and the winter months (October to the end of April) are considered high season. Especially during the skiing season, the guesthouse is generally booked solidly, even on weekdays, so be sure to book well in advance. Prices for a double room with a fireplace start at €90 per night in the high season (€150 during weekends), but the rest of the year they are considerably lower, starting at about €65 per night (breakfast not included). Parking is not always easy during the skiing season, and the closest place to leave your car is a couple of minutes away on foot. The common areas of the guesthouse are non-smoking. Credit cards: Amex, MasterCard and Visa.

Getting there Arahova is barely two hours by car from Athens. The first 50 km or so are on the National Road (in the direction of Lamia). You take the exit for Thiva and start following signs for Delphi. It is about 80 km (good secondary road) to Arahova. About 500 m after you enter Arahova, you will see an old school building on your left (just before the road curves to the right). Leave your car and go down the steps between the school and the taverna (Agnadio). Take a left after you pass the church, and you will see the guesthouse a bit further on, on your right. If you make a phone call to the guesthouse from the main road, someone will come to help you with your luggage.

Amfiklia is just a short drive away from the popular ski resort of Parnassos, and yet, even during the most perfect powder snow/blue sky winter weekend, you will not find much of a ski crowd flocking to the village. This is not because it lacks charm; on the contrary. It is just that for most skiers the hip spot, *the* place-to-be, is Arahova, situated on the opposite side of the mountain.

Even so, Kiriaki Deligeorgi has no trouble filling up her guesthouse. There are plenty of weekenders looking to relax and unwind, rather than show off their ski gear at breakfast. For many, a stroll through the village, a drive through the area and a dip in the swimming pool is enough, and they prefer staying in a guesthouse so full of charm rather than being in the hub of all the action.

How did a young woman like Kiriaki end up spending most of her time in a small mountain village? She grew up and studied in Athens, and sailing was always her greatest passion. All her spare time she was at sea, except during the winter holidays, which she spent with her family in Amfiklia. Kiriaki still can't quite explain why suddenly she gave up sailing, initially to take up mountain climbing (not enough talent, she claims) and then white water kayaking (more success — with her team she became Greek champion), seizing every opportunity to spend time in the mountains of Parnassos.

Kiriaki had the idea to open a guesthouse in the village about ten years ago, when she invited a bunch of Athenian friends to her family's holiday house in Amfiklia for New Year's Eve. It took a few years to take shape, until in 1999 she finally started building her guesthouse on the site of a dilapidated house, right at the top of the village. At first she wanted to restore the old building, but it turned out to be beyond repair. So she tore it down and rebuilt it, following the original architecture and even using much of the old stone.

KIRIAKI

350 02 Amfiklia
Fthiotida
Tel. 22340-29011

While the reconstruction took place with much respect for tradition, there was no attempt to create an illusion of age. This is particularly apparent inside, where walls are painted in pastel colours and traditional furniture is mixed with contemporary urban style items. The result is cosy enough, but probably far lighter and airier than the original house ever was. In the lower floor, in the sitting and dining room, comfortable sofas and fauteuils flank an open fireplace. The charming bedrooms have beautiful parquet floors and timbered ceilings that are painted in soft colours, just like the walls. Curtains, upholstery, bedspreads and pillows have all been carefully chosen in matching tones.

The care that went into the décor is extended to the guests as well. It is all summarised nicely by something Kiriaki said during my stay. I was enjoying a fantastic breakfast and reaching the point of having eaten far too much, when

8.30 to 11.30) including a choice of fresh juices and excellent homemade pies. The grand finale, that huge pancake with fruits, is brought to your table. Throughout the day you can order drinks and snacks. If you want an evening meal, you have to ask for it a day in advance. Keep this in mind, because there is not an overwhelming choice of restaurants in the village.

Bring the children? Children are welcome in the guesthouse and cots are available. In the summer they will enjoy the pool, and the area offers plenty of options for child-friendly activities.

To see and do Your first impression of Amfiklia may be that there is not much at all happening, and that you'll mainly be relaxing by the pool (or fireplace) of the guesthouse. Actually, the village is a great base for all sorts of outdoor activities. The ski slopes of Mount Parnassos are only about 18 km away, and options for other sports include mountain biking, treks, kayaking and climbing. With Kiriaki's experience in mountain climbing and white water kayaking, you obviously have the right person to confer with, if you want to try some of these activities yourself.

Good to know Guesthouse Kiriaki is open all year. During the summer period (July to mid-September), which is considered the low season, prices for a double room start at €85 per night. The rest of the year, rates start at €85 on weekdays, and €120 on weekends, breakfast included. Facilities at the guesthouse include a sitting room with a fireplace, terraces and a heated outdoor swimming pool. Dogs are not allowed. Credit cards: Diners, MasterCard and Visa.

Getting there The fastest way from Athens to Amfiklia is to follow the National Road towards Lamia until Kastro (120 km from Athens). From Kastro you follow signs for Orhomenos (but don't go into Orhomenos – stay on the main road), Heronia and Amfiklia. You will see signs for the guesthouse in the centre of Amfiklia. You can leave your car in the street at the back of the guesthouse, and take the steps down to the entrance.

Kiriaki came to the table with this enormous pancake topped with whipped cream and fresh fruits. Looking quite serious, she started saying "this is what we give to guests we want to impress". This kind of worried me – I didn't want to get any special treatment. But then, a huge smile came over her face, and she added: "and that is each and every single one of them!"

Where you'll sleep The six double rooms and two triple suites are on the top two floors of the house. They are comfortable and well-proportioned, and they have an impeccable en suite shower, a telephone, an internet connection, a television, air conditioning, and a hairdryer; the suites also have a mini-bar. Some of the rooms have a fireplace that you can use.

When you feel hungry Breakfast in the guesthouse is particularly good. There is a well-assorted buffet (from

First impressions can be very telling. When you see Dadi - Arhondiko Parnassou ("Mansion of Parnassos") from the road, it is impossible not to be taken by this immaculate, 19th century, neoclassical mansion. The neat symmetrical design, soft-coloured walls, blue shutters and even, if you look carefully, white, lace-trimmed curtains behind the arched windows, all exude charm. It does not look like a hotel, but more like a house you wish was yours.

Wishing it was theirs, was exactly what Kaiti and Antonis, a couple from Athens, did when they noticed the mansion in Amfiklia, the village they often visited for the weekend. It was totally rundown, and from the moment they laid their eyes on it, they started restoring it in their dreams. They were elated when one day they heard it was for sale. They decided to go for it and convert it into a little guesthouse.

The mansion used to be the residence of one of the richer families of the village and later operated as the village school. By the time Kaiti and Antonis bought it, it was in such a poor state that they had no choice but to redo it – completely. The only parts they managed to salvage were the outside walls and another one on the inside; everything else they had to rebuild from scratch. But they saw it as a chance to make their dream come true, and they managed to do so, miraculously, in less than a year.

DADI - ARHONDIKO PARNASSOU

350 02 Amfiklia
Fthiotida
Tel. 22340-29040

Arhondiko Dadi has become a wonderful place to stay. Inside it feels a lot like the home it once was, even though what you see today was in fact never there before. It does have many of the charming features you find in old houses (even though they are all new), while, at the same time, it offers more contemporary comforts such as double glazing, an excellent heating system, and even a sauna tucked away in the basement. The large sitting room is at the extended part of the house, and due to the open kitchen, it has a more modern feel to it. Exposed stone walls and the open fireplace give it a rustic aspect though, and there are enough books and board games to spend leisurely evenings.

Where you'll sleep The eight bedrooms, named after flowers, are fresh and pretty, with pinewood floors, pastel colour schemes, and spotless modern bathrooms. Some of the double rooms are on the small side, but there are also two larger family suites on the ground floor (both with a fireplace), and the lofty triples on the top floor are also

more spacious. The rooms are fitted with air conditioning, a telephone, a television, a mini-bar and a safe (except in the double rooms), and a hairdryer. Three rooms also have a CD player. The en suite bathrooms in the loft rooms have showers with hydro-massage.

When you feel hungry For breakfast you will find a well-assorted buffet (up to 12.00) with lots of homemade products. There is no restaurant in the guesthouse, but if you ask in advance, you can order evening meals. In the village there are some places to eat, but the choice is not overwhelming.

Bring the children? Children are welcome in Guesthouse Dadi, and the two quadruple suites on the ground floor are very convenient for small families. When the parents want a little 'time-out' they can ask for DVD's to be played in the room.

To see and do Amfiklia is a quiet village, visited by people looking for peace and calm. The surroundings are great for outdoor activities like walking and mountain biking, and in

the winter you can go skiing in the nearby Parnassos Ski Centre. A great day-trip is to drive to the Vagonetto – Fokis Mining Park for a guided tour in the old mining shafts, then continue to the ancient site of Delphi and its museum, and make a final stop in the lively mountain town of Arahova, before crossing back the mountain to Amfiklia.

Good to know Guesthouse Dadi is open all year. The high season is from the end of October until the end of May, when the price per night for two persons starts at €120 on weekends and €80 on weekdays. In the summer the price for a double room is €100 on weekends and €70 on weekdays. Prices include breakfast. Credit cards: MasterCard and Visa.

Getting there From Athens you take the National Road towards Lamia. After about 120 km you take the exit for Kastro, from where you follow signs for Orhomenos (but don't go into Orhomenos – stay on the main road), Heronia and Amfiklia. You will see signs for Dadi before you reach Amfiklia.

Greece's second biggest island, Evia, is one of its most beautiful, and also one of the least discovered by tourists. There are some beach resorts and larger hotels – none particularly attractive (generally, appealing architecture is not what Evia is best known for), but most of this mountainous island has remained blissfully wild and unexploited.

Some ten years ago, Marina and Stefanos Vallis relocated with their children from Athens to Rovies, a seaside village in northern Evia, to manage the family olive grove estate. Thoroughly enjoying this simpler and healthier outdoors lifestyle, they thought of sharing it with others. Most villagers did not think much of their plan to create an agro-touristic guesthouse up on the hill, a good 500 m far from the sea, arguing that no one could possibly be interested in staying at such an 'enormous' distance from the beach. But Marina and Stefanos saw things differently, knowing from their own experience, that for people who spend their lives in the city, space and tranquillity can be more important assets than staying right on the edge of the water.

And so the couple picked a spot in the middle of the beautiful, 36-hectare, Eleonas olive grove, to create a wonderfully quiet, rural retreat. The buildings, Mediterranean villa style, were not designed to impress, but simply to please, and that is how they were done inside as well. There are no fancy or fashionable design elements, nor did the two of them go on a hunt for antiques to fill the place up. Instead they opted for tasteful, simple pine furniture and a light and attractive decoration, in which the olive element is omnipresent. The living room has a roaring fireplace in the winter, while in the summer it opens up to a large terrace overlooking the impressive expanse of the olive grove below, which stretches all the way to the sea.

Let there be no misunderstanding about the agro-touristic aspect of Eleonas: the idea is not that you can work here in exchange for board and lodging. You are simply staying at a working olive grove estate, but *you* are on a holiday, and *others* do the work. Of course, if you are interested, you can watch and learn a few things, and when they are not too busy, Marina and Stefanos will be more than happy to show you around. Call it whatever you like, but Eleonas is simply an unassuming, honest, lovely place, where you can relax and enjoy a slower pace of life.

ELEONAS

Rovies
340 05 Evia
Tel. 22270-71619

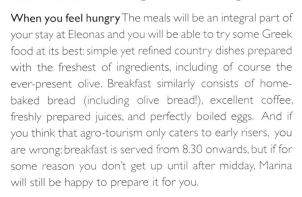

Where you'll sleep The ten double bedrooms are in the bigger of the two buildings. They are comfortable (excellent beds, all twin though), very well cared for and nicely done, with little touches such as the old photographs from the early days of oil production back in the sixties, but there is no excessive decoration or luxury here. Rooms can be interconnected to make up quadruple family accommodation with an internal staircase, and can also take an extra bed (cots are available). All rooms open onto a private balcony or veranda. They have an en suite shower or bathroom, and are equipped with a telephone, an internet connection and air conditioning. Most have a refrigerator.

When you feel hungry The meals will be an integral part of your stay at Eleonas and you will be able to try some Greek food at its best: simple yet refined country dishes prepared with the freshest of ingredients, including of course the ever-present olive. Breakfast similarly consists of home-baked bread (including olive bread!), excellent coffee, freshly prepared juices, and perfectly boiled eggs. And if you think that agro-tourism only caters to early risers, you are wrong: breakfast is served from 8.30 onwards, but if for some reason you don't get up until after midday, Marina will still be happy to prepare it for you.

Bring the children? Eleonas is the perfect place to come with children: there's lots and lots of space for them to play and the only thing you might worry about is not to lose them somewhere among the 4000 (or so) olive trees! It is hard to imagine, but should they ever grow tired of playing outdoors, there is a playroom with children's books, toys, a television and even (not quite in the general spirit of the place) a PlayStation.

To see and do You can use Eleonas simply as a base for relaxing beach holidays, and make trips to nearby fishing villages (Limni is particularly attractive), the mountains, waterfalls and forests. Don't miss Edipsos, a small, kind of old-fashioned town, famous for its hot mineral springs. At Eleonas you will find an outdoor fitness circuit where you can exercise (a great, healthy alternative to the urban, indoor fitness centre). At night, if romantic stargazing is not enough for you, there is a telescope you are welcome to use. And last – but not least – remember that while you stay at Eleonas you can discover a thing or two about olive production and processing. In the fall, during the olive harvest, Marina and Stefanos organise a special week with the

olive as its central theme, with excursions, demonstrations, workshops and lessons.

Good to know Eleonas is open all year. Prices for a double room start at €80 per night, and they include breakfast. There is a small community of cats living on the estate, so guests are kindly requested not to bring their dogs. Credit cards: MasterCard and Visa.

Getting there If you come from Athens, there are two ways to get to Rovies. The first way is to take the National Road towards Lamia. After about 60 km you turn off in the direction of Halkida, where you cross the suspension bridge to Evia. From Halkida you follow signs for northern Evia, Agios Ioannis, Kirinthos, Limni and Rovies. It is a beautiful drive through mountains and forests, but the road is quite winding. Alternatively, you follow the National Road up to Arkitsa and take the ferry to Edipsos (45 min), and from there you take the coastal road towards Rovies. There is a ferry service every two hours, and more frequently during weekends and the summer. From Rovies you call Eleonas, so Marina or Stefanos can come and pick you up.

KORYS AND ANATOLI HOUSES

Even though the largest part of the Greek mainland is covered by mountains, the country is hardly known as a destination for mountain holidays. Most foreign visitors come for a fix of sea and sun, and sadly, probably never realise what a spectacular scenery exists beyond the famous 'white and blue' of the islands. Densely forested mountain slopes, fast-streaming rivers, crystal-clear lakes, flower-filled valleys and breathtaking gorges can be found in nearly every part of Greece, and if this is what you are interested in discovering, you have an awesome number of mountain ranges to choose from.

The mountains of Evritania in the centre of Greece, offer just about everything you could hope for: unspoilt nature, picturesque villages and great opportunities for outdoor activities (skiing included), as well as a handful of centuries-old monasteries thrown in for good measure. Most of the visitors are Athenians, who come during winter weekends for a bit of skiing. Usually, they stay in the town of Karpenisi, where they happily parade their four-wheel drives and colourful snowsuits, but unfortunately fail to experience all the other aspects of mountain life.

Koryschades, a small and peaceful village just a few kilometres away from Karpenisi, is better suited to those who seek to unwind and enjoy the outdoors. It is a village steeped in history, but due to a rapidly declining population, it might have ended up totally abandoned, had it not been for Konstantinos Lappas and Maria Apostolidou, who renovated several gorgeous stone mansions and turned them into guesthouses. They infused a lot of good taste to

them – initially in a simple, traditional manner, which turned more and more stylish as they went along. The Korys and Anatoli Houses stand out.

The Anatoli House is all the way up at the top of the village. It is an old, restored family house with a converted barn next to it. Inside, house and barn are both done in a cosy, unfussy style. The bedrooms have stone and wood floors, thick bare stone walls, and they are furnished with a blend of rustic pieces and antiques. One of the great things about staying here is that right at your doorstep, there is a recently built house with a small indoor swimming pool and an inviting bar/sitting room.

KORYS AND ANATOLI HOUSES

361 00 Koryschades
Evritania
Tel. 22370-25102

The more recently opened Korys House stands out in terms of comfort and style. Its main appeal is probably the large, beautifully decorated sitting room. Furnished with marvellous country-style antiques and comfortable sofas, it is the kind of place that just makes you wish for bad weather so you have an excuse to spend your day sitting by the fire. There is also a pleasant dining room where, on special occasions, breakfast is served. (During the day, guests can use the kitchen to prepare coffee or tea.) The bedrooms are no less alluring. They are far more elegant than the kind of rooms you usually find in guesthouses and totally inviting for long lie ins and lazy afternoons.

Where you'll sleep The Anatoli House features 17 rooms all together (doubles, triples and quadruples), some of which open directly onto the terrace. Each one is different and when you book your room, you should explain what is important to you: lots of space, a fireplace, sweeping mountain views or having somewhere private to sit out-

side. The Korys House is smaller and has only five rooms: one single, two doubles and two quadruples. The rooms in both houses are equipped with a telephone, a television, a mini-bar and an en suite bathroom. One of the rooms in the Anatoli House has a Jacuzzi bath inside.

When you feel hungry Meals are served in the only restaurant of the village, on the central square. This is also run by Maria and Konstantinos. It opens early for breakfast – a rich buffet that includes scrambled eggs, sausages, bacon and cake. The lunch and dinner menu features typical Greek dishes, including traditional pies, salads and a variety of grilled and cooked meat.

Bring the children? This is a great place to come with children, who will not only enjoy the pool, but also the central square of the village, where they can freely play and run around. Many of the larger rooms and suites are well laid out for families with children. Cots are available. If you stay in the Korys House, you will of course have to respect the peace of your fellow guests, but for larger groups with children, the perfect solution is to rent the entire house.

To see and do Don't come only for the skiing. This is a superb area to visit all year round, and to go hiking, horseback riding, rafting, canoeing, canyoning or river trekking.

Good to know The guesthouses are open all year, but the winter is considered high season. Prices for a double room start at €80 in the low season, and €120 in the high season, and they include breakfast. Facilities include an indoor swimming pool and a small meeting room. Credit cards: Amex, MasterCard and Visa.

Getting there The drive to Koryschades takes around three hours from Athens. From Lamia you will follow signs for Karpenisi (it is a beautiful drive but there are some parts with lots of bends). Drive through the town of Karpenisi, bearing left after you pass through the centre, and look out for signs for Koryschades and Megalo Horio. The turn-off for Koryschades is a few kilometres from Karpenisi. The reception for the guesthouses is at the restaurant at the village square.

HELLAS COUNTRY CLUB

The idea of a 'country club' in a small mountain village in the middle of Greece may seem a tad puzzling. If you go for a few days to the Greek mountains, shouldn't you choose a charming, authentic little place to stay? Well, spend a weekend or two in a guesthouse where authenticity is omni-present, but charm, let alone comfort, is hard to find, and then, a stay in anything like a country club will become a very enticing prospect. Needless to say, there exist traditional guesthouses that are not bad at all, but the Hellas Country Club is a different offer altogether. It has qualities you find in the upmarket, chic ski resort hotels in the French Alps, and it is not surprising that it has been a hit since the day it opened.

When you first arrive at the Hellas Country Club, you might for a moment wonder what all the fuss is about. From the outside the building looks like a straightforward, Alpine-style hotel. Stepping inside, however, you will understand. Your first impression will be of the huge sitting room, decorated in a classic-meets-ethnic style, with a large roaring fireplace in the middle and candles lit in every corner. There is nothing typically Greek about it, but it has a tremendously welcoming feel. You won't be disappointed either when you check into your absolutely-not-traditional (but very comfortable!) room, or when you discover all the spots to hang out in the hotel: a large bar and playroom, a cosy, elegant restaurant, a gym, and also a lawn dotted with teakwood garden chairs.

HELLAS COUNTRY CLUB

360 75 Mikro Horio
Evritania
Tel. 22730-41570

Where you'll sleep The Hellas Country Club has 20 double and four triple rooms, as well as five suites. They are decorated in an attractive, almost urban style with strong colour schemes reflected in thick carpets, wallpaper, curtains and bedspreads. Bathrooms are great and the rooms are equipped with a television, a telephone, an internet connection, a mini-bar, a hairdryer and a safe, and they all have a balcony.

When you feel hungry In the morning you are welcomed by a well-assorted breakfast buffet. For lunch and dinner you will find a few little restaurants at walking distance, and if you take your car you can try several more nice places

along the Karpenisiotis River, some serving excellent fresh trout. If you are not in the mood to go out at all, you can order a light meal at the hotel (sandwiches, salads, cold plates, etc).

Bring the children? Children are welcome and there is always enough space for a happy cohabitation of families and the children-free. There are no typical family rooms, but the triples and the suites have space for one or two extra beds, and some of the double rooms can interconnect.

To see and do In winter, most people come to this area for a few days of skiing (the nearby resort of Mount Velouhi has 12 runs). But there is a lot you can do all year round.

The area is great for all sorts of outdoor activities: walking, horseback riding, climbing, mountain biking, river trekking, rafting and canyoning are among your choices.

Good to know The Hellas Country Club is open all year. Prices for a double room range from €110 (summer weekdays) to €205 (winter weekends) and they include breakfast. Dogs are not allowed. Credit cards: all major.

Getting there Follow signs for Karpenisi from Lamia. Bear left after you pass through the centre of Karpenisi and follow signs for Koryschades and Megalo Horio. You will see the turn-off for Mikro Horio after about 15 km, and from then on the hotel is clearly signposted.

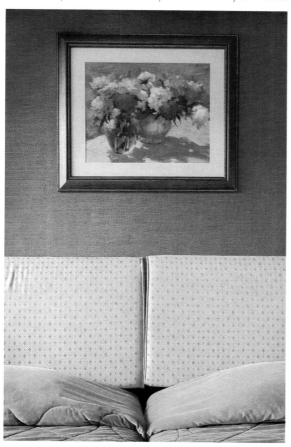

Anerada Inn, a tiny guesthouse in the mountains of Evritania, is the perfect destination if you are planning a little lovers' escape. The cream-coloured house takes its name from a local fable about *anerades*, elves who seduce old men who rest in the shade of chestnut trees, and indeed, seduction is what Anerada Inn is all about. Hidden under the leaves of, guess what, an old chestnut tree, just outside the village of Megalo Horio, it doesn't look anything like a traditional mountain house – in fact it is newly built – and it has definitely a kind of fairy-tale quality.

Just imagine, you arrive at the inn after dark, and you find burning candles showing you the way to the entrance. Then picture being welcomed into a living room (also lit by candles) which is so charming, that you might as well just drop your weekend bag and collapse straight away on the couch in front of the fireplace. And how about finally settling in a room that is so pretty and immaculately cared for, that you could just imagine the *anerades* personally preparing it for you, trying to tempt you to spend your entire weekend in there? Wouldn't you feel instantly seduced?

I admit, I don't quite believe in fairy tales, but Maria Giannakou, the creator and owner of the guesthouse, definitely has some *anerada* qualities. (I am quite sure though that she leaves the old men in the village alone!) It's as if she touches her guesthouse with a magic wand every time she passes by: "*Ting*", the white armchairs have stripes; "*ting*", the curtains have a colour to match; and "*ting*", tiny lights twinkle behind them. Maria simply cannot stop playing with the decoration and every time *I* pass by, the interiors are

a little different. The changes are always for the better and the style is consistent: soft and feminine, refined, sweet and playful, a far cry from the traditional look and feel you might expect to find in a little hotel in the mountains. There is something absolutely enchanting about Anerada Inn, and it is just wonderful that every time you come back, you find another sprinkle of magic added.

ANERADA INN

360 75 Megalo Horio
Evritania
Tel. 22370-41479

Where you'll sleep The Anerada Inn has four double rooms, one double suite and a garden house for two people. They all have an en suite shower and are equipped with a telephone, a television, a CD player, a mini-bar and a hairdryer. Some rooms have a fireplace that you can use. The garden house has a kitchenette. Opening onto the garden, the rooms are great for an independent stay, and ideal for a few days (or rather nights) of romantic cocooning. They have comfortable beds, made with crisp linen and feather down duvets most year round, and everything, bathrooms included, is styled with incredible attention to detail.

When you feel hungry You are not expected to get up early in Anerada Inn, where breakfast is served from

9.00 to 11.00. You will find a delicious spread of, among other things, croissants, scrambled and boiled eggs, cheese pies, crêpes and homemade cake. The smallish sitting room, with two tables only, calls for a bit of choreography if all guests decide to come for breakfast at the same time, especially on days too cold to sit outside, but in the summer you can take your breakfast out to the terrace. In the afternoon Maria serves drinks and tea with home-baked sweets. For lunch and dinner you will have to go out: there is one place to eat in Megalo Horio and you will find several other restaurants in the nearby villages and along the shores of the Karpenisiotis River.

Bring the children? I stayed at the Anerada Inn with my husband and children, all of us squeezed into one room. It was in the middle of the summer, so we spent most of our time outdoors, which was all very pleasant, but if it had been winter, it wouldn't have been so comfortable. Anerada Inn is a romantic getaway and, as Maria once mischievously put it to me: "a good place to make children, but not to show up with them".

To see and do If indeed you come to Anerada Inn for a romantic splurge, your agenda probably won't include much outdoor activity. The area around Karpenisi, however, is great for nature sports. The options include skiing, hiking, river trekking, canoeing and rafting.

Good to know Anerada Inn is open all year. Winter weekends and holiday periods are considered high season, with prices for a double room starting at €150. During weekdays prices start at €90 per night. They include breakfast.

Getting there From Karpenisi, follow signs for Koryschades and Megalo Horio. You will see Anerada Inn at about 15 km from Karpenisi, on the left side of the road, a little bit before the central parking area of Megalo Horio.

When Andreas was 18 years old, he had a dilemma. He had saved a bit of money from a summer job, which was just enough to buy the second-hand motorbike he so much wanted to have. But he had also set his eyes on a ruined house in Katouna, a tiny and virtually abandoned village up in the hills of Lefkada, the island where he was born and raised. The price of the house was the same as that of the bike. Most boys his age would have sped off on the bike, but Andreas loved the idea of having his own little place in such a dream spot, so he went for the house, or whatever was left of it.

Around the same time, Maria, a young Athenian fashion photographer (her grandparents were from the island) bought some other ramshackle houses at the opposite side of the village, and started doing them up. It was only a matter of time before Andreas and Maria met and became partners in their restoration projects. Both had developed a passion for Katouna, and they rebuilt several houses not so much with the purpose of living there, but more as a way to contribute to the conservation of the village. They turned them into a country retreat, a village hotel, which Maria now runs.

The houses were in a state of total dereliction when Maria and Andreas first started 'attacking' them and had to be rebuilt practically from scratch. Preserving whatever they could (some of the old fireplaces are particularly impressive), they gave each house a character of its own, so that some of them have the look of a traditional farmhouse, with bare stone walls and dark wood beamed ceilings, while others, with white washed walls and pale wood floors and beams, have a more contemporary country style.

PAVEZZO
COUNTRY RETREAT

Katouna
311 00 Lefkada
Tel. 26450-71782

What is most remarkable is the attention to detail noticed in every house. Andreas overlooked every aspect of the reconstruction (and participated in much of it whenever he could take time off from his regular occupation as air traffic controller – his passion for machines never left him after all!). At the same time Maria was already planning the decoration, rummaging around flea markets and antique shops. A marble sink from a hammam became part of a kitchen as well as a set of beautiful antique tiles found in France. Old utensils were collected to adorn the original fireplaces. Antique furniture was combined with simple traditional pieces and with some handmade ones by Andreas. All in all, a perfect balance of tradition, contemporary aesthetics and excellent comfort was created.

The setting of the houses is equally appealing. Located at the edge of the village, they nestle among greenery in a haven of absolute tranquillity. From the terraces you get sweeping views over the mountains and a small swimming pool completes the picture of bliss. In the old local dialect, *pavezzo* means shelter, or safe haven. The choice of the name could not have been more appropriate for this exceptional retreat.

Where you'll sleep The Pavezzo Country Retreat consists of seven adorable mid- and late-19th century houses (some share the same roof, others stand free), all with their own veranda or garden. Every house (except the smallest – the Ligaria Cottage) has a fully equipped kitchenette and dining area, and one or two bedrooms. Most of them are for two persons, though some can take one or two extra beds. Villa Honeymoon, a house with its own garden and pool at a few minutes' walk from the others, and Mirtia Villa, have both two bedrooms and can comfortably sleep four people, with the possibility for even two extra persons. Apart from the kitchenettes, the houses are equipped with en suite bathrooms with a shower (some are quite small), a television and a DVD player, a CD player, a hairdryer and a safe. All but two have a fireplace you can use on chilly nights early or late in the season.

When you feel hungry Though the Pavezzo Houses are basically self-catering, you will be treated to an excellent breakfast (including hearty pies, croissants, homemade biscuits and cake, and fresh orange juice) served on the terrace or in the sitting room. Other meals you can prepare yourself in the kitchenette of your house (except if you stay in the Ligaria Cottage) or you can walk over to the cute village taverna.

PAVEZZO
COUNTRY RETREAT

Bring the children? Unless you stay in "Villa Honeymoon", which has total privacy, it is probably not such a good idea to show up in the Pavezzo Country Retreat with kids in the "run around and make noise" age group. Children are welcome (and cots are available) but you should keep in mind that the place is a retreat, and that it is best to respect the peace and quiet of your fellow guests.

To see and do Lefkada is a wondrous green and mountainous island. The coast offers several stunning sandy beaches as well as protected little coves, while the inland is a heaven for walkers. If you want, you can find plenty of 'action' on the island (both in terms of water sports as well as entertainment and nightlife), but the Pavezzo Country Retreat is a place that will best appeal to you if you are looking for quiet and relaxation.

Good to know The Pavezzo Country Retreat is open from mid-March until the end of October, and during the rest of the year it works 'on request'. Prices for two people start at €90 in the low season, and €150 in the high season, and they include breakfast. Facilities include an outdoor pool, and a spa centre where you can get a massage or use the Jacuzzi and sauna. Credit cards: Amex, MasterCard and Visa.

Getting there Lefkada is an island you can drive to – it is connected to the mainland by a long and narrow causeway and a floating bridge. The drive from Athens takes about four to five hours. You can also fly to the nearby airport of Preveza: there are domestic flights from Athens several times a week and in the summer quite a few international charters fly directly to Preveza. After you cross to the island, you should follow signs for Nidri from the town of Lefkada. After about five km you take a right for Katouna (it is at three km from the coast). Once you arrive in the village, you will see a small sign for the Pavezzo Country Retreat.

If I had to describe the island of Corfu in a few words, I would say it is a bit like Tuscany, but with the sea all around it. Tuscany conjures up compelling images of rolling landscapes, vineyards and olive groves interspersed with cypresses, dozy villages and old manor houses, and indeed, that is precisely what Corfu is like. It is a wonderful place to enjoy simple pleasures, like a walk in the hills or a good meal. The island's coastline is absolutely stunning (though parts are so popular that they have developed into small tourist ghettos you should definitely avoid!), but to me it is the inland that makes Corfu really special.

The Pelecas Country Club (no connection to the other four "Country Club" hotels in Greece) is a great place to stay if you want to experience the rural aspect of Corfu, but still have the sea nearby. It is a late 18th century family estate, used in the past as an olive and wine production unit, which, in the early nineties, was converted into a marvellous country hotel.

The main mansion, sitting in the middle of the 30-acre property, was barely touched and especially on the outside, it has kept the looks of a typical Corfu farmhouse. There is nothing polished about this building, but that adds even more to its charm. The top floor hosts the 'Presidential Suite' and on the ground floor you will find the dining room and the sitting room. The outbuildings – the stables and the original olive press – were more radically refurbished and now house the comfortable guestrooms.

Perhaps "hotel" is the wrong word to use for the Pelecas Country Club, as it doesn't feel like one at all (nor do terms like "guesthouse", "inn" or even "club" describe it properly). There is something more 'private' about it. The service offered and the level of comfort you will experience are of a very high standard, but the atmosphere is quiet and laid-back, friendly and uncomplicated. This is not so by chance: owner Nikos Velianitis wants his property to be a place where people feel relaxed and at home. This aspect of 'informal luxury' has attracted quite a few public figures over the years, but no one has ever come here searching for the high life. Leisurely brunches, a large pool with sun beds, a tennis court, horses to ride, a helicopter pad, can all bring up images of 'look-at-me' jet-setters going about, but in fact, quite the opposite is true. The Pelecas Country Club is an excellent place to just be yourself and do your own thing without anyone bothering you.

PELECAS COUNTRY CLUB

Pelekas
491 00 Corfu
Tel. 26610-52917

Where you'll sleep The ten guestrooms are furnished with fabulous family heirloom pieces and charmingly decorated with old chests, lots of big candles, dried flowers, baskets with books and magazines, and so on. They range from spacious studios for two people, to suites with two bedrooms and a sitting room, for up to five people. Each has its own terrace, some with a beautiful view over the garden and the fields. All rooms and suites have an en suite bathroom or shower, a (simple) kitchenette, a television, a telephone, an internet connection, and a hairdryer.

There is also a magnificent Presidential Suite with four bedrooms, a sitting room, a dining room, a kitchen and an office, occupying the first floor of the main mansion. Guests staying here have the exclusive use of the ground-floor dining room and the adjacent sitting room, and of a private garden.

When you feel hungry Days at the Pelecas Country Club start with some of the most lavish brunches you can imagine. It is served until 12.30 in the dining room of the old mansion on a large wooden table. After a spread of omelettes, sausages, savoury pies, salads, crêpes, yogurt, fresh fruits, cakes and sweets, you *may* want to skip lunch anyway. You can have drinks in the garden house near the pool (which, incidentally, Nikos doesn't even bother to add to the bill) and for dinner you can drive a few kilometres to the village or to the town of Corfu.

Bring the children? Though the Pelecas Country Club is not a typical family place, it does has plenty to offer to children. The grounds are just wonderful to play in and run around, though of course do keep in mind that guests without children would appreciate a bit of peace and quiet. Also, because of the pool, you'll need to keep a watchful eye if you have young children who do walk about, but do not know how to swim yet. The suites are very convenient for families, and cots are available. Babysitting can be arranged.

To see and do A swimming pool, (two) horses to ride and a tennis court on the premises. Countryside that is great for walking. Fantastic beaches nearby. An 18-hole golf course at nine km. One of Greece's most beautiful towns only about ten km away. A 6th century fortress, Byzantine churches, museums, archaeological sites. Do I need to go on?

Good to know The Pelecas Country Club is open from Easter until mid- or late October. Prices for two people start at €190 per night, and they include brunch. Facilities include the outdoor swimming pool, a tennis court and a helicopter pad. There are also stables on the premises, so if you own a horse, you can take it with you on your holidays. Credit cards are not accepted.

Getting there Follow signs for Paleokastritsa and Pelekas from the town of Corfu. After about seven km, you turn left towards Pelekas. The entrance to the Pelecas Country Club is on your right, after about two km. Last time I went, the sign had disappeared, so the best I can tell you is to look out for two red brick pillars and an iron entry gate, and to have your mobile and the hotel's number at hand.

Describing Villa de Loulia is not a difficult task. The recently restored Venetian-style mansion is situated in the middle of Peroulades, a quiet, coastal village which has a pleasant, low-key feel to it and has not suffered from tourist development (despite the fact that the coast here is famous for its glorious sunsets). The mansion was built over 200 years ago by a prominent member of the local community (it was a present to his gorgeous wife Loulia) and it has been in the same family ever since. Some years ago it was converted into a hotel, run by the family, with Alexandros Mataragas in the leading role. On the outside, the terracotta-coloured building is beautiful to look at, and inside it is decorated and furnished with style and restraint. It has a walled garden, full of flowers and fruit trees, ideal to laze about, with shady sitting corners, sun beds scattered over a beautifully kept lawn, and a large and inviting swimming pool. In a nutshell: this is a perfect place for relaxing summer holidays.

But, there is more to Villa de Loulia than meets the eye. It also has an intangible quality, something that is much harder to convey. It is what makes most people who arrive as guests, leave as friends and come back for their next vacation. A lot of it has to do with the kind of person Alexandros is, and the way he runs the hotel. Alexandros does not hold a degree in hotel management – his background is in film making. He runs Villa de Loulia in a way that he simply feels is right, with a spontaneous, enthusiastic and very personal approach. He looks after his guests with great attention, always making sure they enjoy themselves and caring much less for being a 'correct' hotelier. He is just himself and has succeeded in creating an atmosphere that is best described as "*bon enfant*": easygoing, friendly and cheerful.

There is also something about the music played at Villa de Loulia. Somehow Alexandros seems always able to guess the mood his guests are in (or at least I was in) and find the perfect music for them. Or perhaps he just fools us all into believing this is the case, whereas in fact it is he, who, with his music *and* strong presence, manages to put us all in the mood he wants us to be in – blissfully happy and relaxed!

VILLA DE LOULIA

Peroulades
490 80 Corfu
Tel. 26630-95394

Where you'll sleep The nine double rooms and the two suites (for up to four people) are all in the old family mansion. They are done in a simple, elegant style, without any extravagance or clutter. Colour schemes are carefully chosen and most furniture is antique; several rooms have charming brass beds. If you have the choice, ask for a room that has its own space to sit out. Set under the eaves, the second-floor rooms have the best views, but probably stay least cool during hot summer days. All rooms have an en suite shower or bathroom and they are equipped with a mini-bar, a telephone, a television and a hairdryer.

When you feel hungry It is unlikely that you will ever get hungry at Villa de Loulia. A daily varied breakfast is served from 8.00 onwards, with mostly local and homemade products: fresh bread, excellent jams, village eggs, yogurt, fruits, juices and sweet treats. Later during the day you can order a snack or a salad (with ingredients harvested straight from Villa de Loulia's own garden), or walk over to one of the nearby restaurants. Do come back for dinner though: there is no better way to dine than sitting out by the pool for a candle-lit, home-cooked meal. Prepared by the family, the food is a praise to everything pure and fresh and a celebration of traditional cuisine at its best.

Bring the children? Villa de Loulia is the kind of place enjoyed mostly by couples, and, even though there is no strict 'no kids' rule, families with young (or rather, noisy) children are not encouraged to book here.

To see and do Corfu offers most of the things that summer holidaymakers want, and appeals to many different kinds of people. If you are looking for action you're in the right place (a few kilometres away, the touristy village of Sidari has quite a bit of it, though not necessarily the kind you might be after), but if you want peace and quiet you won't be disappointed either. Villa de Loulia will appeal to those who seek tranquillity; walking, reading and swimming are the recommended activities here. Also, if you enjoy what you eat at the hotel, you can ask for cooking classes. I am still trying to reproduce the marvellous tomato sauce Alexandros served for an impromptu (pasta) lunch, and I am kicking myself now for not having taken any of his classes.

Good to know Villa de Loulia is open from the Easter holidays until mid- or the end of October. Prices per night for a double room start at €200 (breakfast on top), but sometimes there are special offers for early bookings or packages. Credit cards: Amex, MasterCard and Visa.

Getting there Peroulades is at the north-western tip of Corfu. From Corfu town, follow the road signs for Sidari, and then continue towards Peroulades. Villa de Loulia is on your left as you enter the village. The drive takes about 45 minutes.

248

Zagori

The Zagorohoria, the group of nearly 50 settlements in the mountains of Epiros in the northwest of Greece, are among the most beautiful and unspoilt villages in the country. Some are very small and have only a handful of year-round residents, and others are more developed and attract quite a few visitors, some even by the busload.

Situated at the end of a 12 km long mountain road, with a series of impossibly sharp turns (at least for buses!), Papingo is among the most captivating villages on the entire Greek mainland. It features immaculately restored stone houses, narrow cobbled lanes, small churches and shady little squares. Instead of having been spoilt by tourism, this village has been revived by it. While a few decades ago there were no more than a couple of *kafenions*, you now find several nice little cafés and places to eat, and the atmosphere, while still quiet and laid-back, has become just pleasantly lively.

Nikos Saxonis and his wife Poly, where among the very first to start this positive development, when, about 20 years ago, they decided to turn their back on their busy life in Athens and restore three 150-year-old stone houses, in order to turn them into a small hotel. They meticulously preserved their original character and rendered them simple and unpretentious, in a tasteful style. They have also put in a lot of effort into landscaping, and the terraced garden, ablaze with flowers, may well be the most idyllic spot in Papingo.

The Saxonis Houses swiftly became the Zagorohoria's premier place to stay and even though back then the drive from the capital was much more demanding than it is today (the roads have considerably improved), Athenians didn't hesitate to 'go for it', even for as little as a three-day break. Its success inspired many others to also open guesthouses in Papingo, and nowadays,

the Saxonis Houses, slightly worn at the edges (the small winter sitting room in particular could be made a little more inviting), are no longer the place to stay. However, thanks to the peaceful ambience and the no-nonsense attitude of Nikos and Poly, who do everything by themselves without a single member of staff, it is still one of the nicest addresses in Papingo.

SAXONIS HOUSES

440 16 Papingo
Zagori
Tel. 26530-41615

Where you'll sleep The Saxonis Houses feature three double and five triple bedrooms. They are tastefully sober, in keeping with the local tradition and the spirit of the guesthouse in general. There are no televisions or any other amenities in the rooms, but they all have a very decent shower or bathroom. (With the exception of one, they are all en suite.) Most rooms have local-style wood-built beds positioned under the windows. The cosiest of all is probably room number three, which is slightly different in style, with a double bed placed under an arched niche.

When you feel hungry Breakfast, served from 8.30 to 11.30 on the terrace or in the snug dining room, is maybe not a grand affair, but in all its simplicity, it is just right. Everything is fresh: the orange juice, the bread, the perfectly boiled eggs, the home-baked cake, the yogurt with honey and the homemade jams are all just delicious. For your other meals you have to walk – no more than a couple of minutes – to the village centre.

Bring the children? The Saxonis couple are really trying to offer their guests a quiet and peaceful getaway; therefore they do not encourage visits from families with children. The place is ideal for singles or couples who want a few days of total tranquillity, whereas some other places in the village are much more suitable for families.

To see and do You'll have to agree with Nikos and Poly: if peace and quiet is what you are looking for, you're in the right place. But this doesn't mean you should sit still. Walking is the number one activity in the area (anything from a little stroll to serious hikes), while you can also go rafting and fishing. In the summer you can go for a swim in a natural rock pool near Papingo.

Good to know The Saxonis Houses are open all year. Prices per night for two people are between €65 and €85, including breakfast. Dogs are not allowed. Credit cards are not accepted.

Getting there From Ioannina, take the road in the direction of the airport and Konitsa. After 40 km, turn right towards Aristi and Papingo (lots of sharp turns during the last 11 km). Normally you can drive into Papingo, though when there is snow you sometimes have to leave your car at the parking lot just outside the village. Take a left about 50 m after the big church (with the bell tower), and turn left again, then follow the narrow stone path (cars can just about pass) for about 80 m. Just before the path turns slightly to the right you will see Saxonis Houses, on your right. You can drive all the way to the gate to unload, but at other times it is best to leave your car at the entrance of the village, just a few minutes by foot.

Staying in the village of Papingo is very appealing, but staying right outside it, can be even better, especially at the side where the road ends and nature starts. George and Markella Papaevangelou, who just like the Saxonis couple, have 'escaped' from Athens, picked one of the best sites imaginable for their guesthouse in Papingo. It is a very beautiful spot at the end of a dirt road, after the last house of the village, and it has stunning mountain views. Though it is only a five-minute walk from the centre, it feels like it is in the middle of nowhere.

The guesthouse consists of several buildings. They are recent constructions but, because they are made entirely out of natural stone, wood and old materials, they don't feel new at all and they look just like the original Papingo houses. The interiors portray a similar 'old house' feeling, though they don't have the very low ceilings you find in the traditional houses of the area. (In the past people did whatever they could to keep warm, but the dependable central heating system of our days allows for higher ceilings).

The large living room is a major drawing card for the guesthouse. The wooden floors and ceilings, bare stone walls, a big fireplace and country-style decoration give it a particularly cosy and warm atmosphere. You can really tell how much energy and enthusiasm George poured into this space, a reflection of the way he runs the guesthouse: by enjoying every minute of it.

PAPAEVANGELOU

440 16 Papingo
Zagori
Tel. 26530-41135

Where you'll sleep The ten bedrooms (doubles, triples and quadruples) are in the main building. They are done in a traditional, no-frills style with wooden floors, ceilings and built-in beds, and they have en suite showers. Point out what you are interested in when you book, because some rooms have a fireplace, others don't; most have beautiful views on the rocks of Mount Gamila, but some rooms look out over the terrace; and some have double beds, while others have singles. There are three studios (for up to three persons) in small, separate houses. They are nicely proportioned and slightly cosier in style, and have a large bathroom, a kitchen corner, a television and a DVD player.

When you feel hungry George serves a generous breakfast (fresh orange juice, boiled or scrambled eggs, cheeses, traditional pies, homemade jams, yogurt, fruits and cakes) from 9.00 to 11.00. If later in the day you have a small

craving you can also order snacks, but there is no restaurant at the guesthouse. If you are staying in a studio, you can prepare yourself a bite to eat 'at home', otherwise the nearest taverna is about five minutes on foot.

Bring the children? Guesthouse Papaevangelou is probably one of the best places to stay in Papingo with children, not only because of its location (perfect for kids to roam around), but also because of the unfussy interiors (no worries about things breaking) and the easy-going atmosphere. Several rooms can function as family rooms and cots are available.

To see and do Papingo is a destination for all seasons, with many choices for outdoor activities (walking, hiking, swimming, rafting, fishing…) and, of course, for tours in the surrounding villages.

Good to know The guesthouse is open all year. Prices for a double room start at €90 during holiday periods, long weekends and the month of August. The remainder of the year they start at €70, breakfast included. Credit cards are not accepted.

Getting there From Ioannina, follow signs for the airport and when you get there, take the road towards the direction of Konitsa. About 40 km after Ioannina, turn right in the direction of Aristi and Papingo (lots of sharp turns during the last 11 km). Normally you can drive into Papingo, though when there is snow you may have to leave your car at the entrance of the village. When you are in it, go straight until the road forks (there is a small church on your left). Stick to the right until you reach a tiny square, and then turn left into an unpaved road. You will find the guesthouse at the end on your right.

Kyriakos Griveas, the founder of the miniature chain of "Country Club" hotels in Greece, has a nose for gaps in the market. He launched his first Country Club when he detected a rapidly increasing demand for smart and genuinely comfortable weekend destinations, and after the success of the first, he created several more. Each time he opened a new Country Club it became an instant hit and *the* place to be seen.

Recognising how Greeks like to go on excursions and generally move along in packs (the parea, Greek for "clan of friends", is a big thing in this country), Kyriakos came up with a new idea. He purchased two neighbouring historical mansions in the village of Papingo, but instead of converting them into a typical Country Club *hotel*, he decided to respect their original layout as houses, and to operate them as such, though with a level of service you only find in top hotels.

The concept of the Archontikon Country Club cleverly addresses a clientele looking for a fusion of hotel and villa-rental, offering the convenience of full service, but without the less appealing sides of a hotel. There is no reception desk, no room numbers and heavy key holders (let alone these not-credit cards you have to stick in the wall to be able to switch the light on), no strict hours, no half-finished breakfast buffets, and most of all, no other guests to consider (or to bother you...). Spaces you would have to share with strangers if you were in a hotel are yours only – you have full privacy – while at the same time, very attentive staff will cater to your every whim.

But of course, there is a lot more to the Archontikon than just a clever concept. Kyriakos brought some unheard of elegance and luxury to the area of the Zagorohoria where the majority of places look gorgeous on the outside, but are either blindingly kitsch or sadly sober inside. The Archontikon is neither. Its interiors are absolute eye catchers. Although the décor is undeniably heavy, it is in tune with the local style: warm colours, wide floor boards covered with antique rugs, low, intricately carved ceilings, and a period fireplace in most rooms. Antiques are combined with traditional furniture; silver buckles from local traditional dresses adorn the walls; and upholstery is made of the finest fabrics.

ARCHONTIKON COUNTRY CLUB

440 16 Papingo
Zagori
Tel. 26530-41002

The two mansions that make up the Archontikon date from the 19th century: the larger of the two was built in 1873, and its neighbour dates back to 1865. Both houses have a sitting room with a fireplace that will be lit for you in the winter evenings, a dining room and a vaulted kitchen that the guests can use. The Archontikon 1873 is the most majestic in style (for instance the bedrooms all feature majestic king-sized beds), while the other mansion is a bit smaller and has a more traditional touch (with built-in beds).

Where you'll sleep The Archontikon 1873 has four double bedrooms on the first floor and a magnificent suite on the ground floor, each with its own bathroom. The other – smaller – house has three bedrooms (all on the first floor), one that has en suite bathroom and two that share one. There is also a garden house with two more bedrooms with en suite bathrooms that can be rented in conjunction with Archontikon 1865. All bedrooms are equipped with a television, a telephone and an internet connection. Some rooms also have DVD and CD players. Hairdryers are available.

When you feel hungry Breakfast will be waiting for you on a big table on the vine-covered terrace or in the dining room, and is based pretty much on the-eat-as-much-as-you-can principle. In theory breakfast is served from 8.00 to 10.30, but if you inform the staff the night before what time (roughly) you intend to get up, you can have it any time you'd like.

For lunch and dinner you have your choice of local restaurants, but with such a great kitchen at your disposal, why not occasionally prepare your own meal? If you give the staff prior notice, they can even do the grocery shopping for you in Ioannina. The ultimate relaxing dinner solution is to have it catered, so that without lifting a finger (or opening a cookbook), you can enjoy traditional dishes in the privacy of your house or garden.

Bring the children? Children are welcome in all of the Country Clubs and the Archontikon is no exception. Of the two mansions, the Archontikon 1865 is probably the best choice for families. The more 'grand' style of the other one may not be very comfortable with small children (plus all the beds are doubles). Cots are available in both houses.

To see and do The best way to enjoy your stay in the Archontikon is to come with a group of friends. Many of the activities offered in the area, like rafting and going for hikes through the mountains or the Vikos gorge, will also be more fun when you are with a bunch of people. The best activity, however, may well be just hanging out at your house in the garden or, in the winter, in the cosy sitting room by the fire.

ARCHONTIKON
COUNTRY CLUB

Good to know The Archontikon is open all year. The (extended) winter (October until the end of May) is considered high season. Depending on the season, prices per night for the Archontikon 1865 range from €300 to €600 (for three rooms), and from €600 to €1150 for the Archontikon 1873 (for five rooms). All prices include breakfast. Bookings for smaller groups or individuals are also accepted, though normally not during long weekends and holidays. Dogs are not allowed. Credit cards: all major.

Getting there From Ioannina, take the road that goes past the airport in the direction of Konitsa. After 40 km, take the turn-off for Aristi and Papingo (lots of sharp turns during the last 11 km). Normally you can drive into Papingo, though when there is snow you may have to leave your car at the entrance of the village. Take a left about 50 m after the big church (with the bell tower), and turn left again, and then follow the narrow stone path (cars can just about pass) for about 150 m, and you will see the entrance to the guesthouses on your right.

Situated on a plateau at an altitude of nearly 1000 m, Ano Pedina is not the most typical of the villages in the mountains of Zagori. It is not as striking as some of the other "Zagorohoria" – as they are called – but it is unquestionably pretty with its distinctive 18th and 19th century houses made of natural stone and slate roofs, and it has more of a rural ambience. Also, in a way it feels more 'real', as it does not attract all that many visitors (and certainly not day-trippers). The village counts around 70 permanent residents, 12 of whom are children, an adult-child ratio you rarely come across in such small villages, which tend to get abandoned by young families who prefer the easier life of the city, while the older generations stay behind.

Sophia and Christos Stratsianis, an economist/architect couple living in Ioannina, enjoyed so much coming to Ano Pedina during their weekends, that about ten years ago they bought a house at the top of the village. Built in 1870, it needed substantial work in order to be a comfortable place to stay – everything inside (floors, walls, ceilings, fireplaces) had to be redone. After a two-year restoration, the family used it for a little while as a holiday home, but soon started a new round of works to convert it into a guesthouse.

Primoula could easily have become 'yet another' typical Zagori guesthouse, but Christos and Sophia went out of their way to make their place something special. Excellent taste, great care and devotion, and the willingness to invest some extra money all make for a winning combination, and in the case of Primoula, you can tell that all three elements were present. Your first impression will be of the courtyard, which in the summer is ablaze with flowers. Upon entering the building you are in for more visual treats: everything inside, from the architectural design and the selection of furniture, to the smallest decorative detail, all reflect the loving, elegant touch of a couple addicted to perfection!

Sophia is not usually there to personally welcome her guests. She manages the guesthouse from a distance – a caretaker lives on the premises – but she regularly shuttles up and down between Ano Pedina and Ioannina, to make sure everything is in perfect order. It so often happens that carefully conceived guesthouses gradually lose their charm due to sloppy upkeep, but in Primoula everything looks as fresh as day one and you invariably find the guesthouse in an impeccable state.

PRIMOULA

455 00 Ano Pedina
Zagori
Tel. 26530-71133

Where you'll sleep The feeling of special attention and perfectionist care carries on to the bedrooms, which are all different, though equally enchanting. They are romantic and slightly nostalgic in feel, but not overly retro. It is as if Sophia, who was the key spirit behind the interior design, wants to offer her guests a different experience every time. So in one room you can sleep in an antique brass bed and in another you'll find a canopied bed. There is a room with an old-style wooden bed, and one where you will simply find a mattress on top of a wooden sleeping plateau. All bedrooms have so much charm that it is simply impossible to designate a favourite among the five double and the two triple ones, though when you book you may want to ask for a room with a view. Three rooms are in the house itself and the others are in two smaller buildings in the courtyard. You can also stay in a little house for two or three persons, a bit further up. It used to be a donkey stable, but later it was converted into a "Hans and Gretchen" type of cottage. All bedrooms, and the cottage, have a television, a telephone and an en suite shower, and most have also a fireplace you can use.

When you feel hungry Breakfast is served from 8.00 to 12.00 (or even later). When the guesthouse is full, you can help yourself from a buffet, otherwise a procession of bread, croissants, (village) eggs, fresh juice, pites, cake, homemade marmalade and spoon-sweets will end up at your table. Though Primoula does not have a restaurant, you can ask the staff to prepare you a cold plate or a light meal for later in the day, and you will also find several traditional places to eat in the village.

Bring the children? Although the romantic character of the guesthouse makes it particularly suitable for couples, families with children are welcome. Several of the bedrooms, and the cottage, can take an extra bed (and cots are available as well), but if you travel with more children it is better to take two double rooms. (Ask for two adjacent rooms in the main building, if your children are small.)

To see and do The village of Ano Pedina enjoys quite a 'strategic' position in Zagori: it is easy to reach – the drive from Ioannina takes no more than 40 minutes, on good roads – and it is a perfect base from where to explore the other Zagorohoria. For instance Papingo and Tsepelovo are just over half an hour by car, and Monodendri is barely ten minutes. Just outside Ano Pedina you can visit the monastery of Evagelistria (built in 1786) and the monastery of Saint Paraskevi (dating from 1750). Also, if you are interested in outdoor action (walking, rafting and in the winter even skiing), the village is a good starting point.

Good to know Guesthouse Primoula is open all year. Prices per night for two persons start at €115 during holiday periods and long weekends, and at €90 during the rest of the year, and they include breakfast. Credit cards: Diners, MasterCard, Visa.

Getting there From Ioannina, take the road in the direction of the airport and then Konitsa. Turn right about 13 km after the airport towards Tsepelovo (20 m after the iron footbridge). After 11 km, rather than turning right towards Tsepelovo, continue straight in the direction of Ano Pedina. Take the road into the village, and turn left up the hill into the narrow road across the church. You will see the guesthouse at the end on your right.

When Dutch-born Rita Berends gets an idea in her head, there is no stopping her. Twenty years ago, her doctor in Holland told her it would be good for her health to live in a warm and dry climate. A few weeks later she was on a plane to Rhodes, where a tour operator had offered her a job as a tourist guide. (Never mind that she didn't speak a word of Greek and had zero knowledge of the country.) Rita arrived with a bag filled with summer clothes in early spring, which happened to be the coldest in years. So much for the warm climate… But a positive outlook and a willingness to learn can take someone a long way, and dressed in several layers of summer T-shirts, Rita settled in fast. Meeting Yannis Kirlinkitsis definitely helped. He became her best friend and, three years later, her husband.

After they married, Yannis and Rita gave up the warm weather of Rhodes to move to the cooler north of Greece, where Yannis started a restaurant in the town of Ioannina. It was another brave decision, given that he had no experience in the restaurant business whatsoever. But he too turned out to be a fast learner.

Eight years later the next challenge came along, when the couple (by now with two children) decided to take up the offer of running a guesthouse in the mountain village of Ano Pedina. Again, this was an occupation in which they had no expertise, but hospitable by nature and happy in their work, they made this guesthouse, to Spiti tou Oresti, into one of the most welcoming and homely places in the area.

Their only regret during the eight years they spent running it, was that it was not their own, and so they couldn't keep it up exactly the way they would have liked to. But then again, a new dream had already begun to take shape in their minds, one you probably guessed: to start a place of their own. They found a lovely mid-19th century mansion for sale that was just perfect. It used to be the residence of the village doctor, until in the fifties it became a boarding school where girls learned the arts of weaving, embroidering, sewing and knotting rugs. When Yannis and Rita bought it in 1999, it had been abandoned for 25 years, and it was ready for a thorough restoration.

PORFIRON

Ano Pedina
455 00 Zagori
Tel. 26530-71579

The project took a little longer than expected, not only because this is typically what happens when it comes to construction works in the Greek countryside, but also because the couple was not willing to make any compromises at all, even when that implied waiting for weeks or months for the most skilled of labourers to show up. Yannis had been dreaming of a large, state-of-the-art kitchen to work in and a beautiful dining room for guests to enjoy his food, and would have it no other way. Rita was set on giving every bedroom its own colours and character, so instead of ordering from the hotel furniture catalogue, she collected antique beds for some of the rooms, and had traditional wooden beds made by hand for others, while fretting over colour schemes.

When I visited a few weeks before Porfiron was finally going to open, Yannis was still waiting for the delivery of his kitchen equipment and Rita was putting up the curtains (different fabrics for each room), but the guesthouse already had a 'happy' and welcoming feel to it, making me wish to be one of their first guests.

Where you'll sleep The guesthouse features eight bedrooms. The largest is a family maisonette (for up to five people) with a triple room on the top level and below it a smaller room where two children can sleep. The other rooms are triples and doubles, one of which is quite small and usually rented as a single room. All of them are equipped with a telephone, an internet connection, a television and a refrigerator (except the single room), and have a (smallish) en suite shower. Several rooms have a fireplace, and you can ask for wood if you want to use them.

When you feel hungry With Yannis' background as a restaurateur, you will probably never get a chance to feel hungry. In the morning you will be served a nice breakfast with fresh bread, homemade marmalades, eggs, yogurt, cake and fresh juice in the winter, and, if you smile sweetly, Rita may also prepare genuine Dutch pancakes for you. At lunchtime you can order from a small menu and for dinner you can try some traditional home-cooked food. Usually there are about three dishes to choose from, including a vegetarian option. If you go out hiking for the day, you can ask for a lunch pack.

Bring the children? Friendly and easy-going, Porfiron is an ideal escape for you and your children, especially if they enjoy being in the countryside. The two sons of Rita and Yannis who have been living in the village since a very young age, already have announced to their parents that they "never want to leave" and, after a few days of happy outdoor living, yours might just say the same. Apart from the maisonette room (ideal for families), two large triple rooms on the first floor can interconnect and become totally convenient for people with children. Cots are available.

To see and do Think again if you believe that in a small, unspoilt village there will be very little for you to do. The Zagori area is great for excursions and outdoor activity, and Rita is always in the know of things to do in or around the village. Some interesting people live in Ano Pedina and Rita pushes them to organise activities, so with a bit of luck you may end up collecting mushrooms with a well-known Greek chef, taking a master class in photography, having a professional weaver teach you some tricks of the trade, or relaxing with your own yoga teacher.

Good to know Porfiron is open all year. Prices for a double room start at €60 in the low season (the summer months), and €90 in the high season (Christmas and Eastern holidays), and they include breakfast. Credit cards: MasterCard and Visa.

Getting there From Ioannina, take the road in the direction of the airport and then Konitsa. Turn right about 13 km after the airport towards Tsepelovo (right after you pass under a footbridge). After 11 km, rather than going right towards Tsepelovo, continue straight in the direction of Ano Pedina. Take the road up into the village, and you will see the terracotta-coloured building on your left.

Dilofo is only about ten kilometres from Ano Pedina, but it is a wholly different proposition. Unspoilt and off the main tourist track, both villages have a lot of charm, but of a different kind. Ano Pedina is spread out and has a rural and open feel to it; Dilofo lies hidden amongst the trees on the mountainside, and houses are tightly clustered together. Ano Pedina is visible from a distance, but its charm will only unveil itself once you are in the village, whereas to get to Dilofo, you follow a narrow winding road amidst dense greenery, until the village suddenly looms in front of you; needless to say, the moment you see it, you love it.

As much as a cliché this may sound, in Dilofo you really get the sense that time has long stood still. With only a handful of year-round residents (the current figure stands at seven!) and little on offer in terms of services or entertainment, most visitors to the area are drawn to better known villages like Monodendri and Tsepelovo, where indeed at weekends they arrive en masse. But in Dilofo, once you leave your car and walk over the uneven stone paths, past the large school building (dating from 1860), the churches, a small square with a little *kafenion* and the centuries-old, slate-covered stone mansions, you realise you have the whole village to yourself – except if it is a long weekend, when understandably there are a few more people around.

Some years ago, when it became the location site for filming a Greek television series, Dilofo started getting some attention; pretty soon it was talked about as one of the most authentic villages in the country. Fortunately, this didn't affect its character, though it definitely created a 'market' for an appealing guesthouse. Arhondiko Dilofo, which opened in the summer of 2005, was just what the village needed. It consists of two adjacent houses that open onto a shared courtyard: a very small one, dating from 1633 and a larger one that was built in 1864 and was inhabited until 1995. Even though the buildings were not in a terribly bad condition, it took the new owners, George Kontaxis and his cousin Andonis, two years to renovate them and convert then into a guesthouse. (All the materials were carried to the construction site by mules from the entrance of the village!)

ARHONDIKO DILOFO

Dilofo
450 70 Zagori
Tel. 26530-22455

During the renovation, George was careful to preserve as much as he could, and he even managed to salvage and restore three 19th century frescos he found in the house. Assisted by his wife who took care of the interior decoration, he created a sweet, unpretentious place that truly feels part of the village. It is not fancy or anything, but it is cosy and inviting. The old winery has been converted into a snug sitting/dining room, and in the summer the courtyard is a lovely 'sit out' spot.

Where you'll sleep Arhondiko Dilofo features nine rooms. Four are strictly doubles and the other five have an extra bed. Furnished and decorated with a lot of care (soft colours, hand-painted fireplaces, some antique beds) they certainly are lovely. Each one has its own character, but the most appealing ones are those on the first floor, on the "summer side" of the house, overlooking the village. The "winter rooms" at the backside, and a few rooms that open onto the courtyard, have a very cosy and inviting feel to them, but they have smaller windows and lack the views. The rooms are equipped with a telephone,

a television and a refrigerator, and they have a good en suite shower. Most have a fireplace that you are welcome to use.

When you feel hungry Breakfast is served from 7.00 to 11.00. It is a small buffet with fresh eggs, traditional pies and home-baked cake, and if you want it can be brought to your room. There are two places to eat in the village (though I doubt both are open all year round), and of course there are plenty more options in the nearby villages.

Bring the children? Children are welcome, but keep in mind that it is impossible to go around in the village with a pushchair, so it might not be a good idea to bring children under the age of two (though cots are available). Otherwise, the car-free pathways make the village a wonderful place for your little ones to roam around.

To see and do Dilofo is yet another attractive spot from where to explore the Zagorohoria and enjoy nature. An additional advantage of staying in Arhondiko Dilofo is that George coop-

erates with a professional guide who can take you hiking, canyoning and caving. He also organises two-day canyoning and cave exploring courses for beginners (*and* he helps out in the guesthouse as well!).

Good to know The guesthouse is open all year. Prices for a double room start at €70 in the low season, and €100 during holiday periods and long weekends. They include breakfast. Dogs are not allowed. The nearest place to park your car is a few minutes on foot over uneven pathways. Credit cards: MasterCard and Visa.

Getting there From Ioannina, take the road in the direction of Konitsa (in Ioannina, follow signs for the airport). Turn right about 13 km after the airport in the direction of Tsepelovo. The turn-off for Dilofo is at 14 km from the main road. Park at the entrance of the village and continue on foot. Walk up for about 100 m and then take the stone path down to the right, towards the village square, where you take a right again. After 20 m you go left, and you will see the guesthouse on your left.

ARHONDIKO ALEXIOU VERGOULA

Situated in the north of Greece, Kastoria, a charming Macedonian town, is hardly ever included in the itineraries of foreign tourists, nor do people living in Greece consider it a mini-escape destination. It is just too far out of the way. This is a pity, because the town has a lot going for it. It enjoys a great setting, on the shores of a magnificent natural lake surrounded by mountains. The biggest part of the town is actually built on a peninsula that stretches far into the lake; over there you will also find its most charming neighbourhood: the historical district of Doltso, well known for its superb 18th and 19th century noble houses. It is a neighbourhood with a wonderfully calm, almost village-like atmosphere with kids playing freely in the narrow cobbled streets and alleyways, where cars only just manage to pass through.

Tassos Sfinarolakis spent a great deal of his childhood in this part of town, living in a glorious 150-year-old mansion that was used as a boarding house for kids living too far out to make the daily commute to school. When years later, he was offered the chance to buy that same mansion, he leapt at it and decided to convert it into a hotel. Carrying out a meticulous restoration, he left all of its beautiful old elements intact, and then added an oriental touch, with Asian furniture he collected during his travels in the Far East, and aged teakwood pieces he designed himself, mainly in Indonesian style. He chose beautifully simple designs, which indeed blend perfectly with the traditional Macedonian character of the mansion. The overall effect is stylish and impressive, and despite the admiring gasps the interiors do elicit from new arrivals, the atmosphere is rightly maintained low-key, quiet and relaxed.

ARHONDIKO
ALEXIOU VERGOULA

14 Editras St.
521 00 Kastoria
Tel. 24670-23415

Where you'll sleep The large and comfortable bedrooms (two doubles, three triples and four quadruples) are on the top two floors of the mansion – most have a view over the lake. They have style and character, but they are not too obviously decorated nor do they offer any superfluous luxury. You will find good beds, a fireplace (in some rooms) and a telephone, but no television (though if you are really desperate for one, it will be brought to you). Each room has an en suite shower, but in some rooms it is tucked away in the old wardrobes and really tiny!

When you feel hungry Breakfast and dinner (and lunch upon request) are prepared with the freshest ingredients, straight from the farm of Tassos' family, and are served in an intimate dining room on the lowest floor. Late sleepers will be delighted that breakfast is served up to 14.00.

Bring the children? Children are welcome in the mansion, but there are no special facilities for them. So unless you are planning to spend most of your time outdoors, bring your own supply of books, toys and games, or you will probably end up asking for that television to be brought up to your room.

To see and do You should 'do' Kastoria on foot. It may put a little strain on your leg muscles – some of the alleyways are pretty steep – but it will give you a chance to see up to 70 tiny Byzantine churches (if you manage to find them all), the oldest dating from the 9th century. There are two museums, both worth a visit: the Byzantine Museum displaying a small but impressive collection of icons, and the Folklore Museum where you get an idea of the way wealthy fur merchants in Kastoria lived and worked over 200 years ago. A further walk (or drive) along the winding road around the peninsula will take you through a lovely forest by the water, past the 11th century Mavritissas Monastery.

The surroundings of Kastoria are great for nature and sports lovers. The lake itself offers a multitude of things to do (fishing, canoeing, sailing…) while the mountains nearby are terrific for hiking. In the winter you can even do a bit of skiing.

Good to know The mansion stays open all year. Prices for a double room start at €60, breakfast included (extra charge for the use of the fireplace). Credit cards are not accepted.

Getting there It is not easy to explain how to get to the hotel. If you are lucky you'll drive straight to it (as I did the first time I went there), but you might also go round a few circles until you find it (as it happened to me the second time). Start by following signs for the centre of the town, and try and find the Metropolis Cathedral (on Manolakis Street). After you pass the Cathedral, you should see a sign for the hotel on your left.

Nymfaio is unique. This is not only because it is so pretty (it is indeed known as the most beautiful village in the north of Greece), nor because it is set, at an altitude of 1350 m, in absolutely stunning scenery in the Vitsi mountain range. It is not because of its history, even though it ranked among the most prosperous settlements of the region for over 500 years. It is not because of the horses that wander around freely and not because of the bear sanctuary at the edge of the village either. All these are just part of what makes Nymfaio such an amazing place altogether. But what makes it truly unique, is its development in the last 15-odd years, which tells a fascinating story of how the vision of two men can alter the fate of an entire area.

Nymfaio was a village in decline until Yannis Boutaris, Greece's best-known wine-producer, together with writer/journalist (and now also elected mayor) Nikos Mertzos, set in motion a chain of events that led to its revival. It all started with the restoration of dilapidated properties – only about one third of the village was actually standing at the time. The two men also realised that the village needed a *raison d'être*. It somehow had to attract visitors, and prettiness alone wouldn't do the trick. Boutaris had two excellent ideas, both of which put Nymfaio back on the map.

The first was to create Arkturos, a sanctuary for bears confiscated from their (mainly Roma) owners, after the cruel practice of bears dancing for public entertainment was banned. Now, a decade later, the once-tiny non-profit organisation has mushroomed into a cross-border project that tracks the movements of the estimated 150 endangered bears that roam Greece's northern frontiers. Bears were soon joined by wolves and today Arkturos is perhaps the best known environmental initiative in Greece.

Boutaris' other idea was to set up a place to stay, so stylish and inviting, that it would be a reason in itself to come to the village. He built a beautiful house – new, but modelled after his great grandmother's house – that, soon after it opened in 1993, was accredited as one of Greece's best. Indeed, La Moara ("watermill" in the local, Vlach dialect) offers superbly spacious and comfortable bedrooms, beautiful decoration – art deco elements are juxtaposed with traditional furniture and design elements – plenty of space for guests to relax by the fireplace, and great home-cooked meals. In line with his general ideology, Boutaris didn't staff La Moara with 'professionals', but with people from the village. In fact, it has been managed by the same couple since it opened, and this gives it the atmosphere of a family-run guesthouse.

LA MOARA

530 78 Nymfaio
Florina
Tel. 23860-31377

Where you'll sleep La Moara has some exceptional bedrooms. Two are suites, done in a modern 'chalet' style, each with a double bed set under the sloping roof and a large bath… in the room itself. They are great 'cocoons' for a cosy, romantic winter escape. The style of the other six rooms is different: they offer the perfect blend of luxury and tradition, each with a wonderful bed, a sitting corner with a television, and a set of wardrobes hiding everything else, including the shower and a small refrigerator.

When you feel hungry When I eat out, I like not to have to choose. So I always particularly enjoy dinner at La Moara, a set, four-course meal, served in an elegant dining room, where I have only the wine to think of. Everything is home-cooked; it is traditional fare, but of a high standard, and it all tastes very good. Dinner, however, is only served on Fridays and Saturdays (daily during the holiday periods), but of course there are plenty of restaurants in the village. For breakfast (8.00 to 10.30) you can help yourself from a well-assorted buffet, with home-baked cake, generous amounts of fresh orange juice, and perfectly boiled, free-range eggs.

Bring the children? Nymfaio is a fantastic place to come with children and of course they are more than welcome at La Moara. In the six spacious bedrooms, two divans can be used as single beds. Cots are available too. The basement of La Moara features a large playroom (for young and old – there is also a billiard table) with games and toys, and a selection of videos.

To see and do Most Greek guests consider Nymfaio a place to visit during winter weekends (and La Moara fills up!), which is a pity, because this is a great place to go all year round. The summer is perhaps even the best season to be here: to go for walks through the endless forests, to go horse-riding, and certainly to visit Arkturos. (Keep in mind that the bears sleep during the winter months!)

Good to know La Moara is open all year, except for one month in the summer, usually July. During holiday periods and the month of August it is open seven days a week, but the rest of the year it closes on Mondays and Tuesdays. Prices for a double room range from €125 (week-days except holiday periods, breakfast included) to €210 (in August, holiday periods and weekends in the winter, half-board basis). Credit cards: Amex, Diners and Visa.

Getting there Nymfaio lies (roughly) between Kastoria and Edessa. Look out for the village of Aetos, from where you take a spectacular winding road up the mountains towards Nymfaio (nine km). As you arrive at the village, turn left onto the 'ring road' after you pass the parking lot, and you will see the guesthouse after a few bends.

LA SOARE

Recently, the Boutaris family opened another mansion, in a building dating from 1925. La Soare, as it is called, is not a guesthouse as such, but a private residence that can be rented in its entirety, with a few services provided such as cleaning (every other day) and, upon request, grocery shopping. The interiors of this house also reveal an interesting combination of art deco and traditional elements, and the overall feeling you get is that of a lovely, old-world family home (which is of course exactly what it used to be – and not much has changed). It is maybe not as smart as La Moara, but it is certainly full of character.

La Soare features a sitting room, a dining room and four bedrooms: two doubles, one single, and one with two built-in double beds, all sharing two bathrooms (fairly simple, with showers). However, the (fully equipped) kitchen, a quaintly old-fashioned, large and sunny space, is my favourite spot in La Soare. I can just imagine how wonderful it must be to come here with a bunch of friends (and a car loaded with groceries) and spend long afternoons in that kitchen cooking, chatting, and of course eating.

Good to know La Soare can accommodate up to nine people (but that is with four people sharing one room). The rental price for the entire house starts at €250 per night. It is open all year round. Amenities in La Soare include a television and a washing machine.

Try and list the most amazing places in Greece. The caldera of Santorini, the Acropolis in Athens (of course), the Byzantine settlement of Monemvasia, the monasteries at the Meteora – these make up just the beginning of a list that would cover every province of Greece. The choice is so abundant that it is not surprising that some of the most stunning sites have stayed entirely off the beaten (tourist) track.

Take the Prespes Lakes, all the way in the far northwest of the province of Macedonia, right at the borders with Albania and former Yugoslavia. Situated at an altitude of over 800 m, covering thousands of hectares (and spread over three countries!), the two lakes rank among the most beautiful wetlands in Europe. The biodiversity found in and around the lakes is amazingly rich and the ecological importance of the area is immeasurable. It has more international laws protecting it than any other site in Greece.

Of course the lakes are not going completely unnoticed and they do get their share of Greeks on excursion (foreign visitors barely make it to this far-off corner), but the area remains unspoilt. Fortunately there are no big hotels; instead you find just a handful of traditional guesthouses. Most of them are in Psarades and Agios Germanos, two picturesque villages, but even though they might look pretty on the outside, none stands out for being particularly stylish or tastefully done on the inside. The little 'find', however, is in a sunny spot in Laimos, a quiet little village just a few kilometres from the lakes.

At first glance, to Liakoto, as it is called, looks nice enough, but not spectacular. The building is a new construction and owner Dimitris Noulis did not try to conceal this when he designed his dream guesthouse. The allure of this place lies in its interior. At the centre of the house is a massive, high-ceilinged living room, filled with an eclectic collection of furniture and decorative objects. Plush sofas flank a massive fireplace; a chandelier is hung from the wood beams; there are piles of magazines and books to read; a chess board is set up at a small table waiting for players… It has an inviting lived-in feeling without being cluttered. The emphasis is on space and light but the atmosphere is intimate all the same. When you arrive here you might simply forget you came to see the lakes and be tempted to spend much of your time huddling around the fireplace or, in the summer, sit out on the wooden veranda to enjoy the views.

TO LIAKOTO

530 77 Laimos
Florina
Tel. 23850-51200

Where you'll sleep To Liakoto has eight rooms with en suite showers (four doubles, two triples and two quadruples). They are spacious and tasteful – each room has its own colour scheme – though a bit sober in their decoration. Several have a balcony looking out over the lakes, and some have a fireplace. All the rooms have an internet connection and a telephone.

When you feel hungry Before moving to Prespes, Dimitris lived in Thessaloniki where he owned a restaurant. Though he claims his days as a chef are long gone, he clearly has not lost his culinary skills. In addition to a good breakfast (served any time you like), he prepares fantastic three-course dinners for his guests, using mainly local, organically cultivated ingredients, which he turns into refined meals that he serves in an elegant candle-lit setting. Keep in mind that the guesthouse does not offer a regular restaurant service and that you should 'order' your meal in advance. Otherwise, in Laimos there is one taverna and there are several more restaurants in neighbouring Agios Germanos. There are also some great places where you can have a meal by the lake, in Psarades and on the little islet of Agios Achilleios. Beans are a local specialty (you can even find sweet bean preserves!) and of course you should also try some fish fresh from the lake.

Bring the children? You can safely bring your children to the guesthouse. Dimitris is a father of four (all boys!) who thoroughly tested (and approved) the place for child-friendliness. Don't worry though if you come without children that there will be kids running all over the place: there is a large playroom and a TV room in the (semi-) basement of the house where children tend to find each other. If you travel with a baby, you have to bring your own cot.

To see and do Prespes is paradise for nature lovers and birdwatchers, but even if you don't count yourself in that category, you will find that it is a marvellous place to escape to for a few days. If you have the slightest interest in birds you should bring along binoculars. More than 250 bird varieties are found in Prespes, including some rare types of pelicans.

The lakes are also quite nice to swim in – despite the altitude, the water reaches pleasant temperatures during the summer months. Furthermore, you can take a boat to see the frescoes painted by hermits some 500 years ago on the cliff side near Psarades. The islet of Agios Achilleios, which you access via a floating pedestrian bridge, is a wonderful spot to wander around for a few hours, so you can visit its Byzantine chapels and take in the atmosphere of the small, traditional farming settlement.

Good to know To Liakoto is open all year round. The winter months (October – May) are considered high season, with prices for two people starting at €75 per night. During the rest of the year, the rate for two persons starts at €50 per night. Breakfast is not included in the prices. Credit cards are not accepted.

Getting there Laimos is about 50 km from Florina and 55 km from Kastoria. You simply follow signs for Prespes and as you get to the lakes, you drive towards Agios Germanos. Laimos is just a few kilometres before it. Drive to the village square, from where you can follow signs for the guesthouse.

The town of Edessa enjoys an exceptional setting in the foothills of Mount Vermion, on the edge of a plateau more than 300 m high. A maze of streams runs through it, leading into a waterfall park, right beside the old centre of the town. The falls are quite spectacular and have made the little Macedonian town popular with day-trippers. With virtually no walking required to go see the falls, and with lots of places to eat nearby, this is a perfect spot for Greek family outings!

Hotel Varosi, a fairy-tale pretty, restored stone house, is just five minutes' walk from the waterfalls, in a narrow street in the quiet historical district of Edessa. It is a small, family-run place with only eight bedrooms. Inside, the house has a warm and cosy feel. The style is traditional, but, thanks to the use of soft colours and simple wood furniture (some antiques), not overwhelmingly so. Don't expect any luxury, but the essentials are there: a cosy sitting/dining room as you come in and a second sitting room on the first floor; small terraces for the summer and fireplaces for the winter; and probably most importantly, an unassuming, homely atmosphere, created by Anastasia Salahora, the charming hostess, and her two beautiful daughters, Katerina and Eleni, who work alongside their mother.

VAROSI

45-47 Arhiereos Meletiou St.
582 00 Edessa
Tel. 23810-21865

Where you'll sleep The eight bedrooms, all doubles, are small but sweet. They are painted in soft shades and furnished with antique brass beds, made with hand-embroidered sheets and pillowcases, and covered with soft, velvety blankets in the winter, and fresh, white cotton bedspreads during the warm summer months. All rooms have an en-suite shower, a telephone, a television and air conditioning. Some have an internet connection.

When you feel hungry You can start your day with an excellent breakfast (served to your table) that includes fresh juice, homemade jams, boiled or scrambled eggs, pies, yogurt, fresh fruits and cake. For lunch and dinner you'll find several traditional places nearby, and you can also walk to the waterfalls and take the cliff-side elevator down, to have a meal in a trendy restaurant in a converted rope-weaving factory.

Bring the children? Children are welcome, and some of the rooms can – just about – fit an extra bed. There are also two rooms that can be used together as a family unit. Cots are available.

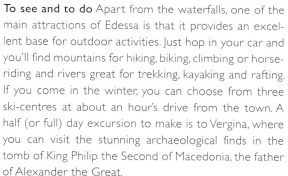

To see and to do Apart from the waterfalls, one of the main attractions of Edessa is that it provides an excellent base for outdoor activities. Just hop in your car and you'll find mountains for hiking, biking, climbing or horse-riding and rivers great for trekking, kayaking and rafting. If you come in the winter, you can choose from three ski-centres at about an hour's drive from the town. A half (or full) day excursion to make is to Vergina, where you can visit the stunning archaeological finds in the tomb of King Philip the Second of Macedonia, the father of Alexander the Great.

Good to know Guesthouse Varosi is open all year. Prices for a double room start at €70 per night. Breakfast will be added to the bill. Dogs are not allowed. Credit cards: MasterCard and Visa.

Getting there Edessa is halfway on the road between Thessaloniki (80 km – an easy drive) and Florina (78 km over a beautiful, but winding road). The road passes through Edessa, and as you enter the town, you should look out for signs for the waterfalls. Follow these until you reach the sports stadium, take a right and then twice a left, and you will see a sign for the hotel.

This country still has so many hidden corners: mountains where you can hike for hours without ever bumping into another human being, charming little villages where time seems to have come to a standstill, lakes that serve as a safe haven for some of the rarest bird species rather than motor boats… the list goes on and on.

A perfect example is the village of Ano Poroia in the northern province of Serres, close to the border with Bulgaria. It is situated at the foot of Mount Belles, at an altitude of 400 m, from where it has sweeping views over Lake Kerkini that lies below it. The artificially created lake and the adjacent (nature protected) area support a rich bird population. Even though over the past years it has become quite well known among Greeks and a few modest tourist lodgings have opened near the lake, it is still definitely a destination that is off the beaten track.

That, however, has not always been the case for Ano Poroia. Once upon a time it was on the route followed by caravans between Constantinople and Monastiri (in today's Skopje), and travellers used to stop in the village for the night. Viglatoras was built almost a hundred years ago as a so-called *hani*, a travellers' inn with bedrooms on the first floor, and space for camels (yes, camels!) on the ground floor. Later, when camels were no longer used as a means of transport in this part of the world, it became a family home.

The owner of Viglatoras, Stelios Kalessis, grew up in the house and when he was a young adult, he left to study in Thessaloniki. Years later, he and his wife Phylli decided to move back to Ano Poroia and turn the property once again into a guesthouse. They built a second residence next to the original one, in the local traditional style, in order to offer a higher level of comfort than what was probably the case in the past, and converted the ground floor of the old lodgings into a homely living and dining room.

VIGLATORAS

620 55 Ano Poroia
Serres
Tel. 23270-51231

When you arrive, Stelios or Phylli will invite you in, and you will be overcome by a sense of well-being. It might be the genuine warmth in their welcome, or the roaring fireplace in the winter, or the pot of tea with freshly baked cake they'll treat you to, or even simply their choice of music. But whatever it is, you instantly sense that you have come to a wonderful place and feel blissfully at home. (When I arrived, the music of the movie "Il Postino" was playing and a chocolate cake came straight out of the oven – this is definitely the way to win *my* heart!)

Where you'll sleep Bliss continues once you see your bedroom in the new building. There are eight rooms in total: two family apartments on the ground floor, two standard doubles as well as two large doubles that can take an extra bed, on the first floor, and two loft rooms on the second floor. They have a refined traditional style, and manage to combine the intimate atmosphere typical of a guesthouse, with the comfort you usually find only in luxurious hotels. They have excellent beds and immaculate bathrooms. Amenities include a television, a kitchenette (in the apartments and the large doubles; the other rooms have a refrigerator), a CD player, a hairdryer and air conditioning (except in the apartments, which stay cool anyway), and some rooms also have a fireplace.

When you feel hungry Viglatoras is almost perfect. Its only flaw is that for lunch and dinner you have to go away from it to a restaurant (there are several at walking distance). Breakfast though *is* perfect. It is served on elegantly set tables, and you will be treated to delicious traditional pies, warm bread with marmalades, perfectly boiled eggs, home-baked cakes and fresh juice. There's no need to get up early in order to catch breakfast – service doesn't stop until 12.30.

Bring the children? Children are welcome at the guesthouse and the two apartments are convenient for families, also because in there you'll have your own little kitchen. Cots are available. The area is great for kids of all ages, although teenagers in search for some nightlife may be disappointed.

To see and do Stelios will give you plenty of ideas for walks, and you can also go horse-riding in the mountains. Lake Kerkini is of course a destination by itself: you can go for a boat tour or explore it by canoe.

Good to know Viglatoras is open all year. Prices for a double room start at €70 on weekends and holidays; for the other nights there's a 10% reduction. Breakfast is included. Credit cards: MasterCard and Visa.

Getting there Ano Poroia is at an easy driving distance from Thessaloniki (about 100 km). You follow signs for Kilkis and Lake Doirani, and about 28 km after the turn-off to Lake Doirani, you turn left towards Kato Poroia and Ano Poroia. Viglatoras is on the parallel road you will see below the central square. There is a sign at the entrance of the village.

Granitis
Kato Nevrokopi
660 33 Drama
Tel. 25230-21050

In the north of Greece, close to the Bulgarian border, there are some spectacular areas that, despite the natural beauty they offer — hills and mountains, rivers and lakes, forests and wildlife — have remained almost entirely untouched by tourism. This is not really surprising: this part of the country is a long way to go to and, more important probably, there are no appealing places to stay. Why bother driving for so long if you end up spending the night somewhere that makes you wish you were home?

Sometimes, however, all it takes to put an area on the map is an attractive hotel. The recently opened Hotel Granitis has all the potential to do just that for the area of Kato Nevrokopi, in the province of Drama. Whether you've spent your day on the slopes of the nearby ski centre, or walking in the mountain tracks, or kayaking on the lakes of the Nestos River, Hotel Granitis is a comfortable place to recuperate afterwards.

The stone building sits at the edge of the village Granitis, a location that affords it magnificent views over the mountains. Inside, the tone is set by stone, wood and warm colours, while high ceilings, large windows and plenty of space (the main floor is essentially one large room opening up to a veranda) create a pleasantly airy ambience. Add the friendly service to all of this and ultimately you have a package worth the extra kilometres drive!

Where you'll sleep The 11 bedrooms (doubles, triples and quadruple suites) are not excessively decorated — the furniture is unadorned and straightforward — but they are cosy, spacious, and most of all, very comfortable (with an excellent heating system for the winter and impeccable marble bathrooms). Each has its own balcony or terrace. The rooms are equipped with a telephone, a television, a mini-bar and a CD player.

When you feel hungry A decent buffet breakfast awaits you in the morning from 7.30 to 10.30. The hotel's restaurant, serving standard Greek fare, is open all day on weekends and holiday periods. At other times you will have to rely at the few places to eat in the village, just a few minutes on foot.

Bring the children? Children are welcome and most rooms are designed as family rooms. Cots are available as well. It is a great area to bring children to; they will enjoy the outdoors.

To see and do The main attraction of Granitis is the ski centre at Mount Falakro. It was recently expanded and now has nine ski lifts. It is still not very big, but it has become one of the best ski resorts in Greece. Unfortunately, however, the lifts only work from Thursday to Sunday (and during holidays). But skiing is not the only reason why people come to Granitis. It is a distinctly beautiful mountain area, great for walking and hiking, and excellent also as a base for excursions: don't miss the caves of Angitis, and the stunning lakes of the Nestos River.

Good to know The hotel is open all year, but winter is definitely the high season. You can safely assume that you will always find a room on weekdays or during the summer months, but not during winter weekends and holidays, unless you book well in advance. Prices for a double room start at €60 in the low season, but go up to €120 during the winter holidays. They include breakfast. Dogs are not allowed. Credit cards: MasterCard and Visa.

Getting there Follow signs for Kato Nevrokopi from Drama. After about 30 km you pass through the village of Granitis, where you will see a sign for the hotel.

Just a few years ago, the city of Kavala would have seemed a somewhat odd choice as a holiday destination. It has a lot going for it, but it is out of the way, and most travellers consider it more a point of departure (boats to the islands of Thassos and Samothraki leave from here) rather than a town to spend time. This has changed with the recent opening of the Imaret. Travellers now have a destination in Kavala and once they settle in the hotel, they have no desire to leave.

A stay in the Imaret is an amazing experience from the moment you arrive. There is of course the unavoidable moment of check-in formalities, but afterwards, rather than being escorted to your room, you will get a private tour through the property. Any tiredness from your trip or desire to freshen up first will evaporate once you are led into the courtyard, where you will start to take in the immense beauty of the building.

The tour will take you back in time to the days of the Ottoman rule in the early 19th century, when a local tobacco trader, Mohammed Ali, joined the military and was assigned to fight the French invaders in Egypt. He was quickly promoted to the highest army ranks, and in 1805, he became the Ottoman Sultan's viceroy and pasha of Egypt. Later, he made several donations to his birthplace Kavala, including a boarding school where boys studied the Koran. The building became known as the Imaret, "hostel for pilgrims" in Turkish.

As you are shown around peaceful inner gardens, silent contemplative spaces and elegant terraces, history rolls out in front of you, and you may find it hard to imagine that ten years ago the Imaret was at the point of collapsing. After the holy school stopped operating in the early 20th century, the building became a shelter for Greek refugees of Asia Minor, but its upkeep was totally neglected. (Apparently, the poverty-stricken inhabitants at some point even burned the old books in the old teaching room to warm themselves.)

The story of the Imaret might have ended there, had it not been for Anna Missirian, who was pained to see how the monumental building was crumbling into dereliction. In the 1990s, its cells were used by local tradesmen to store their ware and to grill souvlakia, and the courtyards, marred by plastic chairs, had become a local hang-out, but nobody lifted a finger to take care of the building. In 1995, Anna went on a crusade to rescue the Imaret, still Egyptian property. It took her seven years to work her way through a maze of bureaucratic tangles and negotiate a 99-year lease with the Egyptian government. The task of restoration that then confronted her was one of colossal proportions, but she managed to transform the Imaret into a hotel that can only be described by using superlatives.

IMARET

6 Th Poulidou St.
651 10 Kavala
Tel. 2510-620151

Your tour will take you through the inner courtyards, one with an immensely high pine tree overgrown with wisteria flanking a pool – not the kind to dive into or play a match of water polo, but one where you can quietly refresh on hot summer days – and two other courtyards with internal gardens full of fruit trees, herbs and strawberries. You will be taken to the old, high-domed teaching room, now used as a reading lounge, to the elegant sitting room, to the hammam, to the old food storage room (left untouched), to the long archways leading past the old cells, and, the ultimate revelation, to the cistern where you can swim by candlelight under the domed ceilings.

As the Imaret unfolds in front of you, you will appreciate how during its transformation into a hotel, Anna stayed as close as possible to its cultural identity. She changed no more than necessary and did not sacrifice any of the original features for the sake of modern comforts. The decoration is appropriately pared down: spaces are not overloaded with eye-catching antiques or heavily oriental ornaments, so that nothing distracts you from the grandeur of the building.

When later you are brought to your room, you find candles lit and bunches of freshly picked herbs and flowers. A superbly comfortable bed made with pure linen in the summer (and warmed with deep-coloured velvet throws in the winter) awaits you, and you know that you are going to be spoiled rotten. In the Imaret, you get exactly what you want before you even realised you wanted it. There are no waiters and bellboys dashing around and asking you every five minutes if there's anything you need. Service, while smooth and efficient, is ever so discreet and the luxury aspect, while omni-present, is of the unobtrusive, nearly 'invisible' kind.

In general, you will find that the Imaret calls for sensuality, simplicity and contemplation. The optimum way to enjoy your stay is to let yourself be carried away by the tranquillity and subtle oriental spiritualism permeating the place. The Imaret is not a venue where people go to show off. Your main spectators will be the seagulls, their incessant chatter sometimes the only sounds to be heard. There is no need to show up jewellery clad – a discreet necklace will do, just like espadrilles are more appropriate shoeware than stiletto heals (take one look at the delicate wooden floors and you will understand why) and if you carry your mobile phone with you, you'll want to put it on silent mode. Similarly, if you feel like parading your designer gear at the dinner table, make it Armani rather than Versace, though really, a crisp white linen shirt will be just right for the occasion.

Where you'll sleep Every room (there are 30 doubles in total), be it the smallest double or the largest suite, is amazing. Most of them are in the original cells where almost two centuries ago the pupils used to sleep. Dome-shaped ceilings, earthy colours, subdued lighting, hand-

IMARET

made upholstery in the finest fabrics, elegant furniture and a delicately oriental decoration set the tone in the rooms that either look out over the courtyards, or to the dock that lies below. Bathrooms are partially open-plan with copper washbasins and (in most rooms) a sunken bath. Rooms are fitted with a telephone, a television and a DVD player (in a few rooms, where they couldn't be hidden, they will be brought to you upon request), a CD player, an internet connection, air conditioning, a mini-bar, a safe and a hairdryer.

When you feel hungry The lounge and the restaurant of the Imaret are the only areas where outside visitors are welcome. People from Kavala regularly drop in to catch a glimpse of the interiors, to then be seduced by the menu, offering fine Mediterranean cuisine with a subtle oriental flavour in some of the dishes.

Breakfast is served until 12.00 wherever you would like it (and later in your room). It is an elegant affair presented on the finest china, with emphasis on quality rather than

abundance: the bread is warm, the egg is perfectly boiled, the juice is fresh, the cake is delicious, and the little pies and yogurt with honey add a Greek traditional touch.

Bring the children? Every once in a while even the most dedicated mums and dads need a moment without their little darlings. The Imaret is the perfect place to make the most out of such an occasion. Children are only accepted if they are above the age of 12, but no matter what their age is, it is better to just be with your other half.

To see and do The hammam, the pool, the reading room, the soothing ambience inviting you to simply relax in exquisite surroundings, might be enough to stop you from even putting a foot outside the Imaret during your entire stay. The hammam treatment in particular, a three-hour affair including a scalp treatment, skin scrub, and a full body massage, is not to be missed. Swimming in the old cistern is another amazing experience – it works by appointment so you will have it all to yourself.

If you can eventually bring yourself to leave the compound, the old part of Kavala is worth exploring. There are beaches not far away and a ski resort at one hour by car (yes, people use the Imaret as a base for skiing holidays!), and the mountains of Drama are generally great for outdoor activity.

Good to know The Imaret is open all year. Prices for a double room start at 220€, regardless of the season. Breakfast is not included. Facilities at the Imaret include an indoor swimming pool, a hammam, massage treatments, a reading lounge, a conference room and a hall for receptions. Credit cards: all major.

Getting there Kavala is situated 140 km east of Thessaloniki. There is an airport less than half an hour drive from the town. When you get to Kavala, you should drive in the direction of the port, and you will see signs for the Kastro, the House of Mohammed Ali and the Imaret.

In France, almost every little town has its "Hotel de la Poste", just like in the British countryside most villages have their "Country Inn" next to the local pub. In Arnea, a small and charming town in the mountains of Halkidiki, in the north of Greece, the Alexandrou Traditional Inn, opposite the town hall, has the same kind of feel — the centrally located inn where travellers stop to spend the night. This is not surprising, since until the forties, the now almost 200-year-old building was used as a resting point by pilgrims and traders on their way to the Holy Mount Athos.

Inside, however, the Alexandrou Traditional Inn is nothing like an ordinary travellers' lodging — it is infinitely more stylish and exquisite. After the original inn was closed, it became the home of the Alexandrou family. The current owners, Dimitris and Vassilis Alexandrou (two architect brothers), grew up in the house (as did their father and his nine siblings). Eventually, all members of the family moved away and for many years the house was used only during the weekends and on the occasional holiday. The two brothers, who are specialised in the restoration of monumental buildings (they are members of the team restoring the Byzantine monasteries on Mount Athos), saw that the house badly needed repairs and realised that rather than fixing just a few things, they should carry out a complete renovation.

Dimitris and Vassilis decided to give the building a future based on its past, and turned it into one of Greece's most beautiful guesthouses. They retained all its magnificent old features, like the superb timbered ceilings, while adding refinement, striking a perfect balance between cosy/ traditional and elegant/stylish. Every aspect — the antique furniture, the delicate wall paintings, the utmost care for

detail — indicates that the brothers sought perfection and did not settle for less. The result is a gorgeous travellers' inn that feels like a warm and hospitable home. It is no longer just a stopover. It has become a destination.

ALEXANDROU TRADITIONAL INN

Patriarhou Vartholomeou 1st Sq.
630 74 Arnea
Halkidiki
Tel. 23720-23210

Where you'll sleep The six lovely bedrooms are on the first floor. Two are strictly doubles and don't have much space beyond the large, antique bed; the others have room for a third person, but keep in mind that this is more the kind of guesthouse for romantic twosomes. The care for detail is taken to extremes in the rooms and the only criticism you could possibly mutter, although admittedly this is a question of personal preferences, are the very firm mattresses. There is no excessive luxury – 'gadgets' are limited to a telephone, a television and a hairdryer – but little touches like crystal water glasses on a silver tray, will make you feel spoiled anyway.

When you feel hungry As in any true travellers' inn, you can have your meals on the premises. The dishes are traditional Greek, but they are executed and served with a finesse that definitely surpasses tradition. The same applies to breakfast, which you can have until the quite civilised time of 11.30. Drinks can be ordered throughout the day, and in the summer you can sit out on a small terrace next to the house.

Bring the children? This is probably not a good idea if your kids are small or need a lot of space to run around and play. There is no garden outside and inside there are quite a few things that could break. You don't want to have to worry about any of that.

To see and do The great thing about staying in a place like Arnea is that you can experience a combination of culture, mountains and sea. You could go walking or mountain biking in the morning and swim in the sea in the afternoon. (Beaches are only 15 km away from the town.) At just three km from Arnea, you can visit the ruins of an ancient civilisation – Profitis Ilias Hill – with a recently excavated *acropolis*.

But by far the most interesting place to see is Holy Mount Athos, the world's oldest surviving monastic community. However, it has strict admittance policies and you can't just drop in for a visit. Women are simply not allowed (!) and men have to go through an extensive application procedure (only ten non-orthodox visitors are allowed per day and they have to have a good reason for their visit – "just curious" won't do it). Don't despair: from Ouranopolis (about one hour by car from Arnea), you can take a boat trip around the peninsula and admire the monasteries from the sea. It is worth it.

Good to know The inn is open all year round. Only holiday periods are high season, when the price for a double room is €115, otherwise the charge per night is €85 on weekdays, and €100 on weekends. The prices include breakfast. Credit cards: Diners, MasterCard and Visa.

Getting there Arnea is at a very easy driving distance from Thessaloniki (just 70 km away), from where you will follow signs for Halkidiki, Polygiros and Arnea. You will find the Alexandrou Traditional Inn on the main road through Arnea, on a small square opposite the town hall.

Not many people have heard of Smixi, a tiny village situated at an altitude of 1240 m in the spectacular Pindos mountain range. It is not hard to reach, but at the same time it is quite far from nearly everything, apart from a small ski resort. In the winter the village attracts a handful of skiers, mostly during weekends; the rest of the year Smixi seems to disappear from people's minds altogether. In fact, that is what makes it all the more attractive — as a place to escape to (*especially* when there is no snow) and to have all to yourself.

Valia Nostra, a newly built hotel at the entrance of the village, fits the bill of the almost private, almost secret getaway, very well. A haven full of comfort and cosiness, it is a great example of the new breed of mountain retreats that are becoming increasingly popular with Greek city dwellers. But contrary to some other, similar places, Valia Nostra is relatively small and largely family-run, and it has a friendly and easy-going atmosphere. It is designed with emphasis on comfort rather than style, but it certainly does not lack character — the nicely proportioned bedrooms especially, have a warm, somewhat alpine feel to them.

The concern about the guests' comfort is also evident in the shared spaces: there is a large, nicely furnished sitting and dining room on the entrance level of the building, a bar on the floor below, and an adjacent space with an inviting swimming pool, flanked by loungers. Valia Nostra caters to all moods: the bedrooms are great for romantic cocooning; in the sitting room you can curl up by the fireplace with a book; if you want a little more action you can have drinks in the lively bar; the pool will do if you want to burn a few calories; and for some indulgence there is a large Jacuzzi, a hammam and a massage parlour.

VALIA NOSTRA

510 00 Smixi
Grevena
Tel. 24620-80151

You could do the same as many others: book well in advance and stay at Valia Nostra during the ski season. But if you want to enjoy the place at its fullest, and have it more or less to yourself, the thing to do is to go off-season.

Where you'll sleep There are six double rooms in Valia Nostra, five suites (two with a mezzanine) and two 'loft' suites. All rooms are large and have plenty of space to keep you in, and the mezzanine-suites have a fireplace (you get an ample supply of firewood). The rooms are equipped with a telephone, a television, a refrigerator and a hairdryer, and the en suite bathrooms have a bath or shower (several with hydro massage).

When you feel hungry Valia Nostra has a restaurant that serves typical Greek dishes, but it opens only for dinner, and only during the high season (basically winter week-ends and holidays), and, for groups, upon request. You can order sandwiches or cold plates at any time. There are a few places to eat in the village as well. Breakfast is a buffet, served every day till 10.30.

Bring the children? The hotel is definitely child-friendly. The bedrooms all have an extra sofa-bed (two in the suites) and you can ask for a cot as well. The carpeted floors in the rooms are convenient for toddlers to play and crawl on, and older kids will enjoy hanging out in the bar, where movies are shown on a big screen. And of course there is the swimming pool…

To see and do So yes, during most of the winter you can ski nearby (it is a small resort with six lifts and some 15 runs), but don't let that be the only reason to come to Smixi. The area is great for walking and hiking, and you can also go horse-riding, rafting and mountain biking. The amazing monasteries of the Meteora make a great day excursion.

Good to know Valia Nostra is open all year, but usually fills up only during winter weekends. Prices for a double room start at €150 during the high season (winter holidays and weekends), and €110 for other nights. They include breakfast. Facilities at the hotel include an indoor swimming pool, a sauna, a hammam, a Jacuzzi and a massage parlour. Credit cards: Amex, MasterCard and Visa.

Getting there From the centre of Grevena, follow signs for Doxaras, Mavranei, Anavrita and Smixi. You will see the hotel as you approach the village. It is a beautiful drive from Grevena that normally takes less than an hour.

PYRGOS MANTANIA

If you love the great outdoors, then Pyrgos Mantania is the place for you. You don't easily find hotels in Greece that are in the middle of absolutely nowhere, but this one certainly is. It is situated in the mountains, at a distance of about 40 km from the village of Pertouli, a well-known mini-break destination. Pertouli is generally considered as the final station, no one really wanders beyond this point. But sure enough, the road continues. It follows a small river but doesn't seem to lead anywhere, which is just as well, as it keeps traffic to a minimum. If you keep on driving through this blissfully unspoilt green and mountainous area, you reach "Tria Potamia", the point where three rivers meet, and a little further on you see Pyrgos Mantania.

The fantastic location is of course a big selling point of Pyrgos Mantania, but it is not the only one. When Lambros Papageorgiou and George Babos, the two friends who own the hotel, started to develop their plans, they realised that the only way to attract people to this far-from-everything spot, would be to create a distinctly comfortable, spacious and particularly inviting place, ultimately matching the great outdoors with equally great indoors. So they included a large and beautiful sitting room in the main building, but to be certain that there would be enough space for people to hang out, even with a full house, they constructed a second building to house the restaurant, which also functions as an extra sitting room. Likewise, they made sure the bedrooms would be large and inviting enough for private daytime relaxing.

The final touch for the creation of an outstanding place is the good atmosphere. This is not easy to plan. Getting friendly, efficient and professional staff and working alongside them, was the sensible first step Lambros and George took. And it did the trick, completing the package of a wonderfully unpretentious, comfortable and easy-going nature escape retreat. But these two are not going to stop here; they plan to take things much further: detached cottages for private stays, little shops selling traditional local products, a meeting room and an indoor pool, sauna and spa are in the works. This story is to be continued...

PYRGOS MANTANIA

Asprospotamos
422 00 Kalambaka
Tel. 24320-87351

Where you'll sleep The 16 rooms spread over two floors (two are small doubles; the others are larger and can also be used as triples and quadruples). They are equipped with a telephone, a television and a hairdryer, and they have an en suite shower. They are painted in warm colours with some pretty, flowered decorative detailing, and tastefully styled with simple, traditional furniture and a few modern touches. In the winter, you should definitely ask for a room on the first floor where you will have a fireplace with a supply of wood at your disposal. Most rooms have a striking view over the mountains, but the best part of it is probably what you hear when you open your window: nothing, except for the sound of water flowing in the river that flows right below.

When you feel hungry If you consider breakfast as the most important meal of the day, you will be delighted with the spread that awaits you on two sturdy, old farm tables in the morning (till 10.30). This is a breakfast meant to prepare you for an active day outside, with home-baked bread, eggs and bacon, ham, olives, cheeses, sweets and cakes, and, to be absolutely sure you will take in enough calories to burn, a large pot with porridge.

There is nowhere to eat nearby, so the restaurant of the hotel stays open all day long. Orders are taken in taverna style: there is no menu, but a waiter (or sometimes even the cook himself) will come to your table to recite the choices of the day. It may sound like fairly standard fare, but when your order is brought to you, you'll be pleasantly surprised – the quality of the food (extremely tender meats, rich salads) is outstanding.

Bring the children? This is a great place to come with children. The garden and the mountains provide an endless playground for your little ones, and older kids will enjoy the river sports they can do nearby. In the living room there is a convenient play corner with games and toys. Cots are available.

To see and do Pyrgos Mantania is definitely an all-year-round destination. It is ideal as a cosy winter escape, as much as it is great for active summer holidays. The surroundings are perfect for hiking and river sports; you can do rafting and kayaking at several different places nearby. In October you can go out into the forest with a mushroom specialist to learn to identify and collect mushrooms, which later in the day you can taste in dishes prepared following traditional recipes. Also, in June and September, walks are organised during which you can collect herbs for mountain tea infusions. Finally, the Meteora (enormous rocks rising from the plains, with an out-of-this-world collection of monasteries perched on top), are a bit over an hour by car, and make a day-trip obviously not to be missed.

Good to know Pyrgos Mantania is open all year. Prices for a double room start at €75 per person, and they include breakfast. Credit cards: MasterCard and Visa.

Getting there It is a bit of a drive to get to Pyrgos Mantania (about 400 km from Athens), but it is absolutely worth it. From Athens the best way to get there is via Lamia, Karditsa and Trikala, after which you follow signs for Elati, Pertouli and Asprospotamos. You will see the hotel about 40 km after you pass Pertouli. It is impossible to miss as there are no other buildings or villages for miles around. Try to plan your trip so that you do the last 70 km by daylight – you will feel more comfortable on the mountain roads, and it is also an extremely beautiful drive.

ARHONDIKO HATZIGAKI

The Arhondiko Hatzigaki is a resplendent mansion that was originally built in the 19th century. It was burned to the ground during the Second World War – an act of revenge by the occupation forces after they found out it was being used by Greek resistance fighters. Half a century later, Dimitris Hatzigakis undertook an ambitious restoration of the family property and opened it as a luxury guesthouse. It only took a few months for it to become a point or reference for Athenians wishing to escape the capital for a few days.

The mansion overlooks Pertouli, a mountainous village in the heart of the Greek mainland. The area is wonderful. With densely forested mountain slopes and sparkling snow-white peaks, it has the potential to develop into a gigantic ski resort, but luckily, that is unlikely to happen any time soon. The nearby three-lift ski centre is fun for a couple of hours of skiing, but thankfully it is too small to attract the masses.

However, it is not just the beauty of the area that attracts people to Arhondiko Hatzigaki; it is also the appeal of the place itself. Dimitris Hatzigakis has succeeded in bringing the mansion back to its full glory, with elaborately timbered ceilings, dark wood, antique tiled floors and lots of fireplaces. He brought in a mix of antique and country style furniture, and created interiors that feel comfortable and inviting while being utterly stylish and elegant.

ARHONDIKO HATZIGAKI

420 32 Pertouli
Trikala
Tel. 24340-91146

There are several sitting rooms in the lowest floor of the mansion (including one with tables to play cards and another with a tiny bar). They are cosy and charming, but small. In separate housing you will find the restaurant and a much larger sitting room with many sitting corners and comfortable couches and, of course, a massive fireplace. In a way, the only thing that is missing these days is the presence of Dimitris Hatzigakis himself, to give you the scoop of the family history. He is often around, but he leaves it to his staff to welcome and take care of the guests.

Where you'll sleep With 22 rooms and suites, each of them different, there is a lot to choose from. All rooms are large and comfortable, and very stylish. Those that are in the mansion itself are the most grand in style, but the rooms in the converted stables are also very attractive. All rooms have a television, a mini-bar and a safe, and the modern, marble-clad bathrooms are equipped with hairdryers.

When you feel hungry In the morning you will find a buffet breakfast waiting in the large living room in the outhouse (until 10.00) and if you are in a lazy (or private) mood, breakfast can also be brought to your room (until 11.00; there is an extra charge). For lunch and dinner, traditional home-cooked meals are served in the taverna-style restaurant and there are several more places to eat at walking distance in the village.

Bring the children? Even though the atmosphere and style of the Arhondiko Hatzigaki is ideal for romantic escapes, children are very welcome. Most rooms can sleep up to four persons, and cots are available.

To see and do The area is great for outdoor activities (river canoe, kayak, rafting, hiking…), and during the winter months – usually from Christmas to the end of March – you can try the tiny ski centre (six km from the village). The Meteora, a group of incredible rock formations with centuries-old monasteries perched on top, make a day excursion you shouldn't miss (a bit over about half an hour by car). The monasteries are open to the public. Ladies should be aware of the dresscode: no bare shoulders or trousers (most monasteries let you borrow skirts you can wear over your trousers).

Good to know Arhondiko Hatzigakis is open all year. The winter weekends and holiday periods are considered high season. Prices for a double room start at €140 in the summer, at €220 during long weekends and holiday periods, and at €190 for the remainder of the year, and they include breakfast and dinner. Facilities include a large room that can be used for meetings, seminars or other events, a health centre with a sauna and a gym, a playroom for little people, another room where bigger people can play billiard and table tennis, and an outdoor swimming pool. Credit cards: Amex, MasterCard and Visa.

Getting there The 360 km drive from Athens takes at least four hours, and yet, Athenians don't hesitate to head for Pertouli on Friday night for a less-than-48-hours escape from the capital. If you can, however, try and do the drive during daytime. Especially the last 30 km road stretch is so beautiful (it takes you through a gorge where you drive along the river), that it would be a pity not to be able to see the scenery. From Athens the fastest way is via Lamia, Karditsa and Trikala – from Trikala you follow signs for Elati and Pertouli. There is a sign for the hotel at the entrance of the village.

Metaxohori, literally "Silk Village", was once a flourishing community where families made a comfortable living out of (home) silk production. Today, the little silk worms are long gone; what remains is a small settlement full of charm, with a central square shaded by immense leafy trees and old stone mansions scattered on verdant mountain slopes. The area is absolutely beautiful and the sea is not far (there is an endless sandy beach at barely 20 minutes by car), but luckily, the village has yet to be discovered as a holiday destination. For the time being, entertainment, nightlife and shopping facilities remain limited to just one *kafenio*, one taverna and one old-fashioned grocery store. Metaxohori is a place you should get to before everybody else does.

The village has also a perfect *auberge de charme*: Arhondiko Soulioti. Dating from 1850, it is one of the oldest silk mansions. When Theodore Souliotis bought it in the late nineties, it had not been used for a long time, let alone maintained. In fact, it was barely standing, and had to be rebuilt practically from scratch. Theodore, however, who is a civil engineer from neighbouring village Agia, saw it as a good opportunity to create a wonderful guesthouse, and in doing so, to also contribute to the preservation of Metaxohori.

Ultimately he did an excellent job, and Arhondiko Soulioti became a beautiful place. It looks adorable on the outside and feels cosy and comfortable inside. The simple, traditional decoration is in tune with the architectural design; a collection of reproductions from the work of the Greek cartoonist/painter Bostatzoglou (who used to have a house in the village) in the living room adds a special touch.

The service is particularly friendly. Theodore runs the guesthouse with his sister and a bunch of young, local staff; together they all take good care of their guests. The only thing that could possibly be better in Arhondiko Souliotis is the sitting area. During the summer, you can sit out on the lovely terrace, but in the winter there is limited space to relax inside. The only common room is more dining than sitting room, and even though there is a fireplace, there is no comfortable sofa to go with it. Theodore is planning to restore a second old village house just across the street, which, he promises, will take care of this small problem.

ARHONDIKO SOULIOTI

Metaxohori
400 03 Agia
Larissa
Tel. 24940-22040

Where you'll sleep The guesthouse has eight rooms (two doubles, five triples and one quadruple) that are all equipped with a telephone, a television and air conditioning, and they have excellent en suite bathrooms. Most rooms have wooden floors and beamed ceilings (some have bare stone walls) and are tastefully appointed with a combination of traditional local and old-style Asian furniture. They vary somewhat in size, but they are all cosy and comfortable.

When you feel hungry In Metaxohori you don't have many choices for places to eat (the village taverna offers basic fare), but you can have all your meals at the guesthouse. For breakfast you will find a small buffet (7.00 to 11.00), while lunch and dinner (non-fussy, traditional food) are home-cooked by two women from the village.

Bring the children? Arhondiko Soulioti is definitely a child-friendly place, but when you book, you should make sure you get one of the larger rooms, especially if you come in the winter, when you will probably spend some more time indoors. Cots are available.

To see and do There are several good reasons to come to Metaxohori. There is of course the village itself, reminiscent of the villages of Pelion, but a tad more quiet and laid-back, and also less developed. In addition, the area is fantastic for all sorts of outdoor activities (such as walking, hiking, canyoning, rock climbing and mountain biking). And while Metaxohori is not considered a typical summer holiday destination, the seaside is not far at all and you can find excellent sandy beaches.

Good to know Arhondiko Soulioti is open all year and prices are the same throughout: the rate for a double room is €85, and for a triple or quadruple room €115 per night. Breakfast is included. Credit cards are not accepted.

Getting there Metaxohori is easy to reach from the Athens-Thessaloniki National Road, and it makes a perfect overnight stop on your way from or to Athens. Take the motorway exit Larissa 2 or 3, and follow signs for Agia, and then Metaxohori. The guesthouse is clearly signposted in the village.

ARHONDIKO VOGIATZOPOULOU

Agios Georgios is the first in a string of villages built along the western slopes of Mount Pelion, overlooking the Pagasitikos Gulf. It is a quiet and charming place with old houses scattered on the mountainside, a small *plateia* shaded by an immense plane tree, one tiny shop and just a few simple tavernas. Arhondiko Vogiatzopoulou stands proudly in the middle of a well-kept garden, bordering the (tranquil) main road. It was built almost a century ago by a family from Volos who used it as a summer home for 30 years.

Some ten years ago, Miltos Spanos, the grandson of the original owner, and his wife Mary, started a (much needed) renovation of the mansion aiming to restore the family tradition of spending summers in Agios Georgios. As the work neared its end, they began to wonder what they were actually going to do with all the space they had created eight bedrooms seemed rather big for them and their two grown-up children. So plans – and much of the layout of the house – were changed, and finally, in 2004, Arhondiko Vogiatzopoulou opened as a guesthouse.

Mary took care of the biggest part of the decoration and opted for a romantic, traditional-meets-contemporary style. She chose imaginative spring-like colour schemes in the flower-themed bedrooms, which she furnished with a successful combination of antiques and modern pieces. On the ground floor there are three warmly decorated sitting rooms. One of them features a bar, which, however, I found somewhat out of place, compared with the more cosy-traditional style of the room.

In the end, the idea of quiet summers in Agios Georgios never materialised for the Spanos family. Mary now spends a lot of her time running the guesthouse, and during weekends and holidays she is joined by her husband and children who help her take care of the guests. Still not quite used to the idea that the renovations are completed, Mary and Miltos are already discussing plans to convert the two smaller sitting rooms into a suite, and add a winter garden-like extension to the mansion in order to create additional sitting space for the guests.

ARHONDIKO VOGIATZOPOULOU

385 00 Agios Georgios
Pelion
Tel. 24280-93135

Where you'll sleep You can take your pick from two doubles, one triple room, and one quadruple suite. There is also a small garden house that has been converted into a studio with an open kitchen (note that the shower is not very practical). The bedrooms are generally on the small side but have quite a luxurious feel (hydro massage in most showers, a hairdryer, bathrobes, slippers, great duvets, a telephone and a television). Most rooms have a sweeping view over the sea.

When you feel hungry Breakfast is something Mary should be particularly proud of: every day, up until 11.00 (or later…) you will find a table spread with home-made cheese or spinach pies, apple (or other wonderful) cake, seasonal fruits and freshly squeezed orange juice. During the day Mary also enjoys preparing little bites for her guests, and if you get inspired by her delicious cooking, you are free to use the kitchen yourself as well. In the village there are a few places to eat, and should they be closed, you can drive to Milies where you will always find a few restaurants that are open.

Bring the children? Children are welcome, but, as the rooms are not huge and the common spaces are on the small side as well, the Arhondiko Vogiatzopoulou is probably not the best choice for families during the winter.

To see and do Pelion is a year-round destination, and walking and exploring are its two main activities. During the winter quite a few people from Athens and Thessaloniki come for a little weekend escape, while in the summer it is an excellent place to go to, if you want to avoid the crowds and enjoy nature, but also be able to go for a swim.

Good to know Arhondiko Vogiatzopoulou is open all year. Daily rates for two people start at €120 during weekends and holiday periods, and at €90 during normal weekdays, and they include breakfast. Dogs are not allowed. Credit cards: MasterCard and Visa.

Getting there Follow the coastal road from Volos in the direction of Avria. Take a left in Ano Lehonia and follow signs for Agios Georgios. You will see the guesthouse on your left about 300 m after the village square.

If you are not a great fan of fashionably minimalist hotels and prefer places where you feel like a guest in somebody's house, then Arhondiko Tzortzi may be just right for you. The almost 150-year-old neoclassical house is situated above the shady little square of Agios Georgios in Pelion. Even though it has been used as a guesthouse for more than 15 years, it has the atmosphere of a private home. You wouldn't imagine a family with young children living in it, but you could easily picture it as the house of an elderly lady, who over the years filled her home with a lifetime's worth of family heirlooms and memorabilia.

Reality, of course, is a little different. Owner Eva Patsiada is still many years away from being that 'elderly lady' and the decoration is something she carefully planned after she and her husband bought the premises. Because it had always been a family home, Eva wanted to keep that same feeling, even though she had to re-create it from scratch. Happy with the result of her work, she does not feel the need to regularly redecorate; instead the house is being kept just as it is. To some, this may create the impression of slight neglect, but in fact, this continuity only adds to one of the major selling points of Arhondiko Tzortzi: its immense old-world charm.

ARHONDIKO TZORTZI

385 00 Agios Georgios
Pelion
Tel. 24280-94252

Where you'll sleep There are five bedrooms (three doubles and two quadruples) in the mansion. They are not fancy, but they have attractive features such as the hand-painted walls and ceiling in one room and an antique iron bed in another. The two quadruple rooms are in the little outbuildings. They are not as charming as the rooms in the main house, but it is not a bad idea to book those if you come with young children and you don't want to worry about breakable items or the peace and quiet of your fellow guests. All bedrooms have an en suite bathroom or shower, and there are two that have a working fireplace.

When you feel hungry Breakfast in Arhondiko Tzortzi is by itself worth the stay. Served every morning until 12.30 in a small house in the garden, it is a never-ending parade of treats like warm bread with excellent home-made marmalades, savoury pies, hot cheese-breads, sweet pies, chocolate cake, and extras like oven-baked cinnamon apples with whipped cream. Every time you think you can take no more, something else will be brought to your table that smells and looks so good that you just have to try… and finish it. So, in all likelihood, you will skip lunch. For dinner you can choose between several traditional tavernas in the village (the restaurant of guesthouse Dereli, just across the street, is recommended), but sometimes they are closed on weekdays. In nearby villages, you will find several restaurants that are always open.

Bring the children? The sitting room of the mansion is not really suited for small children, but the two quadruple rooms in the garden houses are very convenient for families, and the little breakfast house is a good place for playing games after a long day in the open air. Cots are available.

To see and do After that amazing Tzortzi breakfast, you may want to burn some calories. So before jumping into the car to tour the peninsula, why not sign up for a hike with the walking guide recommended by Eva?

Good to know Arhondiko Tzortzi is open all year round. Prices for a double room start at 80€ in the winter season, but in the summer they are brought down. Normally they don't include breakfast. Note that dogs are not allowed. Parking is available in the street, at one minute from the guesthouse. Credit cards: all major.

Getting there Follow the coastal road from Volos in the direction of Avria. Take a left in Ano Lehonia and follow signs for Agios Georgios. The guesthouse is just above the village square (you will see a sign).

Vyzitsa is among the most picturesque and characteristic villages in Pelion, featuring some of the finest examples of the distinctive architecture of the area. Built on the forested slopes of the peninsula, it is famous for its tall, mesmerizing mansions, the so-called *arhondika*, constructed during the commercial boom of the 18th century. Because of its immeasurable charm, the village is very much in vogue as a mini-break destination, and especially during winter weekends, cars with Athens and Thessaloniki number plates compete for the limited parking space under the central square.

At first glance, nothing distinguishes the majestic Santikos Mansion from its neighbours. It is a typical Pelion-style three-storey high *arhondiko*, built out of stone and wood. Its first two floors have rather small windows (in the past they were used as storage space and winter rooms) and the third floor (where the living quarters used to be) is a slightly larger construction with big windows on three sides.

The mansion had suffered the same fate as many *arhondika* in the area, that, though famed for their beauty, over the years had crumbled into dereliction. Fortunately, in the seventies the Greek government stepped in and started to provide aid for their restoration. Quite a few were then converted into guesthouses, some run by the Greek Tourist Organisation, others privately, with interiors varying from sober and traditional to flamboyant and even bordering on the kitsch. Indeed, on the outside they all look impressive, but the interiors are a different story – the level of comfort and aesthetics varies widely.

SANTIKOS MANSION

370 10 Vyzitsa
Pelion
Tel. 24230-86765

The Santikos Mansion used to be one of the *arhondika* that were run as simple, traditional guesthouses. (In the past it was known under a different name.) A few years ago, however, it was bought by the Santikos family who transformed it into a warm and stylish retreat. Seasoned hoteliers (the family already owned two top-notch island hotels), the new owners considered the mansion their pet-project – a place were they were planning to spend many of their weekends (as indeed they do). They went out of their way to create a décor that would do full justice to the magnificent original features of the mansion. Stylish furniture, upholstery in warm colours and elegantly draped curtains were used to wondrous effect, creating an atmosphere of tradition mixed with understated luxury.

It is this perfectly accomplished combination of authentic Pelion style with a high standard of comfort that makes the Santikos Mansion unique in the area. It is not just the décor though, the place excels at all levels: young local staff is friendly, professional and efficient (but not fluent in English!); breakfast consists of local products, but is prepared with finesse and served with flair (wherever and whenever you want it); wooden beds are in the traditional built-in style, but they are up there with the world's most comfortable; and from the terrace you will enjoy splendid views to the sea, with soothing music playing in the background. It is not surprising then, that some of the guests that come from far away to see Pelion, in the end barely leave the premises!

Where you'll sleep The Santikos Mansion has six spacious double rooms and one triple. Some of the double rooms can combine to function as suites. The small outhouse has been converted into a maisonette for two persons. All rooms have a telephone, an internet connection, a television, a mini-bar and a hairdryer.

When you feel hungry A great breakfast is served up to 13.00, and if later in the day you feel like having a bite of something, you can order small snacks. There is no restaurant in the mansion, but there are several places to eat in Vyzitsa and in nearby Milies.

Bring the children? The Santikos Mansion is the perfect romantic escape for couples, but that doesn't mean you cannot stay here if you travel with children; on the contrary, they are very welcome. The rooms are suitably large, so even if it is too cold to spend much time outside, your children will have enough space in the room to play. Cots are available for babies and toddlers, and the suites are very convenient for families with older children.

SANTIKOS MANSION

To see and do Vyzitsa is a perfect base if you'd like to go for walks over the stone-paved tracks connecting the villages of Pelion, drive to the sea for a swim, and visit the craft museum and the library in neighbouring Milies, the village where on Sunday you can take a ride on the old steam railway.

Good to know The mansion is open all year. The winter months (October-April) and the first three weeks of August are considered high season, and prices for two people start at €140 per night (breakfast included). The rest of the year, prices start at €90 per night. The house can also be rented in its entirety on a weekly basis

(Sunday to Sunday), at better rates. Keep in mind that you cannot drive all the way to the mansion – you will have to leave your car in the street and walk up (over a cobbled path), but it only takes a couple of minutes. Credit cards: Diners, MasterCard and Visa.

Getting there Follow the road from Milies to Vyzitsa (three km). Leave your car on the street below the central square of the village, then walk up to the square, where you will see a sign for Santikos Mansion. When you arrive, you can give a phone call to the mansion, and someone will come down to help you with your luggage.

Where else would you find the Lost Unicorn, but hidden behind the village square with the, reputedly, oldest and largest plane tree in Greece? The tranquil *plateia* of Agia Paraskevi in Tsangarada, famous for its magnificent 1000-year-old tree (with a perimeter of about 17 m!), is an enchanting spot, and provides the perfect setting for this small and homey hotel. When Clare and Christos, a young British-Greek couple, during their holidays in Greece, came to Pelion for the first time and passed by the little square, they instantly fell for the idyllic *plateia* and the soft-coloured building. They had a chat over the fence with the British-American owners, but never even went inside.

Back in England, Clare and Christos started dreaming of doing something similar and maybe open a small hotel somewhere in Greece. One day, just for fun, they looked on the Internet for properties for sale, and the first that popped up on their screen was the Lost Unicorn. They took this as a sign they had to pursue their dream, and, to cut a long story short, a year later they had become the proud owners of the little hotel.

The century-old building isn't quite as grand as most historical Pelion mansions, but inside it is absolutely lovely. It first started operating as a hotel in the fifties and even though it closed its doors twenty years later, it still carries an old-fashioned feel about it. But be prepared: with the exception of the original *terrazzo* flooring there is little typically Greek or even Mediterranean about it – in fact, it looks more like an elegant British country-house hotel. And to some extent, that is just what it is.

The previous owners, who had bought it in 1995, had filled the large living room, the dining room, the library, as well as the bedrooms with gleaming English Victorian antiques, and served their guests English breakfast and afternoon tea with scones. After Clare and Christos took over the property *and* all of its contents (including quite a collection of unicorn statues!), they decided to continue in the same spirit, but added a fresh dose of enthusiasm. Clare and Christos receive their guests as friends, spoiling them with excellent breakfasts, high teas, drinks by the open roaring fire or on the flowered terrace, and wonderful candlelit dinners.

THE LOST UNICORN

370 12 Tsangarada
Pelion
Tel. 24260-49930

Where you'll sleep Six double bedrooms are on the first floor, and there are two more rooms on the penthouse-like second floor. The bedrooms are small but charming with antique beds and elegant, British-style bedding. They are equipped with a telephone, a television and a hairdryer, and every room has its own little balcony. The en suite showers are a little old fashioned but they are pleasantly large and impeccably clean.

When you feel hungry Clare and Christos serve breakfast in the dining room or on the terrace (from 9.00 to 11.00), and you can choose between full English or scrambled eggs with smoked salmon. On Sunday, you can also opt for a champagne brunch, served between 11.00 and 13.00. If you ask in the morning (or better even, a day in advance or upon booking), you will be served a splendid three-course dinner in the evening. Otherwise, you can order simple dishes *à la carte*. There are also several restaurants within walking distance.

Bring the children? It is better to not show up with young children at the Lost Unicorn. It is not only that the rooms can't fit extra beds, but also the atmosphere is more geared toward grown-ups looking for quiet.

To see and do Pelion is an all-year-round destination. During the summer, there are many gorgeous beaches to choose from, while in the winter you can try out the Pelion ski centre. And of course throughout the year, there is walking; in fact there is no better way to explore Tsangarada than on foot. If you want to make sure you get to see the most beautiful, hidden spots, you can sign up for guided walks.

Good to know The Lost Unicorn is open almost all year round, apart from a few weeks during the winter when Christos and Clare go on holiday. The price for a double room is €100 per night during weekends and holidays, and €85 for all other periods. Breakfast is included. Note that dogs are not allowed. Credit cards: Amex, MasterCard and Visa.

Getting there The easiest way to reach Tsangarada is to follow signs for southern Pelion from Volos. You drive along the coastal road for about 20 km and continue following signs for Neohori and Tsangarada. Tsangarada consists of four small communities. The Lost Unicorn is in Agia Paraskevi, and it is signposted from the main road. When you reach the square, continue along the cobbled lane past the church and leave your car at the end. The Lost Unicorn is about 50 m on your left.

When 20 years ago British-born Jill Sleeman came to Pelion for the first time, she just knew the verdant, mountainous peninsula was the place for her. She found her dream spot in Mouresi, where she bought a 19th century neoclassical house that in the past was used for the cultivation of silk worms, did it up and opened it as a B&B with just four rooms.

The Old Silk Store is an easy-going sort of place, without any fashionable décor elements, let alone luxury of any sorts. But it definitely has something… Jill lives in the house herself and it's her presence that makes the Old Silk Store such a pleasant place to stay. Here, you don't feel like you are just renting a room where you get your set breakfast and that's it — no, you are staying at Jill's. She openly enjoys the company of her guests and she is always in for a chat. Her year-round companions are a somewhat grumpy pony and a sweet, but naughty old donkey (she rescued them both from their previous, unloving owners), and her guests, many of which are regulars and have become her friends, are quite obviously more fascinating conversation partners.

THE OLD SILK STORE

370 12 Mouresi
Pelion
Tel. 24260-49086

Where you'll sleep The four charming bedrooms are on the top floor of the mansion. Painted in soft hues and furnished simply with old brass twin beds, they are bright, comfortable and pleasant. The bathrooms are slightly old-fashioned but perfectly adequate; one of the rooms has its bathroom across the corridor. There are no televisions in the rooms; the only piece of electrical equipment you'll find is a kettle for making coffee or tea. (In the unlikely case you feel the need to watch television you can do so in the living room.) One room has a tiny kitchenette. There is also a small garden house, the Old Barber's Shop, for up to three people, with a working fireplace and an open-plan kitchen – ideal for longer stays.

When you feel hungry Jill prepares a great breakfast for her guests with bread that she bakes herself, homemade jams, fruit juices (some she makes from her own fruits), and

daily varied dishes such as yogurt with fruits, scrambled eggs or baked pears. When the weather is nice, she serves breakfast on the flowered terrace or in the shade of the apple orchard. For your other meals you will find an array of places to eat, some in Mouresi at walking distance, others a little further, near the sea or in Tsangarada.

Bring the children? Children are welcome at the Old Silk Store, although the quiet ambience of the place might not suit families with very small children, especially in the winter, when you share the smallish sitting room with other guests.

To see and do Jill loves hiking and she knows the walking paths of Pelion like the palm of her hand. She regularly organises guided walks for her guests or other groups. There are some beautiful beaches just a short drive away

(in principle you could even walk, but it is quite a climb to get back) and during winter weekends, you can go skiing at the Pelion ski centre near Hania, at 28 km from Mouresi.

Good to know The Old Silk Store is open all year, except February. Prices are the same throughout the year: €60 for a double room and €80 for the Old Barber Store. For breakfast you pay extra. Dogs are not allowed. No credit cards.

Getting there Follow the coastal road from Volos and drive via Agria, Neochori and Tsangarada towards Mouresi. Just before the centre, turn off the main road in the direction of the sea, towards Damouchari and Agios Ioannis. A bit further down you will see the Old Silk Store, on your left, above the road.

Portaria is a charming village situated at an altitude of 650 m, halfway between Volos and the ski centre of Mount Pelion. Easy to reach, blessed with a ravishing setting and magnificent architecture, and with many different places to stay, it tends to attract a fair amount of visitors. Hotel Despotiko occupies a quiet spot at the edge of the village, just a few minutes walk through the narrow, cobbled lanes off the central square.

The main building is a tall and imposing mansion built in 1840 by a wealthy tradesman. Next to it there is a recon-structed old barn, now used as a sitting room. The gun-holes next to the mansion's heavy iron entrance door and the openings above it, for pouring burning hot oil, give you an idea of how unsolicited visitors were handled in the past. Obviously, today things are a little different. The mansion is running as a hotel, and visitors are wel-comed with wide open arms by Evangelia, Panagis and Eleni, three close friends who took over the hotel a few years ago. Young and enthusiastic, they have added a hefty dose of warmth and friendliness to the sober grandeur of the place.

DESPOTIKO

370 11 Portaria
Pelion
Tel. 24280-99046

Where you'll sleep Most of the 21 bedrooms (doubles and triples, and some can take an extra bed) are in the mansion. The best are the ones at the front: they are nicely proportioned and with high ceilings and arched windows, they feel quite grand. The rooms at the back are smaller and have more of a cosy feel. Some more rooms are located on the first floor of the adjacent old barn. Recently repainted in fun colours they are no less attractive than the ones in the main building. All rooms have an en suite shower or bathroom (nothing fancy), a telephone and a television.

When you feel hungry In the morning (up to 11.00) a buffet breakfast awaits you in the spacious living room with a full

range of hearty (and deliciously fattening) options and a few healthier alternatives, such as muesli, yogurt, fruits and fresh juice. There is no restaurant in the hotel, but you'll find plenty of places to eat nearby, including the newly opened Despotiko restaurant. If, however, you don't feel like going out you can ask for meals to be brought to you at the hotel.

Bring the children? By all means, yes! A genuine family atmosphere reigns at Hotel Despotiko, and there is enough space for you not to worry whether your kids disturb other guests. There is also a playroom with a television and a DVD player.

To see and do Walking is the number one activity in this area: the cobbled lanes of Portaria and neighbouring village Makrinitsa lead you past gorgeous mansions, churches and chapels. During winter weekends you can go skiing (with a sea-view!) in the Agriolefkes ski centre near Hania, 15 km from Portaria. It is small (five lifts), but it is known for the good snow quality. It also has a particularly attractive trail for cross-country skiing.

Good to know Hotel Despotiko is open all year. In the high season (October to May), prices for double rooms start at €90; in the low season double rooms are €75 per night (breakfast included). Dogs are not allowed. Credit cards: Amex, MasterCard and Visa.

Getting there From Volos you follow signs for Portaria. When you reach the first houses you should look out for a small sign on your right for Hotel Despotiko. Take a right into the cobbled lane and just follow the signs. It is a narrow lane, but you can drive all the way to the hotel.

What greater challenge can there be for a young architect, specialised in the restoration of historical buildings, than to buy a derelict three-storey Pelion mansion and bring it back to its old glory? Maria Diamond was still in her twenties when she first set her eyes on a dilapidated mansion at the bottom of the village of Makrinitsa, but she never thought of it as a 'challenge'. She simply saw her dream standing right in front of her.

After the mansion became hers, she took charge of its entire restoration. She painstakingly cared for every detail, preserving whatever she could, and recreating in its original form whatever was beyond rescue. Quite often she had to argue with the workers who didn't believe in preservation. (One day, for instance, she caught them just when they were about to chop the magnificent old wooden entry door into pieces – you can still see the axe marks!) But Maria did not compromise, and in 1990 she finally opened Arhondiko Pandora, which remains until today one of the finest and most original buildings in the area.

Staying at the Arhondiko Pandora is an absolute treat – you could just spend your days admiring the sheer beauty all around you: the amazing patterns of the timbered ceilings, the paintings and gravures adorning the walls, the period furniture and antique objects, the wonderfully landscaped terraces and, to complete the bliss, the sweeping views over Volos and the sea. There are no more than seven rooms, but the house usually fills up only during weekends in the autumn and winter (and even then there is enough space for all guests to be comfortable). If you come in the spring or summer, you may have the entire mansion to yourself.

ARHONDIKO PANDORA

370 11 Makrinitsa
Pelion
Tel. 24280-99404

Maria divides her time between Athens and Makrinitsa, but is usually around when she has guests (otherwise, a girl from the village takes care of them). Her English is fluent and if you have any interest in the local traditional architecture, she will enjoy showing you all the exceptional features of the mansion.

Where you'll sleep There are seven attractive rooms and suites – six are in the mansion and one is in an outbuilding. Decorated in character with the mansion, they combine tradition with elegance. They are equipped with a telephone, a television, a DVD player and a safe, and they have nice (but not huge) en-suite bathrooms. One of the suites has a fireplace that you can use.

When you feel hungry A breakfast of fresh and homemade products is served from 9.00 to 10.30 in the dining room or on the terrace, and throughout the day you can order drinks and snacks. (Room service is also possible.) Meals are served in the mansion's private little taverna during holidays and, upon request, for special events. In the village you will find several good places to eat (five to ten minutes on foot); the square of Makrinitsa is a lovely place to have lunch outside.

Bring the children? Even though the rooms are large and the suites can take up to four people, Arhondiko Pandora is not the kind of place where you should come with young children.

To see and do There is no doubt that Makrinitsa is among the most beautiful of the Pelion villages. You will very much enjoy strolling around its cobbled lanes where you can buy local products in little shops. If you stay a bit longer, you can use Makrinitsa as your base to explore more of the Pelion peninsula, and when there is snow, you are only a roughly 15-minute drive from the ski centre near Hania. (Bear in mind, however, that the ski lifts only work at weekends.)

Good to know Arhondiko Pandora is open all year. During the winter months prices for a double room start at €135, and during the summer they start at €120 per night. Breakfast is included. Facilities include a sitting room on the ground floor with a fireplace and a television. The small, private 'taverna' just below the main terrace can be used for meetings and small events. If you have a small dog, it is welcome at the guesthouse, but dogs are not allowed in the sitting rooms. Credit cards: Visa (extra charge).

Getting there Follow the signs for Makrinitsa from the centre of Volos (if you miss them, you can also follow the signs for Portaria). You will find Arhondiko Pandora on your left hand at the bottom of the village. If you come from Portaria, pass the parking area at the entrance of Makrinitsa, follow the road down towards Volos and you will see the hotel on your right.

PERLEAS MANSION

Famous for its *mastiha* production – the sticky, tasty resin of the mastic tree that was used as a chewing gum in ancient times (and in Greece still is today!) – Hios is a fascinating island. Well off the beaten track, it is a great place to visit if you're after a combination of good beaches and places of interest while avoiding the crowds. Even in August, you can still find beaches that are practically empty.

The area of Kambos, some kilometres south of the capital, is one of the most fertile parts of the island, with lovely old Genoese mansions set in verdant gardens and olive, fruit and vegetable producing estates. This is where the Genoese upper class lived during the heydays of the island, and later, the Greek gentry (many Greek shipping magnates still have houses here). A few of the old mansions are now used as guesthouses, and of those, the 17th century Perleas Mansion easily stands out. It is the residence of Claire and Vangelis Tsitsopoulos, who live here all year round, working their estate of over a thousand fruit trees, while also receiving guests.

Claire and Vangelis are not your run-of-the-mill hoteliers. They are the kind of people who would create a warm atmosphere even if they were managing a highway motel, so you can imagine what they are actually doing in a setting that is so appealing to begin with. Vangelis is an artist (he makes amazing sculptures out of scrap iron), as well as a collector of rare objects, and the house displays a scattering of eye-catching artefacts.

The couple has literally opened their own house to guests, so that on the occasional rainy day, early or late in the season, you will have breakfast in the family dining room, or a drink in their sitting room. You will not, however, have the uncomfortable feeling you are invading their private space, and you, as a guest, will also have full privacy. Bedrooms are charming and spacious (a few are on the first floor of the mansion, others are in the smaller houses scattered on the estate), but you will probably spend most of your time outdoors. The grounds of the Perleas Mansion are wonderful, especially the main terrace, with its old well, the wooden water wheel and the marble cistern, which, covered by water lilies, now functions as an elegant, elevated pond.

PERLEAS MANSION

Vitiadou St.
Kambos
821 00 Hios
Tel. 22710-32217

Where you'll sleep There are three double rooms on the first floor of the mansion, and the other rooms are in the garden houses (three doubles and one family unit for up to five persons). Each room has its own personality – most have a fresh romantic look, while a few have a more old-fashioned sort of charm. They all have an en suite bathroom (they are decent, but vary in terms of aesthetics), a telephone, a mini-bar and air conditioning.

When you feel hungry Claire serves breakfast from 8.30 to 10.30, and it includes fresh fruit juice, homemade jams, eggs (boiled, fried, omelette), cold meats, cheeses, yogurt, cake and biscuits. There is no restaurant in the Perleas Mansion, but three nights a week (Mondays, Wednesdays and Fridays) an evening meal is served on the terrace. It is a set menu offering a selection of excellent home-cooked traditional Greek dishes, prepared almost entirely with fresh, organically cultivated ingredients from the estate. Don't plan an evening out on those nights – it would be a shame to miss such a great meal, served in a wonderfully romantic setting. There are a few other places where you can eat in Kambos, and Claire and Vangelis will be happy to give you suggestions for restaurants in Hios town and in nearby villages.

Bring the children? If you have children who love to play outside, you're in the right place. They will have plenty of space to run around, and there are also some cute farm animals they can say hi to. The only thing to be careful about if you come with toddlers is the cistern, although, as it is elevated, it would take a very adventurous toddler to fall in. Several rooms have single beds and cots are available.

To see and do Even though the Perleas Mansion is a great place to relax, there is so much to see and discover on the island that you shouldn't sit around too much! There are scores of amazing villages to visit (the medieval *mastihohoria* like Mesta and Pyrgi in the south, the castle village of Anavatos in the middle of island, picturesque Volissos in the north…), as well as impressive monasteries (notably the 11th century Nea Moni Monastery in the centre of the island). There are also many beaches worth exploring (don't miss the black stone Mavra Volia beach on the south coast). Back at 'home' at the mansion, you can sign up for one of Claire's classes in traditional marmalade making, or take part in the organic farming activities.

Good to know The Perleas Mansion is open from the beginning of March until the end of October. The price per night for a double room is €95 in the low season, and €115 in the high season (mid-June to mid-September), and it includes breakfast. Credit cards: MasterCard and Visa.

Getting there Hios can be reached by fast ferryboat from Piraeus (about six hours) or by plane (several flights per day from Athens). To get to the guesthouse from the town of Hios you should follow the coastal road towards the airport. Take a right immediately after the airport (at the end of the landing strip) and then take a left towards Kalimasia. Turn into the second (narrow) lane on your left after you pass the BP petrol station. At the end of this lane, on your right, you'll find the Perleas Mansion.

When you travel around in countries like France or Italy, you can spend all your nights in medieval *chateaux*, converted monasteries and renaissance *palazzos*. In Greece the choice of historical hotels is much more limited. With a few exceptions, no matter how many kilometres you travel, your journey back in time (as far as sleeping arrangements are concerned) will be no further than 100 to 150 years. Don't be fooled by the Parthenon and the profusion of archaeological sites – these are not places where you can spend the night!

The Argentikon in the Kambos area in Hios *is* historical, and the current owner, a Greek shipping magnate, clearly wants to stress this point. He has filled every space with period pieces to make sure that guests are fully wrapped up in the experience. The estate dates back to 1550, when the Genoese Argenti family (who were present on the island since the beginning of the Genoese occupation in 1346) built it as a summer residence. For hundreds of years the property went from father to son, but after it suffered substantial damage in the 1881 earthquake, the family moved to Genoa.

ARGENTIKON

Kambos
82 100 Hios
Tel. 22710-33111

We owe it to the late Philip Argenti that the Argentikon is not among the Kambos estates that today are still crying out to be restored. About half a century after his father's family had left Hios, Philip returned to the island to revitalise the estate, adding the Castle of the River which became the main residence, and later the Pyrgi house, which he decorated with local-style *xystra*, walls scratched in white and grey geometric patterns. But his foremost project was the restoration of the original *palazzo*, which took several decades.

After Philip Argenti passed away, his son Lorenzo made further improvements to the estate, where he reputedly received royalty and dignitaries from all over. About ten years ago, however, Lorenzo Argenti sold the estate, which, after a costly renovation, entered a new stage in its historical journey, opening its doors as a "luxury suites" hotel in 2005. "Hotel" is maybe not the best word to use, as you will understand the moment you arrive. George Dorizas, the gracious manager of the Argentikon, will welcome you in the Argenti Hall (the old laundry room) offering you a drink as well as a quick run-down of the history of the estate, before showing you around and accompanying you to your suite. And from that moment onwards, your stay will be whatever you'd like it to be.

My first move was to switch off the air conditioning. In order to preserve the antiques, the temperature inside the buildings is kept at a permanently low level – too cool for comfort as far as I was concerned. So I opened the windows instead, to

allow a summer breeze to enter my suite and listen to the intense chirping of the cicadas. Taking in my surroundings, I had to admit that my personal taste is perhaps a little more modest, but I do agree that for anyone looking for an escape to the extraordinary, a few days of reverie, and a full immersion in history and luxury combined, this is the place to be.

To me, the gardens are the best part. Winding pathways lead past rose gardens, shady sitting corners, oleander and cypress trees, old marble statues and columns, carefully maintained hedges, pebble-mosaic terraces, lavender bushes, marble cisterns and wells with the large wooden water wheels, and myriads of fruit trees. And perhaps the most attractive spot of all is the swimming pool, a small

compromise in terms of historic authenticity, but one that is absolutely worth it.

Even though the Argentikon won't remind many guests of their own residence (heads of state aside), George is on a mission to make everyone feel welcome and at home. A small army of staff provide round-the-clock service treating everyone like royalty and surprising them with numerous attentive little touches. Despite what appearances might suggest, you will not experience any snobbery, nor will you get the feeling you must behave like royalty. The Argentikon may be for the more affluent among us, but it is not the kind of place where the rich and famous go to show off and to 'see and be seen' – on the contrary, the estate is a hideout offering privacy and tranquillity.

ARGENTIKON

Where you'll sleep The suites of the Argentikon are found in five different buildings. Two suites are in the oldest residence on the estate: the Palazzo; there are two in the Castle of the River at the far end of the property; the *xystra* house features two more suites; and an old stable has been converted into the Kambos Suite. Every suite has a sitting room, one to three bedrooms, and at least one bathroom (some with Jacuzzi) and is fitted with a telephone, an internet connection, a television, a complementary mini-bar, air conditioning, a hairdryer and a safe. Furnished entirely with antiques, these suites have nothing in common with 'ordinary' hotel suites, but are more like how you would imagine guest suites in royal palaces to be. The décor is overwhelming and uncompromising; the only modern elements are the amenities. The two suites in the Palazzo, as well as the Kambos suites, are probably the most majestic of all; those in the Castle of the River are the most homely; and the suites in the *xystra* house have a more charming side to them.

When you feel hungry All you need to do is dial 133 and the troops will spring into action. Breakfast will be brought to your suite (in theory until 11.00 but in practice as late as you want) and you can ask for just about anything 'within reason' – caviar and champagne included. You can also enjoy lunch and dinner in the privacy of your suite, but a more attractive option is to walk over to the restaurant situated on the lower floor of the Palazzo, where you can sit either on the shaded terrace or inside in the elegant dining room. Meals are a combination of fresh products from the estate (and the sea) and delicacies imported from all over the world. The chef means to impress his guests, and does everything he can to succeed.

Bring the children? Let's face it, if you go somewhere with young kids, you might be happier to arrive at a bungalow furnished with shock-tested Ikea gear, than in a historical mansion filled with precious antiques. But then again, everything is a matter of attitude: of the parents, of the children and of the hosts. As far as your hosts are concerned, they will be more than happy to have you and your little ones. So it's up to you really. If you feel your children will understand that the beds are not to be used as trampolines, by all means, bring them along. And even if inside you may have to utter an occasional "don't touch that", the seemingly endless grounds of the estate, full of winding little footpaths and hiding places, and – not to forget – the swimming pool, make a wonderful playground for children. The wells (a 30 m drop to the water level), George promised me, will be secured, so you will just have to be careful with the pond-like cistern near the *xystra* house, if you have a child that can't swim (but knows how to climb).

To see and do Hios is an island that calls out to be explored, and you will enjoy the *mastihohoria* (the *mastiha* producing, medieval communities) and other picturesque villages, the historic monasteries, and of course the exceptional beaches on the island. Staying at the Argentikon, of course you shouldn't miss the Argenti Museum on the top floor of the Koraï Library in the town, displaying Philip Argenti's personal collection of folk art, old maps, costumes and family portraits. (Philip was a zealous historian and spent much of his life studying and chronicling the island's history and architecture.) Alternatively, Argentikon is a place where you could come with all these books you always wanted to read and just unwind and let yourself be pampered.

Good to know The Argentikon normally stays open all year. Prices for two people start at €550 in the low season, and €790 in the high season, and they include breakfast, and arrival and departure transfers. Facilities at the Argentikon include a (small) sauna, a spa and a massage parlour. There is also a conference hall for up to 130 people (in a separate building dating from 1550), complete with state-of-the-art audio-visual equipment, and the Argenti Hall, which can be used for meetings for up to 45 people. Credit cards: all major.

Getting there You can get to Hios in about six hours by fast ferryboat from Piraeus or in just half an hour by plane from Athens. The Argentikon is barely ten minutes' drive from the airport (20 from the port) – in any case you will be met upon arrival.

ARHONDIKO ANGELOU

When I first heard about the Arhondiko Angelou on the island of Leros and saw some pictures of it, I foolishly, and inexplicably, jumped to the conclusion that this had to be a guesthouse run by a stodgy old granny and that it probably smelled of mothballs. A chance meeting with Marianna Angelou, the owner of Arhondiko Angelou, put me straight. How could I have been so wrong? Marianna turned out to be a charming young woman with whom I hit it off instantly, and, as I found out a few weeks later, when I went to visit her on Leros, if there are any smells lingering in the guesthouse, they are of freshly washed linen and home-baked cake.

The house in the seaside village of Alinda was built in 1895 for Marianna's great grandmother who used it as a summer home. (Apparently she was a severe lady who Marianna's father did not enjoy visiting very much; maybe that's where I got my ideas from!) Already as a child, Marianna spent all her summers on Leros where her parents had a small hotel (on the other side of the island), and some of her fondest memories are of serving breakfast to guests during school holidays, feeling ever so grown-up!

In the seventies, Marianna's father decided to renovate the house in Alinda and convert it into a guesthouse. When it opened, Marianna was 12 years old and immediately started regarding it as her own, working side-by-side with her father. After she finished school, she took over the management while also studying tourism. Now married and a mother of two, she divides her time between Athens and Leros, and just like she once did, her two children spend their entire school holidays on the island. (But they are still too young to serve breakfast!)

Marianna feels a profound fondness for her guesthouse, and takes care of it with great passion and devotion. Every extra profit she makes is instantly reinvested in the house. She recently carried out a complete refurbishment, modernising the bathrooms, laying beautiful wooden floors in the first-floor bedrooms (the ground-floor rooms still have the gor-geous, original floor tiles), replacing most of the furniture that her father had chosen in the seventies with more romantic antiques, and redoing the interior paintwork. She is, however, always looking ahead, and rather than feeling content with what she achieved so far, she is already planning the next improvements. She won't stop until she's got it all perfect.

To me, Arhondiko Angelou is just perfect as it is. Everything looks fresh, romantic and sweetly old-fashioned, and the atmosphere matches the look. There is something so honest about it, something very 'real' you rarely come across. If only every island had a guesthouse like this one…

ARHONDIKO ANGELOU

Alinda
85 400 Leros
Tel. 22470-22749

Where you'll sleep There are seven bedrooms in the house, varying from a smallish double to suites for up to four persons, all with an en suite shower. Telephones and fans are the only amenities, but whatever the rooms do not offer in opulence, they more than make up for in charm. And besides, a window looking out over the flowered garden, total quiet at night, a mattress to die for, aren't these qualities worth infinitely more than a television or a Jacuzzi bath?

When you feel hungry Arhondiko Angelou is one of the rare places where breakfast is just… right. Marianna is not trying to impress you with a please-overeat kind of start of the day, instead she bakes her own bread, lets you taste different homemade marmalades every day (it is one of her specialties), makes fresh orange juice on the spot, and always spoils you with a sweet treat (pancakes, muffins, banana bread, carrot cake, rice pudding…). There is no restaurant in the guesthouse, but if you ask Marianna, she can prepare a picnic basket for you and occasionally she may also cook you a meal. The restaurants of Alinda are just five to ten minutes away on foot.

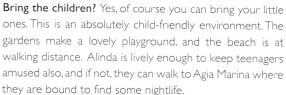

Bring the children? Yes, of course you can bring your little ones. This is an absolutely child-friendly environment. The gardens make a lovely playground, and the beach is at walking distance. Alinda is lively enough to keep teenagers amused also, and if not, they can walk to Agia Marina where they are bound to find some nightlife.

To see and do Leros is definitely off the beaten tourist track and will appeal to anyone who wants to be away from the crowds (though beware: in August the little island gets its share of visitors too). It doesn't stand out for its beaches, but there are lots of places nice enough to enjoy the sea; the villages have charm (in particular Agia Marina and Platanos, the castle-topped *hora*); the hilly landscape is beautiful; the people are friendly and the island generally has an authentic and unspoilt feel to it. It is just perfect for quiet, relaxing holidays, though there is also scope for some activity: you can take lovely walks, there are several museums to visit, and you can go for day excursions to nearby islands (Kalimnos, Lipsi, Patmos…). You can even rent a small motorboat to discover the nearby uninhabited islets and deserted beaches.

Good to know Arhondiko Angelou is normally open from Easter till the beginning of October; upon request, stays are possible during the winter months. Prices for a double room start at €65 in the low season and at €85 in the high season, breakfast included. Credit cards: Diners, MasterCard and Visa.

Getting there The island of Leros can be reached by plane (one daily flight from Athens) and by ferry from the port of Piraeus (8-11 hours). There are also fast boat connections from other islands, and from Rhodes there is even an air connection (three times a week). Keep in mind that in July and August the ferries are often full, so it is recommended to book well in advance. You will find taxis at the airport and in the port, and if you arrive with your own car, you follow signs for Agia Marina and Alinda. When you drive along the coastal road of Alinda, you will see a sign for Arhondiko Angelou.

Tucked away in the Turkish quarters of the old town of Rhodes, among the 14th century city ramparts, the Marco Polo Mansion is one of Greece's most magical places to stay. It is in a narrow, cobbled alleyway where during the day artisans and merchants spread out their trade. The unavoidable pareo, souvenir and art shops are a definite reminder that this is the 21st century, but walk here late at night under the arches covering the alley, and you will feel as if time has stood still for hundreds of years.

If it wasn't for the bright blue entrance, you could easily miss the Marco Polo Mansion. From the outside, nothing suggests that this is a hotel (which in any case, is the wrong word to use – it is a house that welcomes guests). All you see is a small, arty bar with an idyllic back garden. The occasional passer-by, who stops here for a drink or a light meal in the shade of fruit trees, might never realise that this is a place where you can actually spend the night.

The owner, Giuseppe Sala, is an Italian painter, artist, traveller and interior designer. The 'hotelier' addition to his CV happened more or less by chance. Spending part of the year in Rhodes (he also has homes in Rio de Janeiro and Milan) one day, he mentioned to his friend Efi Dede how nice it would be to open a little hotel in the old town. It was a mere thought. That same day, Efi's eye fell on an old building a little further down the road from Giuseppe's gallery, that she'd never really noticed before, with a tiny 'for sale' sign on it. To cut a short story even shorter, within 24 hours Giuseppe was the new proprietor of the 15th century Turkish mansion.

During the renovation, Giuseppe had the good sense to change as little as possible, and thus retain the warm, oriental and slightly mystical charm of the mansion. He simply heightened the appeal by decorating it with eye-catching, deep colours, magnificent fabrics, splendid old rugs, traditional furniture, antique objects from Morocco, Turkey and India, and, of course, with his own water paintings and prints subtly adorning the walls.

Giuseppe asked Efi to become the hostess of the Marco Polo Mansion, a task she happily accepted. It would not serve her right to say she simply 'runs' the place. Efi and her husband Spyros, who later joined in as well, bring warmth to the mansion which far exceeds that of the décor (hard as that may seem). They take care of the place as if it was their own. They personally welcome guests and make them feel at home and ultimately, make most of them come back time and again. The Marco Polo Mansion is not just a charming place to stay – it is an escape, a place to unwind, to take in the atmosphere, the aesthetics, the quiet… and to just dream away.

MARCO POLO MANSION

40-42 Ag. Fanouriou St.
Old Town
851 00 Rhodes
Tel. 22410-25562

Where you'll sleep There are four double rooms on the first floor of the mansion: the large Imperial with its canopied bed overlaid with an Indian sari, the snug Harem (with two single beds), the First Antique with its Turkish hammam, and the Second Antique with a view on an old minaret. Three rooms (Yellow, Green and Pink) are in the old garden house and they open directly to the terrace. A second garden house features two more rooms (Byzantine and Signorina). This is a more recent construction, but it is equally charming. All rooms have en suite showers (some in domed old Turkish baths), a fan and a refrigerator.

When you feel hungry There are plenty of places to eat in the Old Town, but in the end many of Efi's guests barely go out: home cooked meals are served in the garden and the combination of simple but delicious food and a quiet, friendly atmosphere is irresistible, something the restaurants in town simply can't beat. Guests often end up eating together and Efi and Spyros join in regularly. Breakfast is served in the garden as well: you can help yourself from a spread of enticing light and healthy options.

Bring the children? Although the option of staying in the Old Town may not cross your mind when you are planning a family holiday in Rhodes, your children may actually tremendously enjoy the wondrous medieval ambience inside the city walls. Efi, in any case, will welcome your little ones with wide-open arms. Keep in mind that some of the rooms in the mansion have low windows and are not safe for toddlers – clarify that when you make your booking!

To see and do You can either spend a few nights in the Marco Polo Mansion and discover the Old Town (there are plenty of sights to keep you busy for several days), or you can use it as a base for a longer stay on the island, so you can combine culture and history with going to the beach and relaxing. As a major tourist destination, Rhodes has plenty of organised activities as well; golfers for instance can play at the Afandou Golf Course (just 15 km from the town) and there is also a scuba diving school near the town.

Good to know The Marco Polo Mansion is open from the beginning of April until the end of October. Prices for a double room start at €90 in the low season, and €110 in the high season, and they include breakfast. Normally, a minimum stay of three nights applies. Note that with a few exceptions, cars are not allowed inside the city walls, and the nearest place to park your car is a good five-minute walk. Credit cards: Amex, MasterCard and Visa.

Getting there You will have to leave your car at the San Francisco Gate (Agios Athanasios on the map). Inside the town walls, walk down Omirou Street and turn left into Ag. Fanouriou Street. You will see the café of the Marco Polo Mansion on your left. If you arrive by taxi, you will be dropped off at the San Francisco Gate, but if you have a lot of luggage, you should insist that the driver takes you up to Platia Haritou, much closer to the Mansion. Then call the hotel so someone can come and pick you up.

MARCO POLO MANSION, THE GALLERY HOUSE

Just 50 m away from the Marco Polo Mansion is the art gallery of Giuseppe Sala, and above it is the Gallery House, where you can also stay. To get to it, you pass through the gallery, go up steep wooden stairs and the entire first floor is yours. Like the Mansion, the Gallery House is also decidedly oriental in flavour without being too heavy. It exudes the charm of an old house that underwent no more than a minimal renovation – it

speaks for itself. Untreated, rough wooden floorboards, walls washed in deep colours with plaster coming off in a few spots, a bare light bulb hanging from an impossibly high ceiling, an old-fashioned little kitchen with a bare concrete floor – these are small imperfections which, together with the immensely alluring furniture (finds from oriental bazaars as well as precious antiques) and decoration with simple flair, add up to utter perfection.

Where you'll sleep The Gallery House has two bedrooms (the Oriental, a magnificent double room, and next to it the Cycladic Room with two large single beds), a massive hall-cum-sitting room, a small kitchen and a bathroom with

shower. The art gallery opens only a few hours in the morning and in the late afternoon, and if you want the feeling of full privacy upstairs you can close the trapdoor on top of the stairway – but nobody ever bothers.

There also is one room (with a double and a single bed) behind the gallery opening to a lovely little courtyard. It has a fantastic Turkish bathroom and a nice little kitchen, both accessed from the courtyard.

Good to know A minimum of one-week stay applies to the Gallery House, with prices starting at €2300 per week. Breakfast (served at the Marco Polo Mansion) is included.

NIKOS TAKIS FASHION HOTEL

Boutique hotels, fashion hotels, art hotels… Labelling hotels is so *à la mode*. Keep it under 50 rooms, and your hotel is 'boutique'. Bring in a trendy designer, and it becomes 'fashion'. Hang modern paintings on the walls, and you can have it in the 'art' category. It was all kind of intriguing for a while, but quickly became so much of a cliché. So what are we to make of the Nikos Takis *Fashion* Hotel, the latest arrival on the scene? Well, this is a case where the 'fashion' label is actually quite justified.

The hotel's fashion pedigree is beyond question. Having dressed innumerable Greek and foreign celebs and royalty, and running a successful *prêt-à-porter* chain of boutiques, designer couple Nikos & Takis are sort of the Greek Dolce & Gabanna (except that *their* relationship has been a happy one for about four decades now!). In later years they have joined forces with a younger couple, Haris and Ilias, and their creations keep going strong on the Athens catwalks. Ilias, however, had a few ideas that went beyond designing things to wear; the conversion of the Nikos-Takis boutique in the old town of Rhodes into a small hotel was his initiative.

It made total sense. A tiny hotel offering a super friendly atmosphere as well as great luxury was exactly what was missing within the old city walls of Rhodes. The charming and superbly located (at a quiet, sunny spot around the corner of the Street of the Knights) turn-of-the-century townhouse, was just right for what Ilias had in mind. His idea was to create a warm and homely environment so he opted for just four suites and a sitting room.

NIKOS TAKIS FASHION HOTEL

26 Panetiou Avenue
Old Town
85 100 Rhodes
Tel. 22410-70773

Using flamboyant colours and a multi-ethnic melange of furniture, objects and fabrics, he gave the interiors a strong oriental character with a dash of eccentricity. The result is on the borderline between fun and over-the-top, but it clearly, touchingly – and loudly – demonstrates Ilias' enthusiasm about it all.

The four partners now regularly shuttle up and down between Athens and Rhodes, and although they do not run the hotel on a day-to-day basis, they are all closely involved and have created a very easy-going atmosphere. Just like in their regular profession, where their priority is to make those who wear their creations feel good about themselves, in the hotel the designers are also keen on making those who stay feel happy. Guests are not only treated to a wonderful environment, but they are also spoiled with all sorts of attentive gestures. So when you come back from the beach you'll be offered some ice-cream and fruits; later in the day some ouzo and *mezedes*, and in the evening, homemade liquor.

Where you'll sleep There are three nicely proportioned suites (Tzami, Ontas and Vosporus) and one large room (Marokino) in the hotel. Each one is unique and decorated with a lot of flair, and is equipped with a telephone, an internet connection, a television and a DVD player, a CD player, a mini-bar, air conditioning, a safe and a hairdryer. The en-suite bathrooms of the suites have a Jacuzzi, and the Marokino has a marble bath.

When you feel hungry Breakfast is served any time you want it, and the menu changes on a daily basis. Standards include freshly squeezed orange juice, croissants, omelette and home-baked cake – along with the variety of extras. Later in the day the staff will gladly whip up a bite for you to eat, and there is an enormous choice of restaurants nearby.

Bring the children? Ilias did not design the hotel with children in mind, and so it has become more of a place for couples than for families. But children are accepted and some suites have an extra bed, but there are no cots.

To see and do Whether you come for a romantic mini break or for longer holidays, the Nikos-Takis Fashion Hotel makes a superbly comfortable base. Rhodes is mostly known as a summer-beach destination, but the rich history and culture of the island, as well as its beautiful landscape (it is a walkers' paradise) make it a worthy year-round destination. Keep this hotel in mind for a short, romantic winter escape.

Good to know The Nikos Takis Fashion Hotel is open all year. Prices for two people start at 120€ in the summer, and at 100€ the rest of the year. They include breakfast. Credit cards: All major.

Getting there Take a taxi to one of the gates on the north side of Old Town city walls (or walk from the port) and walk along the Street of the Knights. Panetiou is a side street by the Great Magistrate's Palace. The hotel is not hard to find at all; there are also city maps posted on nearly every street corner.

How long does it take to build and equip a not-so-big hotel? Barring unforeseen disasters, if you have a plot of land that is easily accessible, if you don't expect too much in terms of architecture and design, and if you are willing to cut a few corners, you could possibly get it done within a year. But what if you plan to build near the top of a protected village, right below one of Greece's most important archaeological sites, accessed only through steep, narrow alleyways? What if you intend to strictly follow the local, historical architecture and what if in terms of design, only the finest will do? Moreover, what if you are a perfectionist and cutting corners is not your style? Then, it might take a little longer indeed.

Michalis Melenos can tell you *how* much longer a *little* longer can get. Owning a piece of land in his native Lindos, he toyed with the idea of building a small hotel for years. It started as a dream that materialised slowly yet steadily, and was gradually transformed into a vision for a hotel that would not be just an addition to the village, but rather, an integral part of it. He called in the services of Anastasia Papaioannou, a Rhodian architect specialised in the restoration of local, historical houses, to design the Melenos Lindos. The small buildings she created are in absolute harmony with the style of the village, a mélange of Byzantine and Ottoman influences. Especially the limestone main building at the top of the property is undistinguishable from the original constructions of that era. Its impeccable state is a give-away, but you could easily be fooled into believing it is historical.

MELENOS LINDOS

Lindos
85107 Rhodes
Tel. 22440-32222

Forget one year – *this* project took more than 12 years to bring to completion! (And that doesn't include the time spent for the architectural design, nor the delays due to bureaucratic procedures involving all the necessary permissions; let alone the time spent 'dreaming' about it, which was an equally important part of the process.) Maybe it could all have been just a hint faster, had Michalis been a bit more willing to make even the smallest compromise in order to gain time. The truth of the matter is that only the end result mattered to him and he spared no effort, expense or time in order to make his dream come true. He was helped a lot by a close friend, the Australian artist Donald H. Green, who spent five years in Lindos designing the gardens and the interiors.

Just to give you an idea of what this project involved, imagine the effort that went into the pebble mosaic terraces alone. They are made of white, grey and pinkish pebble stones (so-called *hohlakia*) that were collected

from local beaches. Workers had to carry up more than 3000 large bags filled with pebbles, which were then sorted out by size, shape and colour, and laid out with mind-boggling precision in elegant patterns. When you take in the sheer dimension of the surfaces covered, you won't be surprised to know that this was a full-time job for ten people, and lasted nearly three years!

It was not only landscaping that was handled with such diligence and artistry. Every aspect on the inside, from the wooden lattice work and the fine motives in the hand-painted ceilings, to the colourful embroideries and antique objects adorning the rooms, reflects that same eye for

MELENOS LINDOS

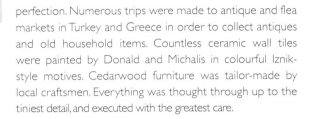

perfection. Numerous trips were made to antique and flea markets in Turkey and Greece in order to collect antiques and old household items. Countless ceramic wall tiles were painted by Donald and Michalis in colourful Iznik-style motives. Cedarwood furniture was tailor-made by local craftsmen. Everything was thought through up to the tiniest detail, and executed with the greatest care.

Staying in a place that offers such a sequence of visual treats (including the amazing views) is a very special experience. Moreover, the impeccable aesthetics are matched by flawless service (friendly, attentive but not overbearing) and great comfort. The Melenos Lindos is one of those rare hotels where you can experience luxury of the highest standards in a pleasantly laid-back atmosphere – a combination that is not easy to find.

Where you'll sleep The 12 generously sized rooms offer a remarkable blend of local tradition and luxury. The style may first strike you as heavy but the overall feeling is nevertheless one of freshness. There are no beds, but superbly comfortable mattresses are placed on elevated sleeping platforms, and made with the finest bed linen. Mod-cons (television, CD player, mini-bar, safe) are fitted into elaborately carved closets (still leaving lots of space for your clothes) – only the air conditioners are visible. Excellent bathrooms are stocked with a great range of bath treats, a hairdryer, slippers, robes and enormous towels. The rooms are doubles, but most can sleep one or two children as well. There is one suite with two separate rooms, for four people. All rooms open up directly to the terrace, and each has its own sitting corner outside.

When you feel hungry Breakfast is served from 8.30 to 10.30 and you can have it wherever you like. You will be asked what you are in the mood for, and a little bit of self-indulgence will not be frowned upon. For lunch and dinner you can try some fine Mediterranean cuisine on the terrace at the top of the property while also having some of the best views you can imagine: from one side you will look over the sea, and from the other at the Acropolis of Lindos.

Bring the children? The calm and romantic mood of the Melenos Lindos makes it more of an environment for adults, but well-behaved kids of all ages are welcome. (Cots are available.) Teenagers will enjoy the fun atmosphere at the beach of Lindos, in particular on Sundays when swinging beach parties are organised, but if you come with young children the problem is that there is nowhere really for them to play in the hotel.

To see and do Rhodes is a multi-facetted island that appeals to beach bums and lovers of art and culture alike, to party animals as well as to anyone looking for peace and quiet. The same applies to Lindos itself, with its lively, sandy beach (and many quieter ones a short drive away), the Acropolis that crowns the village, the little shops, bars and restaurants scattered throughout and, in the midst of all that the Melenos Lindos, offering an oasis of tranquillity.

Good to know The Melenos Lindos is open from the beginning of April until the end of October. Prices for a double room start at around €300, and they include breakfast. Credit cards: Amex, MasterCard and Visa.

Getting there Rhodes can be reached by ferryboat from Piraeus (overnight ferries take about 12 hours), from other islands (Crete, Kos, Santorini, Paros and others) and also from Marmaras in Turkey (one hour away), while Rhodes airport is served by an array of domestic and international airlines. Lindos is about 50 km from the airport and 45 km from the harbour, and can be reached either by bus (cheap, but time consuming) or taxi. In Lindos, you will be met by the staff at the square at the bottom of the village, so you don't have to haul your luggage up to the hotel. Upon request, the hotel can also arrange a private car transfer from the airport.

your
GREECE
NETWORK OF GREAT SMALL HOTELS
www.yourgreece.com